SMALL HOUSES

Philip Jodidio

HOMES FOR OUR TIME
SMALL HOUSES

TASCHEN

CONTENTS

CONTENTS

Philip Jodidio

DRAW ME A LITTLE HOUSE

What is a small house and why is it interesting? The size of single-family houses varies from country to country, for reasons of culture, economics, and other factors such as land availability. At least a note of statistical comparison is useful to understand just where the small homes in this volume fit into "average" sizes in three countries—the United States, Japan, and England. The median size of a completed single-family house in the United States in 2020 was 2261 square feet (210 m^2).[1] Although the statistical base is different, this size can be compared to a similar study concerning the average floor area per dwelling in Japan in 2018. Those figures were 65.9 square meters in Tokyo and 86.9 square meters in Kyoto.[2] Again, starting from a slightly different base, research shows that the average property size in England is 729 square feet (68 m^2).[3]

A Modern Trend

For the purposes of the selection made for this book, "small" was defined as having an interior floor area of less than 100 square meters. One or two houses published here exceed that limit, but others are as small as an amazing seven square meters. It is not an accident that there are quite a few Japanese houses in this book—small houses have long been a trend there because of very dense urban patterns and surely also because the Japanese are used to living in spaces that might be considered too small in other countries ranging from Australia to the United States. Japanese architects have also taken an innovative approach to small houses for many years. Tadao Ando's nearly legendary Sumiyoshi Row House (Azuma House, Osaka, 1976) has a floor area of just 34 square meters with a site area of 57 square meters. And yet that house has been published thousands of times. Its *in-situ* concrete presence is tempered by an unexpected central courtyard that obliges residents to go outside to reach their own bedrooms. And yet the light and breeze admitted in this way brings the house to life and allows "nature" to enter fully despite the urban congestion of Osaka.
Two other remarkable small Japanese houses merit particular attention. One is the Love2 House (Tokyo, Japan, 2019, see page 198) by Takeshi Hosaka, which weighs in at a slim 19 square meters. The architect used Edo-period accounts of the very small *nagaya* (9.6 m^2) homes used for families of four to guide his concept. The architect also refers to Le Corbusier's Cabanon as a source for his tiny home. His concept involves an ingenious system of seven "short walls" that separate the house into three areas for the

kitchen, dining area, and bedroom. A window facing the street can be opened to encourage discussion with passersby. "The front street has a flower bed, so we enjoy it as our garden. In this house we feel that the town is very close." This use of a street-side flower bed is an intelligent extension into community space that makes the very small house seem more generous. Another clever Japanese scheme is the 90-square-meter Toolbox House (Miyakojima-ku, Osaka, 2021, see page 460) by Yoshihiro Yamamoto. The functions of this house are divided between eastern and western zones. Built with galvanized-steel sheet, plywood, tile, oak and Japanese cedar flooring, mortar, tatami mats, and cork, the house is rigorous in terms of its economics and use of space. Another Japanese house that can be listed here is Studio NOA's House in Nobeyama (Nagano, 2017), which has only 38 square meters of floor space but nonetheless includes an entire floor devoted to an "observation room" with a telescope that surveys the night skies through a stainless-steel dome.

Small Is Beautiful

A home, of course, insulates its inhabitants from the outside world—it is a place of comfort and of protection. Might it be that a small house, even in an urban environment, brings residents closer to the natural world? Toyo Ito's own home, the Silver Hut (Nakano-ku, Tokyo, Japan, 1984), was enveloped in perforated aluminum. This iconic house was otherwise largely closed to its chaotic urban environment, aside from the open roof that provided a connection to nature despite the invasive presence of the city. The Silver Hut had a floor area of 138 square meters, so it was rather large by the standards of this book—but it was a clear example of a modest-size residence that responds to the idea of being in direct contact with nature. The economist E. F. Schumacher wrote a seminal book in 1973 called *Small is Beautiful: A Study of Economics as if People Mattered.* That title and book might well be an explanation of why small houses are popular— because they are essentially designed "as if people mattered" and not in the mode of over-sized homes that give too much importance to certain individuals. Schumacher's book contested the idea that "bigger is better," which has often been a leitmotif in architecture. A big house means the owner is important presumably, but is that really the case,

Takeshi Hosaka, Love2 House, Tokyo, Japan, 2019.

Page 2: *Sotamaa, Meteorite, Kontiolahti, Finland, 2020.*

Previous spread: *Barry Connor, Skylark Cabin, Twizel, New Zealand, 2020.*

and is there still room for such displays of ego, whether monetary or architectural? It is clearly time to share, time to think of reducing consumption of space, and of every other resource that the earth will soon run short of.

Prefabricated Wilderness

The constraints imposed by small houses often produce results that are very interesting insofar as the architecture concerned: multiuse spaces, and in short making the most of very little, are powerful engines of investigation and discovery for many architects. Another side effect of the scale of these houses is that there are not many very well-known architects involved. Tadao Ando was not well known in 1976, and in this volume only a few figures, like Bjarke Ingels (BIG), stand out for the size of their offices and the nature of their design and construction portfolio. Tom Kundig of Olson Kundig in the United States also has a high profile, and here we have taken the liberty of including one of his older projects, the 18-square-meter Gulf Islands Cabin (Gulf Islands, British Colombia, Canada, 2008, see page 284). The BIG project is Klein A45 (Upstate New York, USA, 2018, see page 118) which is an effort at prefabricating a luxurious small house (17 m²). Prefabrication is, in fact, a frequent element in the design and construction of small houses, perhaps because it is costly to have bespoke design elements that are produced on an individual scale. Fran Silvestre, best known for his spectacular (large) white houses in Spain,

Croxatto & Opazo, La Loica and La Tagua Cabins, Matanzas, Chile, 2018.

has innovated with his NIU houses—prefabricated residences that range in size from 70 to 160 square meters (see, for example, NIU N70, Valencia, Spain, 2021, page 380). Silvestre demonstrates that much of the ethereal quality of his big houses can, indeed, be translated into smaller formats.

Another prefabricated structure that has already seen several adaptations is the Minimod Curucaca (Santa Catarina, Brazil, 2017, see page 242) by MAPA Architects. Built with cross-laminated timber (CLT) and corrugated metal, this 70-square-meter Minimod is sustainable in almost every respect. It is a sophisticated house that can be placed almost anywhere and used in a PnP (plug-and-play) mode without unduly complex preparation. CLT, which is designed and manufactured digitally, has become quite a common feature in house construction, but it is of particular benefit to small houses where added sophistication in design permits greater comfort and more environmental compatibility. Kynttilä (Savonlinna, Finland, 2020, see page 292) by ORTRAUM architects measuring just 16 square meters uses CLT not only for its structure but also for the entrance door and interior furnishings. Where a skilled carpenter might have labored for weeks to complete such a design, computer-driven machines now allow a broader access to original and carefully crafted wooden forms. Todd Saunders, who has built both in Norway and in Newfoundland, has been actively investigating small, environmentally responsible prefabricated homes. His 17-square-meter XS Micro House (2021) built in a prototype version in Bergen, Norway, is designed to be manufactured in a factory in 12 components and shipped on site. The house includes a kitchen and washroom behind a bed. Rainwater collecting, solar panels, and a composting toilet give it the capacity to be fully off-grid. The architect states that the same system can be used to assemble larger houses, ranging from 50 to 100 square meters in size. Particularly in the guise of weekend retreats, Scandinavians have a substantial tradition of small houses that Saunders references in this type of work.

A Meteorite and Iron Ore

The Meteorite (Kontiolahti, Finland, 2020, see page 404) by Ateljé Sotamaa engages not only the use of prefabricated CLT panels but also a highly unusual form that uses thick walls that actually permit the air gap employed to act as insulation—the house, explain the architects, is "insulated by air and uses natural ventilation." Here and in many other cases, environmental issues have come to the forefront: "sustainability" is the key word whereas, several years ago, architects might not have paid attention to the potential for pollution of various types generated even by a very small structure. The noted Brazilian architect Gustavo Penna has gone so far as to collaborate with a large mining company to determine how iron ore trailings and other mining waste can be used in construction. His 45-square-meter Sustainable House (Ouro Branco, Minas Gerais, Brazil, 2019, see page 298) also uses solar heating, biodigesters, composting tanks, and rainwater collection to underline an ecologically friendly approach not generally associated with mining companies. It might be said that this shows that just about everyone is getting on the bandwagon. Sustainability in a small-scale structure may well be easier to achieve than in a very large building, but the very fact that the issue is raised for small houses is positive and surely productive if enough residences follow known methods to reduce their carbon footprints. A further advantage of small houses is that since they engage relatively small budgets, they may allow a greater degree of experimentation and innovation than their larger "relatives." Alphaville's House of 24 mm Plywood (Kyoto, Japan, 2020, see page 46) is a 43-square-meter experiment in undifferentiated and yet partially divided space. This house, where plywood is the most evident material, can be a residence, a place of work, or even a gallery. Using a typically

Japanese approach to "nature," the architects bring light and even breeze into the house, which is in dense urban Kyoto.

Life in the Woods

Kundig's Gulf Islands Cabin is, of course, representative of an entirely different category of small houses—retreats or woodland cabins that are small by convenience (and sometimes budget), but not because of urban density. Sean Godsell, a well-known Australian architect, imagined his Shack in the Rocks (Victoria, Australia, 2021, see page 182) using an unexpected variety of sources of inspiration. He looked to local haysheds for some guidance in terms of the form of his 32-square-meter refuge, but also to Riken Yamamoto's Yamakawa Cottage (Yatsugatake, Japan, 1977) because of the way in which its single roof shelters both the interiors and outdoor space. Both projects speak to a desire to spend time, or even perhaps to live, in the wilderness. Examples in literature of this attitude abound and might well be related back to Henry David Thoreau's *Walden; or, Life in the Woods* (1854). The cabin that the American poet and philosopher built near Concord, Massachusetts, in 1845, and lived in for 14 months, in many respects symbolizes the reasons that men and women seek refuge in very small abodes, far from the stress and pollution of cities. The idea of returning to nature is all the more prevalent today since what remains of the wilderness is severely threatened by urbanization or by the substances that "modern" life disseminates in the air and water. When excess and "luxury" are driving forces of some societies, more and more people feel the need to scale down to an absolute minimum, to live opposite the rising sun, or to hear the sounds of nature every day. This is not to say that very small houses or refuges cannot offer a good deal of comfort—in fact, most of the cases seen in this book do come with all the amenities of "civilization." Thoreau wrote: "I went to the woods because I wished to live deliberately, to front only the essential facts of life, and see if I could not learn what it had to teach, and not, when I came to die, discover that I had not lived. I did not wish to live what was not life, living is so dear; nor did I wish to practice resignation, unless it was quite necessary. I wanted to live deep and suck out all the marrow of life, to live so sturdily and Spartan-like as to put to rout all that was not life, to cut a broad swath and shave close, to drive life into a corner, and reduce it to its lowest terms." Thoreau's ode to living in nature might well resonate even more today in many countries than it did in 19th-century America.

Art in the Cracks

A number of small houses could more readily fit into the category of works of art rather than pure architecture. Such is the case of Jakub Szczęsny's Keret House (Warsaw, Poland, 2012, see page 438). This house measures just 12 square meters but is also remarkable because its maximum width is 133 centimeters. It is literally squeezed into a crack between two existing buildings in Warsaw. Named after an Israeli author (Etgar Keret), this unexpected presence in Poland surely evokes events of World War II in a poignant way. A model of the Keret House was the first Polish architectural design to be included in the permanent collection of the Museum of Modern Art (MoMA, New York, 2013).
El Sindicato's Parasitic House (Quito, Ecuador, 2019, see page 168) also measures 12 square meters but it is situated on a rooftop. As the architects explain: "Although it is possible to build this type of project in urban or rural sites without existing buildings, ideally its construction should occur on underused rooftops of urban buildings that are structurally sound—buildings where one can connect to the existing water, waste, and electrical grids. In this way, we contribute to the densification of the city at a very small scale, with a minimum investment and use of resources, as well as contributing to the conservation of architectural heritage." A small house in an urban setting can allow "densification" but also provide lodging for people who do not have the means to build larger homes. At this point, the small house becomes an element of social activism propelled by the inventiveness of architects.

Mad Max Goes Off-Grid

Those who are most interested in the ecological future might well venture even further into the wilderness, to the point where there is neither electricity nor running water, where one can be decidedly "off-grid." Australia, with its vast expanses of territory and its independent spirit, is a place where being off-grid is quite

MacKay-Lyons Sweetapple, Enough House, Upper Kingsburg, Nova Scotia, Canada, 2015.

decidedly fashionable. The aptly named Off-Grid FZ (Blue Mountains, Sydney, Australia, 2020, see page 64) is a 94-square-meter house designed by Simon Anderson (Anderson Architecture). Made largely of concrete, fiber cement, and "slide-out, fold-down and roller-down fire shutters," the house is rated FZ for "fire zone." Without being facetious it might seem as though it is ready for the brave new world of "Mad Max." Equally reinforced, Permanent Camping Two (Berry, New South Wales, Australia, 2020, see page 136) by Casey Brown sports a two-story copper-clad tower that can withstand gale force winds and bushfires. Aside from its protective capacity, Permanent Camping Two is off-grid as well, so it uses photovoltaic panels to provide light and power. There is no doubt that this structure has a fortified aspect, especially when entirely closed, and yet it does provide the owners with a splendid view of the sea, and a feeling of security against all dangers, even those of an unstated dystopian sort.

Redoing the Past

Renovation of existing structures, for example small barns or other agricultural buildings, is another source of inspiration to many architects. The Geneva architect Charles Pictet has taken on the challenge of converting an existing tool-shed near his own house into a real residence complete with work area, bed, and kitchen. His Atelier and Residence in a Garden Shed (Geneva, Switzerland, 2021, see page 306) measures 24 square meters (plus a 5 m² chicken coop). The architect has not substantially modified the external appearance of the existing building, but inside he has made it modern and bright, surely a path that other architects are already following. In this instance, Pictet has imagined what might be called a refuge were it not located about five meters from his house not far from the center of Geneva. He is surely at ease in a small space, perhaps even more so than in his larger house? Another case of this kind of conversion is the work of the Spanish architects mar plus ask (Olive Houses, Mallorca, Spain, 2019, see page 250). One of these small structures was also a tool-shed, and the other was newly built. Coloring these structures in pink and purple, they have created a poetic retreat for "architects, artists, and writers." This very aesthetic creation combines the old and the new in a coherence imposed by the architects. Another relatively small house an ocean away is also divided in two. The Cosmos Pavilions (Valle de Bravo, Mexico, 2019, see page 340) by Claudia Rodríguez and Rozana Montiel is made up of a "public" structure and a "private" one, set in a forested site. Logically, the public pavilion is more open—both structures, though, look like they might have been based on existing buildings, perhaps reusing existing stone walls in the case of the private house. This is only an impression though, one of being at home in this green environment, somehow a world away from urban cares.
Two Chinese projects, one of which is published here, engage in an active dialogue with existing neighborhoods. Hutong 02 (Nanluoguxiang, Beijing, China, 2015, see page 124) by B.L.U.E. Architecture Studio involves a conversion of two miniscule (3.6 and 2.8 m²) "houses" in an old, dense residential area of the Chinese capital. Using elements such as an ingenious extendible dining table allows residents to enlarge their dining area into the neighboring courtyard. More ambitious, the renovation of Guangzhou Mengsheng House (Guangzhou, China, 2018) by the larger practice URBANUS measures 96 square meters. It is a renovation of an existing three-story brick-and-concrete building that dates from 1985. The architects cut through the floors and added skylights, bringing daylight into what was previously a gloomy house. They used small pieces of maroon stone with the exterior cladding to make the building continue to fit into its dense neighborhood. In both cases, the very tight spatial layout of Chinese cities was taken on by architects who succeeded in making small (or very small) houses more modern and comfortable.

The allure of tall but still small buildings is expressed where urban sites offer too small a footprint for lower structures. An interesting example of a new build is the 83-square-meter Towerhouse (Amsterdam, the Netherlands, 2021, see page 130) by the Croatian-Dutch architect Lada Hršak. She made use of a tiny (32 m²) site, one of the last available pieces of land in the historic part of the Dutch city. Each floor has a separate function and a selected city view, with the levels connected by a steep wooden staircase. In an unexpected way, the architect, like Sean Godsell in Australia, references modern Japanese architecture as being a source for her design. The rather hard concrete Tower House in Tokyo by Takamitsu Azuma (1966) is, indeed, well known to many architects. Hršak states: "The Azuma house, the 'grandmother' of all Tokyo's pocket houses, is a long-time source of inspiration, due to its mastery of minimal space to provide unexpected spatial richness.

Extravagant Comfort

Whereas many practical reasons have driven a worldwide trend toward smaller houses, there are also deep-seated motivations that have to do with the history of modern architecture. The Cabanon de vacances built between 1951 and 1952 at Roquebrune-Cap Martin by Le Corbusier is an obvious example of this relation. Beginning in 1948, the architect worked nearby on vacation residence schemes called Roq et Rob. Although those projects were never realized, Le Corbusier did create the only structure he ever built for himself, a cabin measuring just 3.66 × 3.66 × 2.26 meters in size in Roquebrune. Prefabricated in Corsica, the Cabanon is located near the famous house of his friend Eileen Gray (Villa E.1027, 1924), and just next to a bar called "L'Etoile de Mer" that belonged to the client for Roq et Rob, Thomas Rebutato. Built with industrial materials, and with a rough, even rustic, wood appearance, the Cabanon was an experiment with Corbu's idea of the Modulor, the system of human proportions that he invented in 1943. Despite its apparent simplicity, the Cabanon is the result of careful thought, with its furnishings arranged in a spiral pattern, for example. In 1954, Le Corbusier bought 1 290 square meters of land from Rebutato, including the Cabanon, and in return he designed and built five "Unités de camping" for his client.[4] The architect clearly

Alphaville, House of 24mm Plywood, Kyoto, Japan, 2020.

liked Roquebrune-Cap Martin and his small cabin. He said: *"J'ai un château sur la Côte d'Azur, qui fait 3,66 mètres par 3,66 mètres. C'est pour ma femme, c'est extravagant de confort, de gentillesse."* (I have a castle on the Riviera that measures 3.66 meters by 3.66 meters. It is for my wife; it is a place of extravagant comfort and kindness.) Surely, a place "where a goddess might trail her garments."

The Way of the Future

It is obvious that a small house, presumably on a small site, or sometimes a rural or wilderness setting, should cost less than a larger residence. Some are imbued with a sense of lightness and economy, like Corbu's Cabanon, while others are more solid. Many today are firmly rooted in new trends of digital design and construction. Many houses published here actively engage with current trends toward sustainability and ecological awareness. While some countries like Japan have a long history of living in small spaces, others like the United States still show a preference for larger homes. And yet economics and the realities of global warming would seem to presage an almost universal trend to decreasing floor areas per person. This kind of fact, or rather statement of simple logic, is an overriding affirmation of the importance of finding ways to create a better small environment. There are too many people on earth to permit so many to occupy so much space; the time of reckoning has already come. There must be more within a smaller envelope; there must be a healthy place of residence that does not spew poison into the world. It is not a political statement to say that a small home will be the way of the future, it is a statement of fact; homes must be smaller the longer populations rise, and the more the resources of the earth are challenged by overconsumption.

It does not require a great deal of prescience to predict that small houses will be more and more present in the future. This is for a series of very clear reasons that, of course, begin with more reasonable costs. A second factor in the popularity of small houses is that they correspond to numerous movements that encourage lowering pollution and the carbon footprint of buildings. The smaller and more ecologically responsible a house, the more virtuous the owners (and architects) can feel. Increasing populations in many countries create a pressure on available land for new construction—this has been the case for a very long time in places like Tokyo but is now a more general phenomenon. It can also be foreseen with a reasonable degree of certainty that the inventiveness of contemporary architects will be expressed very frequently in small houses. Dealing with a single open-minded client, an architect has a much greater capacity to innovate than when opposite a large company or government. It is further to be imagined that small homes will emerge in the future in the place and on the location of existing buildings, whether agricultural in rural areas, or quite simple, unobtrusive, and inexpensive in urban environments. Build on a rooftop like El Sindicato in Quito, convert a toolshed like Charles Pictet in nearly urban Geneva, when it is small, it is easier to realize, and offers the potential for whatever creativity an architect is capable of. There is no Board of Directors or Trustees in charge of the average small house, but, instead, an individual client who may not even be obliged to be wealthy to create an ideal residence—small, discrete, and, with a good architect, innovative.

The small houses published here have also proven to be a fertile ground for the use of the latest techniques in architectural design and manufacturing. Computer-driven systems, like those that can tailor CLT to any form desired, make a modern version of wood construction ideal for the small houses that are being built today. What is astonishing, as hopefully this book demonstrates on its own scale, is that small houses are an international phenomenon, ranging from New Zealand to California and back again. Closer to their sometimes natural settings, easier to obtain and build than larger homes, small houses are also an ode to the ephemeral. A small house, particularly one designed to reduce impact on the environment, can easily be removed without a trace. Prefabrication of various types is also readily applicable to the small home or to the kind of "quasi-home" represented by the kind of pavilion guest room seen in places like the Breitenbach Landscape Hotel—48° Nord (Breitenbach, France, 2020, see page 322) by Reiulf Ramstad or the Paradinha complex designed by Samuel Gonçalves (SUMMARY) in Alvarenga (Portugal, 2021, see page 430). Although these hotel-type "cabins" may not have every characteristic of a real home, they are nonetheless another manifestation of the trend toward small, independent structures for shelter and enjoyment.

Houses designed by architects are, of course, present throughout the world, but the forces that act on small homes seem to be one of the most ubiquitous and significant trends in contemporary architecture. How to resolve the issues of contemporary comfort within the smallest of envelopes; how to make people at ease in the increasingly small homes that rising populations imply. Just as Tadao Ando emerged from the creation of the Sumiyoshi Row House as an influential and ultimately world-straddling architect, so, too, many of the younger architects seen in a book like this one are likely to be the "stars" of tomorrow, formed in the crucible of smallness, ready to prove that the talents of a real architect are important even when the scale of the project is apparently insignificant. Those who imagined small houses as a kind of trifling anecdote in a world of skyscrapers and 3000-square-meter villas are invited to glance at the solutions offered for small homes in this volume. They are invited, too, to run their hands along the smooth and solid concrete walls of Tadao Ando, who offered the solidity and permanence of much larger buildings to his first small houses.

How Small a House do I Need?

Today, the question is no longer "how big a house do I need?" but rather, "how small a house do I need?" World events, including catastrophic climate episodes, and surely the pollution that drives temperature increases, originating in no small part from construction, are triggers for behavioral changes on a nearly planetary scale. The so-called tiny house movement, most firmly established in the United States, is driven in good part by a desire to tread lightly on the earth, to be able to move and adapt to an uncertain future. Population increases, particularly in urban centers, also impose the kind of rigor that the Japanese have long known—living in small spaces, living with the potential instability of the earth itself. In these circumstances, very large homes that might last for generations appear to be creatures of the past. There will always be exceptions; certainly the very wealthy are loathe to abandon the kind of grand image that goes with a big house. Nor should the cost of having even a tiny home in Tokyo seem negligible—scarcity of land drives prices to surprising heights. At the other end of the income scale, the idea of having a house at all is an impossible dream. The dwellings published here are individual houses, almost all intended for four people or less.

Less Is Still More

The question of just how little we need is not a new one; it drove Le Corbusier's Cabanon design and many other efforts to truly adapt habitat to (minimum) human requirements. Elevated today to the status of a work of art, the Cabanon is also an echo of the earliest homes on earth, huts or light constructions made with whatever materials were available. Palaces and stately homes have existed for hundreds, or rather thousands, of years, but so, in parallel, have the smallest of abodes, their trace often swept away by the passage of time. The architects involved in the houses published here may not always be the best-known figures of their generations, but it is certain that they have not reneged on what must be considered their fundamental "duties." Finding ways to make small homes comfortable and, at their best, aesthetically engaging and innovative is very much the task of the architect—how to give us more with less. The dictum "less is more" (Ludwig Mies van der Rohe, 1947) referred most directly to ornament or the lack thereof in modern architecture, yet the same phrase can readily be applied to the very contemporary concerns about architecture. Too much architecture costs too much, pollutes too much, and has become increasingly unfashionable. The key today is still "less is more" but for different reasons and in a different register than ornament. One might speculate that it is

Wonder, Intertwine House, Yanqing, Beijing, China, 2019.

precisely the architects who succeed at making very small homes that open new perspectives, who are arguably the most important figures in their profession today. The same reasoning can, of course, be applied to larger buildings that need to be less expensive and less expansive, but houses are a much more common form of construction than any bigger building type. With an inventive architect and a willing client, a small house can open horizons for the future. The culture of (over-)consumption is burning its own substance and has already begun to encounter fundamental barriers to further expansion. This societal and even scientific fact will continue to drive a worldwide trend toward small homes; they just make sense at every level.

The Only Solution

Without pretention or excessive certainty, it can be said that this book about small houses is really about the future of architecture, and, shall we be so bold, it is about the future of humanity. Learn to live in a smaller house, learn to use fewer resources and to be satisfied with what there is. There was once a dream of industrialized repetitive space, symbolized by the runaway grids implied by the Dom-Ino House of Le Corbusier. There was a political dimension to this idea, one of equality. But stating the virtues of small houses is not even political anymore, it is simply about what is now and will be possible in the future. One obvious fact is that the houses published in this book are of no particular style—instead, they have almost as many styles as there are projects. Small houses are not a matter of fashion or style; they are the result of stronger underlying forces.

Bureau LADA, Towerhouse, Amsterdam, The Netherlands, 2021.

Opposite: *Takaaki Fuji + Yuko Fuji, Bay Window Tower House, Tokyo, Japan, 2020.*

Following spread: *Prentiss + Balance + Wickline, Boathouse, Orcas Island, Washington, USA, 2021.*

Resources are running out, even as (some) populations rise. Short of war and famine, the only solution is to be smaller and more modest. The architects involved in the houses published here demonstrate with some success that small surely does not mean ugly or uncomfortable—it can, on the contrary, be an endless stimulus to creativity. Antoine de Saint-Exupéry's Little Prince asks the narrator to draw him a sheep... ***Dessine-moi un mouton...*** **May the reader ask the architect, draw me a little house.** ***Dessine-moi une petite maison...*** **For the good of the earth and its inhabitants, the small house may not be the ultimate solution, but it is a step in the right direction.**

1 *https://www.census.gov/construction/chars/highlights.html accessed on May 26, 2022.*
2 *https://www.statista.com/statistics/1255411/japan-average-size-dwellings-by-prefecture/ accessed on May 26, 2022.*
3 *https://www.housebeautiful.com/uk/lifestyle/property/a35405209/average-house-price-england-square-foot-yes-homebuyers/ accessed on May 26, 2022*
4 *http://eileengray-etoiledemer-lecorbusier.org/le-cabanon/ accessed on May 26, 2022*

Philip Jodidio

ZEICHNE MIR EIN KLEINES HAUS

Was ist ein kleines Haus und was macht es so interessant? Je nach kulturellen, wirtschaftlichen und anderen Faktoren wie zum Beispiel der Grundstücksverfügbarkeit variieren Einfamilienhäuser in ihrer Größe von Land zu Land. Ein statistischer Vergleich mag uns dabei helfen, die in diesem Band vorgestellten kleinen Häuser in Bezug zu den „Durchschnittsgrößen" dreier Länder zu setzen: So war 2020 ein Einfamilienhaus in den USA durchschnittlich 210 m² groß.[1] Vergleichen wir dies mit einer – trotz unterschiedlicher Parameter – ähnlichen Studie von 2018 über die durchschnittliche Wohnfläche pro Wohnung in Japan, erfahren wir, dass diese bei 65,9 m² (Tokio) bzw. 86,9 m² (Kyoto) liegt.[2] Eine dritte Untersuchung wiederum verweist auf 68 m² als durchschnittliche Grundstücksgröße in England.[3]

Ein moderner Trend

Für die Auswahl im Sinne dieses Buches wurde eine Gebäudeinnenfläche von weniger als 100 m² als „klein" definiert. Während ein oder zwei der hier vorgestellten Häuser diese Obergrenze überschreiten, gibt es andere, die gerade einmal erstaunliche 7 m² messen. Dass für dieses Buch mehrere Häuser in Japan ausgewählt wurden, ist nicht dem Zufall geschuldet. Kleine Häuser liegen dort bereits seit Langem im Trend, zum einen aufgrund der dichten urbanen Bebauung und zum anderen sicherlich auch, weil die Japaner daran gewöhnt sind, in Räumen zu leben, die in anderen Ländern wie Australien oder den USA als zu klein gälten. Hinzu kommt der innovative Ansatz japanischer Architekten in Bezug auf kleine Häuser. Das fast schon legendäre Sumiyoshi Row House (Azuma House, Osaka, 1976) von Tadao Ando misst lediglich 34 m² bei einer Grundstücksfläche von 57 m². Dennoch mauserte sich dieses Häuschen zum Publikationsliebling. Seine harte Betonpräsenz wird durch einen unerwarteten Innenhof abgemildert, den die Bewohner durchqueren müssen, um in ihr Schlafzimmer zu gelangen. Das Licht und die Brise, die auf diese Weise in das Haus eindringen, erwecken es zum Leben und schaffen inmitten des städtischen Trubels von Osaka eine Bühne für die „Natur". Auch zwei weitere ungewöhnliche japanische Häuschen verdienen unser besonderes Augenmerk. Da wäre zum Beispiel Love2 House (Tokio, Japan, 2019, siehe Seite 198) von Takeshi Hosaka, das es gerade einmal auf 19 m² bringt und dessen Konzept zum einen auf Schilderungen aus der Edo-Zeit über sogenannte *Nagaya* zurückgeht, extrem kleine (9,6 m²) Häuser für vierköpfige Familien. Zum anderen diente Le Corbusiers Cabanon dem Architekten als Inspirationsquelle. Hosaka schuf ein ausgeklügeltes System von sieben „kurzen Wänden", die das Haus in drei Bereiche für Küche, Essbereich und Schlafzimmer unterteilen. Ein Fenster kann zur Straße hin geöffnet werden, um Gespräche mit Passanten zu ermöglichen.

„Das Blumenbeet an der Straßenfront nutzen wir auch als Garten. In diesem Haus spüren wir die Nähe der Stadt." Die Nutzung eines straßenseitigen Blumenbeets ist eine intelligente Erweiterung des Gemeinschaftsbereichs, die das winzige Häuschen fast schon großräumig erscheinen lässt.Ein weiteres cleveres japanisches Projekt ist das 90 m² große Toolbox House (Miyakojima-ku, Osaka, 2021, siehe Seite 460) von Yoshihiro Yamamoto, das in östliche und westliche Funktionszonen unterteilt ist. Das aus verzinkten Stahlblechen, Sperrholz, Fliesen, Eichen- und japanischen Zedernholzböden, Mörtel, Tatami-Matten und Kork errichtete Haus gestattet hinsichtlich Wirtschaftlichkeit und Raumnutzung keinen Spielraum. Auch das Haus von Studio NOA in Nobeyama (Nagano, 2017) findet sich in diesem Buch wieder. Trotz seiner lediglich 38 m² Grundfläche, widmet es ein ganzes Stockwerk einem „Beobachtungsraum" mit Teleskop, das durch eine Edelstahlkuppe in den Nachthimmel blickt.

Klein ist schön

Ein Haus möchte zuallererst seine Bewohner von der Außenwelt abschirmen. Es ist ein Ort der Behaglichkeit und des Schutzes. Aber ist es nicht auch so, dass ein kleines Haus – selbst in urbaner Umgebung – seine Bewohner der natürlichen Welt näherbringt? Toyo Itos eigenes ikonisches Haus Silver Hut (Nakano-ku, Tokio, Japan, 1984) war mit perforiertem Aluminium umhüllt, ansonsten aber weitgehend von seiner chaotischen städtischen Umgebung abgeschottet – abgesehen von dem offenen Dach, das trotz der invasiven Präsenz der Stadt eine Verbindung zur Natur herstellte. Silver Hut hatte eine Grundfläche von 138 m², war also nach den Maßstäben dieses Buches ziemlich groß. Dennoch stellte es ein überzeugendes Beispiel für einen Wohnraum bescheidener Größe dar, der den direkten Kontakt mit der Natur suchte. 1973 verfasste der Wirtschaftswissenschaftler E. F. Schumacher ein bahnbrechendes Buch mit dem Titel *Small is Beautiful: Die Rückkehr zum menschlichen Maß.* Dieser Titel und der Inhalt des Buches könnten die Popularität kleiner Häuser erklären, denn entspricht nicht deren Größe einem „menschlichen Maß" und sträuben sie sich nicht gegen den Gigantismus der XXL-Residenzen, die ihren Bewohnern oft zu viel Bedeutung beimessen? Schumachers Buch stellt sich gegen das Credo „je größer, desto besser", ein in der Architektur häufig anzutreffendes

Studio Puisto, Kivijärvi Resort/Niliaitta Prototype, Kivijärvi, Finland, 2020.

Leitmotiv. Ein großes Haus suggeriert, dass darin eine ziemlich wichtige Person wohnen muss. Aber wie viel Sein steckt hinter diesem Schein? Und ist in unserer Welt überhaupt noch Platz für derartige monetäre oder architektonische Selbstdarstellungen? Es ist fraglos an der Zeit, miteinander zu teilen und darüber nachzudenken, wie wir die Nutzung von Raum und jeder anderen Ressource, die auf unserer Erde bald zu Neige gehen, reduzieren können.

Vorgefertigte Wildnis

Die Einschränkungen, die kleine Häuser mit sich bringen, führen oft zu architektonisch sehr interessanten Ergebnissen: Die Notwendigkeit vielseitig nutzbarer Räume und salopp formuliert, aus sehr wenigem das Beste herauszuholen, ist für viele Architekten ein starker Ansporn zu ungewöhnlichen Überlegungen und Entdeckungen. Als weiterer Nebeneffekt tritt hinzu, dass sich eher weniger bekannte Architekten diesen Häusertrends anschließen. Tadao Ando war 1976 noch ein recht unbeschriebenes Blatt, und in diesem Band heben sich nur einzelne Persönlichkeiten wie Bjarke Ingels (BIG) durch die Größe ihrer Büros oder ihres Portfolios hervor. Auch Tom Kundig von Olson Kundig (USA) zählt zu den ganz Großen, wir waren so frei, hier eines seiner älteren Projekte vorzustellen: die 18 m² große Gulf Islands Cabin (Gulf Islands, Britisch-Kolumbien, Kanada, 2008, siehe Seite 284). Von BIG wählten wir Klein A45 (Upstate New York, USA, 2018, siehe Seite 118), den Versuch eines vorgefertigten Luxushäuschens (17 m²). Die Vorfertigung spielt häufig eine Rolle in Planung und Bau kleiner Häuser, womöglich weil die individuelle Produktion

Casey Brown, Permanent Camping Two, Berry, New South Wales, Australia, 2020.

maßgeschneiderter Designelemente zu kostspielig ist. Fran Silvestre, vor allem bekannt für seine spektakulären (großen) weißen Häuser in Spanien, kreierte mit seiner NIU-Reihe Fertigbauten mit Größen von 70 bis 160 m² (siehe z. B. NIU N70, Valencia, Spanien, 2021, Seite 380). Mit diesen Entwürfen zeigt Silvestre, wie sich der ätherische Charakter seiner regulären Häuser auch auf kleinere Formate übertragen lässt. Eine weitere vorgefertigte Struktur, die bereits mehrmals adaptiert wurde, ist das Minimod Curucaca (Santa Catarina, Brasilien, 2017, siehe Seite 242) von MAPA Architects. Dieses 70 m² große Minimod aus Brettsperrholz und Wellblech ist in fast jeder Hinsicht nachhaltig, ein ausgeklügeltes Haus, das fast überall platziert und im PnP-Modus (Plug-and-Play) ohne übermäßig komplexe Vorbereitung genutzt werden kann. Generell hat sich Brettsperrholz, dessen Design digital entworfen und produziert wird, im Hausbau durchgesetzt, erwies sich aber vor allem bei kleinen Häusern von Vorteil, da ein ausgeklügeltes Design mehr Komfort und Umweltverträglichkeit erzeugt. Das nur 16 m² große Kynttilä (Savonlinna, Finnland, 2020, siehe Seite 292) von ORTRAUM verwendet Brettsperrholz nicht nur für seine Grundstruktur, sondern auch für die Eingangstür und Inneneinrichtung. Originelle und sorgfältig gefertigte Holzformen sind nicht mehr nur das Resultat wochenlanger Schreinerarbeit, sondern gehören nun zur breiten Produktpalette computergesteuerter Maschinen.

Todd Saunders, dessen Bauten sowohl in Norwegen als auch in Neufundland stehen, widmet sich intensiv umweltfreundlichen Fertighäuschen. Sein 17 m² großes XS Micro House (2021), als Prototyp im norwegischen Bergen gebaut, ist so konzipiert, dass seine zwölf Teile ab Fabrik an den künftigen Standort versandt werden können. Es bietet – hinter dem Bett verborgen – auch Platz für eine Küche und einen Waschraum. Dank Regenwassertank, Sonnenkollektoren und Komposttoilette ist das Haus komplett netz-unabhängig. Dem Architekten zufolge funktioniert dieses System auch bei größeren Häusern von 50 bis 100 m². Mit XS Micro House verweist Saunders auf die weit zurückreichende Tradition der bei Skandinaviern beliebten Wochenendhäuschen.

Ein Meteorit und Eisenerz

Das Meteorite (Kontiolahti, Finnland, 2020, siehe Seite 404) von Ateljé Sotamaa zieht nicht nur Nutzen aus vorgefertigten Brettsperrholzpaneelen, sondern auch aus seiner höchst ungewöhnlichen Form, in deren dicken Wänden ein Luftzwischenraum als Dämmung fungiert. Das Haus, so die Architekten, ist „durch Luft gedämmt und profitiert von natürlicher Belüftung“. Nicht nur bei diesem Projekt steht die Umwelt an erster Stelle. „Nachhaltigkeit“ ist das Thema der Stunde, während Architekten noch vor einigen Jahren Verschmutzungen, die sogar durch Kleinstbauten entstehen könnten, eher wenig Beachtung schenkten. Der bekannte brasilianische Architekt Gustavo Penna ging sogar so weit, mit einem großen Bergbauunternehmen zu kooperieren, um die Verwendungsmöglichkeiten von Eisenerzrückständen und anderen Bergbauabfällen im Gebäudebau zu untersuchen. Sein 45 m² großes nachhaltiges Haus (Ouro Branco, Minas Gerais, Brasilien, 2019, siehe Seite 298) betont mit Solarheizungen, Biokocher, Kompostieranlagen und Regenwassersammler einen umweltfreundlichen Ansatz, wie er im Allgemeinen nicht mit Bergbauunternehmen assoziiert wird. Die Annahme liegt also nahe, dass so ziemlich jeder auf den Zug mit aufspringt. Gewiss, Nachhaltigkeit mag in einem sehr kleinen Gebäude leichter zu erreichen sein als in einem sehr großen, doch allein die Tatsache, dass das Thema bei kleinen Häusern überhaupt eine Rolle spielt, ist lobenswert und in Verbindung mit etablierten Methoden zur Verringerung des CO2-Fußabdrucks auch nutzbringend. Ein weiterer Vorteil kleiner Häuser besteht darin, dass sie aufgrund ihrer relativ geringen Kosten mehr Experimentier- und Innovationsfreude wecken als ihre größeren „Verwandten“. Das House of 24 mm Plywood von Alphaville (Kyoto, Japan, 2020, siehe

Seite 46) ist ein 43 m²-Experiment mit einem einzigen, nur teilweise geteilten Raum. Bei diesem Haus, das Wohnhaus, Arbeitsplatz oder sogar Kunstgalerie sein kann, ist Sperrholz nahezu allgegenwärtig. Mit ihrem typisch japanischen Naturverständnis bringen die Architekten Licht und sogar eine frische Brise in das Haus, das in Kyoto von gedrängter Urbanität umgeben ist.

Leben in den Wäldern

Wie zu vermuten, repräsentiert Kundigs Gulf Islands Cabin eine ganz andere Häuschenkategorie: Rückzugsorte oder Waldhütten, deren geringe Größe nicht Stadtplanungszwängen, sondern der Bequemlichkeit (und manchmal auch dem Budget) geschuldet ist. Sean Godsell, ein bekannter australischer Architekt, ließ sich bei der Planung seines Shack in the Rocks (Victoria, Australien, 2021, siehe Seite 182) von einer unerwarteten Vielfalt an Inspirationsquellen leiten. Bei der Form seines 32 m²-Refugiums orientierte er sich an örtlichen Heuschobern, aber auch an Riken Yamamotos Yamakawa Cottage (Yatsugatake, Japan, 1977), dessen einteiliges Dach sowohl die Innenräume als auch den Außenbereich schützt. Beide Projekte zeugen von dem Wunsch, Zeit inmitten der Wildnis zu verbringen oder vielleicht sogar dort zu leben. Auch die Literatur trägt ihren Teil zu dieser Lebenshaltung bei wie zum Beispiel Henry David Thoreaus *Walden oder Leben in den Wäldern* (1854). Die Hütte, die der amerikanische Dichter und Philosoph 1845 in der Nähe von Concord, Massachusetts, baute und 14 Monate lang bewohnte, verdeutlicht in vielerlei Hinsicht, warum Menschen sich in einer kleinen Bleibe fernab vom Stress und Schmutz der Städte geborgen fühlen. Der Gedanke, zur Natur zurückzukehren, drängt sich wieder immer mehr in unser Bewusstsein, umso mehr als das, was von der Wildnis heute noch übrig ist, durch Verstädterung oder Luft- und Wasserverschmutzung stark bedroht ist. In einer Zeit, in der Überfluss und „Luxus" als treibende Kräfte auf Gesellschaften einwirken, verspüren immer mehr Menschen das Bedürfnis, sich auf ein absolutes Minimum zu beschränken, dauerhaft von Natur umgeben zu sein oder sie zumindest jeden Tag in irgendeiner Form in ihrem Leben zu spüren. Das bedeutet aber nicht, dass sehr kleine Häuser nicht ein hohes Maß an Komfort bieten können. Die meisten hier vorgestellten Waldhäuschen verwöhnen ihre Bewohner mit

Marte.Marte, Mountain Cabin, Laterns, Austria, 2011.

allen Annehmlichkeiten der „Zivilisation". „Ich ging in die Wälder, denn ich wollte wohlüberlegt leben und nur den wesentlichsten Dingen des Lebens gegenüberstehen", schrieb Thoreau. „Ich wollte versuchen, ob ich nicht seine Weisheiten empfangen könnte, damit ich nicht in der Todesstunde innewürde, dass ich gar nicht gelebt hatte. Nichts anderes als das Leben wollte ich leben. Das Leben ist so kostbar. Wenn es irgend möglich war, wollte ich nicht verzichten. Intensiv leben wollte ich, das Mark des Lebens in mich aufsaugen. Hart und spartanisch wollte ich leben, um alles auszurotten, was nicht Leben war, einen breiten Schwaden zu schlagen dicht über dem Boden. In die Enge wollte ich das Leben treiben und es auf die einfachste Formel bringen". Heute dürfte Thoreaus Ode an das Leben in freier Natur in weiten Teilen der Welt auf offenere Ohren stoßen als im Amerika des 19. Jahrhunderts.

Ritzenkunst

Einige kleine Häuser sind wahre Kunstwerke. So auch Keret House von Jakub Szczęsny (Warschau, Polen, 2012, siehe Seite 438). Nicht nur seine geringe Fläche von nur 12 m² ist bemerkenswert, auch seine maximale Breite von 133 Zentimeter lädt zum Staunen ein. Es zwängt sich buchstäblich in eine Ritze zwischen zwei bestehenden Gebäuden. Auf ergreifende Art gedenkt diese ungewöhnliche, nach einem israelischen Autor (Etgar Keret) benannte Struktur den Ereignissen des Zweiten Weltkrieges. Ein Modell dieses Entwurfs befindet sich als erster polnischer Architekturentwurf in der ständigen Sammlung des Museum of Modern Art (MoMA, New York, 2013). Parasitic House

selgascano, House in Los Rincones (The Nooks), La Vera, Spain, 2021.

von El Sindicato (Quito, Ecuador, 2019, siehe Seite 168) misst ebenfalls 12 m², wurde aber als Dachaufbau konstruiert. „Zwar ist es durchaus möglich, eine solche Struktur in urbanen oder ländlichen Gebieten freistehend zu bauen", so die Architekten, „doch sollte es idealerweise auf ungenutzten Dächern von städtischen, strukturell soliden Gebäuden platziert werden, um deren Wasser-, Abfall- und Strominfrastruktur mitnutzen zu können. Auf diese Weise tragen wir in kleinem Maßstab mit einem Minimum an Investitionen und Ressourcen sowohl zur Verdichtung der Stadt als auch zur Erhaltung des architektonischen Erbes bei." Ferner bietet das Häuschen jenen Menschen eine Unterkunft, die nicht über die Mittel für ein größeres Haus in der Stadt verfügen. In diesem Sinne präsentiert es sich auch als vom Erfindungsreichtum der Architekten befeuertes Element des sozialen Aktivismus.

Mad Max wird netzunabhängig

Ein besonders stark ausgeprägtes Interesse an einer ökologischen Zukunft mag gar die Entscheidung für einen komplett netzunabhängigen Lebensstil befeuern: ohne Strom und fließendes Wasser. Besonders in Australien, einem Land mit endloser Weite und unabhängiger Seele, ist Netzunabhängigkeit ganz groß in Mode. Das 94 m²-Haus mit dem treffenden Namen Off-Grid FZ House (Blue Mountains, Sydney, Australien, 2020, siehe Seite 64) wurde von Simon Anderson (Anderson Architecture) entworfen und scheint einer „Mad Max"-Kulisse entsprungen. Vorwiegend aus Beton, Faserzement und „faltbaren Brandschutzrollläden" erbaut, ist das Haus FZ-gelistet („Feuerzone"). Das ähnlich verstärkte Permanent Camping Two (Berry, New South Wales, Australien, 2020, siehe Seite 136) von Casey Brown wird von einem zweistöckigen, mit Kupfer verkleideten Turm dominiert, der Windböen und Buschfeuern standhält. Neben diesem Schutz bietet Permanent Camping Two auch Netzunabhängigkeit, da für seine Licht- und Stromversorgung Photovoltaikpaneele bereitstehen. Die Struktur ähnelt zweifellos einer kleinen Trutzburg, vor allem, wenn alle Zugänge geschlossen sind, doch bietet sie ihren Bewohnern einen herrlichen Meerblick und das Gefühl, hier vor allen – auch unausgesprochen dystopischen – Gefahren geschützt zu sein.

Vergangenheit – neu interpretiert

Auch der Umbau bestehender Strukturen, zum Beispiel kleiner Scheunen oder anderer landwirtschaftlicher Gebäude, dient vielen Architekten als Inspirationsquelle. Der Genfer Architekt Charles Pictet nahm sich vor, einen Geräteschuppen in der Nähe seines Wohnhauses in ein komplett eingerichtetes Häuschen samt Arbeitsbereich, Bett und Küche umzugestalten. Sein Atelier and Residence in a Garden Shed (Genf, Schweiz, 2021, siehe Seite 306) misst 24 m² (zzgl. eines 5 m² großen Hühnerstalls). Während er das äußere Erscheinungsbild des bestehenden Gebäudes im Wesentlichen beibehielt, gestaltete der Architekt das Innere modern und hell, ein Ansatz, der in Architektenkreisen sicherlich bereits Anhänger gefunden hat. Für dieses Projekt schwebte Pictet eine Art Refugium vor, das zweifellos diese Bezeichnung auch verdienen würde, befände es sich nicht nur 5 Meter von seinem Haus unweit des Genfer Stadtzentrums entfernt. Wir wagen daher die Vermutung, dass er sich schlichtweg auf kleinem Raum wohler fühlt als in seinem großen Haus. Ein weiteres Beispiel für diese Art der Umnutzung ist das Werk der spanischen Architekten mar plus ask (Olive Houses, Mallorca, Spanien, 2019, siehe Seite 250). Eines der beiden Olive Houses war früher ebenfalls ein Geräteschuppen, das andere wurde neu errichtet. In Rosa und Lila gehalten, bieten sie „Architekten, Künstlern und Schriftstellern" einen poetischen Rückzugsort. Diese ungemein ästhetische Schöpfung verbindet Alt und Neu in einer von den Architekten vorgegebenen Kohärenz. Nur einen Ozean von ihnen entfernt finden wir zwei andere, relativ kleine Häuser: die beiden Cosmos Pavilions (Valle de Bravo, Mexiko, 2019, siehe Seite 340) von Claudia Rodríguez und Rozana

Montiel. Die zwei Häuschen, ein „öffentliches" und ein „privates", wurden inmitten einer bewaldeten Landschaft errichtet. Wie zu erwarten, ist der öffentliche Pavillon transparenter und luftiger gestaltet. Beide Gebäude scheinen auf bestehenden Baustrukturen zu basieren, wobei für das Privathaus womöglich bereits vorhandene Steinmauern wiederverwertet wurden. Dies ist jedoch nur eine Vermutung und ein Eindruck, in dieser grünen Umgebung zu Hause zu sein, unendlich weit von allem städtischen Trubel entfernt. Zwei der hier vorgestellten chinesischen Projekte wiederum stehen in aktivem Dialog mit bestehenden Stadtvierteln. Bei Hutong 02 (Nanluoguxiang, Peking, China, 2015, siehe Seite 124) von B.L.U.E. Architecture Studio handelt es sich um den Umbau zweier winziger (3,6 und 2,8 m²) „Häuser" in einem alten, dicht besiedelten Wohngebiet der chinesischen Hauptstadt. Dank der Einrichtungselemente wie des raffinierten ausziehbaren Esstischs können die Bewohner ihren Essbereich in den benachbarten Innenhof ausweiten. Noch ehrgeiziger ist der Umbau des 96 m² großen Guangzhou Mengsheng House (Guangzhou, China, 2018) durch das größere Architekturbüro URBANUS. Im Rahmen dieser Renovierung eines bestehenden dreistöckigen Backstein- und Betongebäudes von 1985 öffneten die Architekten die Böden und fügten Oberlichter ein, um Tageslicht in das zuvor düstere Haus hereinzulassen. Für die Außenverkleidung verwendeten sie kleine kastanienbraune Steine, damit sich das Gebäude optisch in die dicht bebaute Nachbarschaft einfügt. Bei beiden Projekten nahmen sich die Architekten des arg beengten Raums chinesischer Städte erfolgreich an, indem sie kleine (oder sehr kleine) Häuser modern und komfortabel gestalteten. Der Reiz hoher, aber dennoch kleiner Gebäude ist dort besonders spürbar, wo urbane Bauflächen zu wenig Platz für niedrigere Strukturen bieten. Ein interessantes Beispiel dafür ist das 83 m² große, neu errichtete Towerhouse (Amsterdam, Niederlande, 2020, siehe Seite 130) der kroatisch-niederländischen Architektin Lada Hršak. Sie bebaute ein winziges Grundstück (32 m²), eine der letzten verfügbaren Flächen im historischen Teil Amsterdams. Jedes Stockwerk erfüllt eine eigene Funktion und bietet Ausblicke auf die Stadt, wobei eine steile Holztreppe die verschiedenen Ebenen miteinander verbindet. Wie der Australier Sean Godsell überrascht auch Lada Hršak mit ihrem Verweis auf die moderne japanische Architektur als Inspirationsquelle für ihren Entwurf. Doch in der Tat ist das vergleichsweise hart wirkende Betonturmhaus in Tokio von Takamitsu Azuma (1966) vielen Architekten wohlbekannt. „Das Azuma-Haus, die ‚Großmutter' aller Tokioter Taschenhäuser, ist schon seit Langem eine meiner Inspirationsquellen", erklärt Hršak, „denn es zaubert aus kleinstem Raum einen unerwarteten räumlichen Reichtum".

Extravaganter Komfort

Zwar beruht der weltweite Trend kleinerer Häuser auf vielerlei praktischen Gründen, doch wurzelt er auch tiefer in der Geschichte der modernen Architektur. Das zwischen 1951 und 1952 von Le Corbusier in Roquebrune-Cap Martin errichtete Cabanon de vacances entsprang offensichtlich diesem Zusammenhang. Ganz in der Nähe hatte der Architekt ab 1948 an „Roq et Rob" gearbeitet, einer serienmäßigen Herstellung von Ferienhäusern. Dieses Projekt wurde nie verwirklicht, aber Le Corbusier schuf damals das einzige Haus, das er jemals für sich selbst gebaut hat: eine nur 3,66 × 3,66 × 2,26 Meter messende Waldhütte in Roquebrune. Das auf Korsika vorgefertigte Cabanon liegt in der Nähe des berühmten Hauses seiner Freundin Eileen Gray (Villa E.1027, 1924) und direkt neben einer Bar namens „L'Etoile de Mer" von Thomas Rebutato, dem Bauherrn von Roq et Rob. Das Cabanon in rauer, ja sogar rustikaler Holzoptik wurde aus industriellen Materialien errichtet und experimentierte mit Corbusiers Idee des Modulor, seiner auf den menschlichen Maßen beruhenden Proportionslehre von 1943. Trotz seiner scheinbaren Schlichtheit ist es das Resultat sorgfältiger Überlegungen, wie zum Beispiel die spiralförmige Anordnung der Möbel zeigt. 1954 erwarb Le Corbusier von Rebutato ein 1290 m² großes Grundstück, auf dem sich auch das Cabanon befand und bedankte sich bei ihm mit fünf selbstentworfenen „Unités de camping".[4] Roquebrune-Cap Martin und seine kleine Hütte hatten es dem Architekten ganz offensichtlich angetan: *„J'ai un château sur la Côte d'Azur, qui fait 3,66 mètres par 3,66 mètres. C'est pour ma femme, c'est extravagant de confort, de gentillesse."* (Ich habe ein Schloss an der Côte d'Azur, das 3,66 Meter mal 3,66 Meter misst. Es ist für meine Frau; ein Ort extravaganten Komforts und Freundlichkeit). Gewiss ein Ort, „an dem eine Göttin die Schleppe ihrer Gewänder ausbreiten könnte".

Der Weg der Zukunft

Es liegt nahe zu vermuten, dass ein kleines Haus, sei es auf einem kleinen Grundstück, sei es in ländlicher Umgebung oder in der Wildnis errichtet, weniger kostet als ein größeres. Einige Häuschen – wie Corbusiers Cabanon – sind von einem Gefühl der Leichtigkeit und Sparsamkeit durchdrungen, andere geben sich solider. Viele wurzeln tief in den neuen Trends des digitalen Designs und Bauens. Zahlreiche der hier vorgestellten Häuser setzen sich aktiv mit aktuellen Fragen der Nachhaltigkeit und des ökologischen Bewusstseins auseinander. Während einige Länder wie Japan auf eine lange Tradition des Wohnens auf kleinem Raum zurückblicken, bevorzugen beispielsweise die USA nach wie vor größere Wohnflächen. Und doch scheinen Wirtschaft und Klimakrise eine fast universelle Marschrichtung in Richtung immer kleinerer Pro-Kopf-Grundflächen vorzugeben. Solche Tatsachen, oder vielmehr: solche auf simpler Logik beruhenden Feststellungen lassen uns keine andere Wahl, als uns Wege in eine bessere – verkleinerte – Umwelt zu bahnen. Es leben zu viele Menschen auf der Erde, als dass sie weiterhin unverhältnismäßig viel Platz für sich beanspruchen dürften. Die Zeit der Abrechnung ist bereits gekommen. Wir müssen mehr Nutzen aus kleineren Flächen ziehen. Unsere Wohngegenden müssen umweltfreundlich werden und dürfen keine Gifte mehr in die Welt hinausspeien. Wenn ich behaupte, dass kleine Häuser unsere Zukunft sind, dann ist dies kein politisches Statement, sondern eine Tatsache: Solange die Bevölkerungszahlen steigen und je mehr natürliche Ressourcen verbraucht werden, müssen Häuser kleiner werden.

Es bedarf keiner großen Weitsicht, um vorauszusagen, dass kleine Häuser immer mehr an Bedeutung gewinnen werden. Dafür gibt es eine Reihe offensichtlicher Gründe, allen voran natürlich die geringeren Kosten. An zweiter Stelle steht sicherlich ihre Kompatibilität mit den Zielen vieler Umweltbewegungen, die sich gegen Umweltverschmutzung und für die Verringerung des CO2-Fußabdrucks von Gebäuden einsetzen. Und je kleiner und ökologisch verantwortungsvoller ein Haus, desto tugendhafter dürfen sich Bewohner (und Architekten) fühlen. Die wachsende Bevölkerung in vielen Ländern führt zum erhöhten Wettbewerb um verfügbare Grundstücke für Neubauten. In Städten wie Tokio ist dies schon seit Langem der Fall, aber nun stehen wir vor einem globalen Phänomen. Ebenfalls mit ziemlicher Sicherheit absehbar ist, dass der Erfindungsreichtum der zeitgenössischen Architekten immer öfter in Entwürfen kleiner Häuser münden wird. Ein Architekt, der es mit einem einzelnen aufgeschlossenen Bauherrn zu tun hat, kann seine Innovationsfähigkeit viel besser entfalten als gegenüber einem großen Unternehmen oder einer Regierung. Es ist ferner vorstellbar, dass künftig kleine Häuser bestehende Gebäude für sich nutzen, sei es in ländlichen Gebieten oder ganz einfach, unauffällig und kostengünstig inmitten einer Stadt. Ob auf einem Dach wie El Sindicato in Quito oder als Charles Pictets umgebauter Geräteschuppen in Genf – Kleines lässt sich einfacher realisieren und fordert das kreative Potenzial eines Architekten heraus. Für das durchschnittliche Minihaus muss kein Verwaltungsrat oder Treuhänder eingesetzt werden. Es braucht nur einen einzelnen Bauherrn, der nicht einmal besonders wohlhabend sein muss, um sich sein ideales Domizil zu schaffen: klein, diskret und, falls er einen guten Architekten an seiner Seite weiß, innovativ.

Die hier vorgestellten kleinen Häuser haben sich auch als fruchtbarer Boden für die neuesten Techniken in architektonischer Gestaltung und Fertigung erwiesen. Dank computergesteuerter Systeme, beispielsweise zum Zuschneiden von Brettsperrholz in jede gewünschte Form, dienen moderne Holzhausversionen heute als Idealvorlage kleiner Häuser. Erstaunlich ist, dass sich Kleinbauten zu einem internationalen Phänomen entwickelt haben, das von Neuseeland bis Kalifornien und wieder zurück reicht – ein Umstand, den dieses Buch hoffentlich angemessen veranschaulicht. Näher an ihrer (natürlichen) Umgebung, einfacher zu erhalten und zu bauen als größere Gebäude, lesen sich kleine Häuser auch als Ode an das Vergängliche. Ein kleines Haus, insbesondere eines, dessen Konzept die Umwelt so wenig wie möglich belastet, lässt sich leicht und spurlos wieder entfernen. Die verschiedenen Arten der Vorfertigung sind auch für kleine Wohnhäuser oder „Quasi-Wohnhäuser" unkompliziert anwendbar, so zum Beispiel das Breitenbach Landscape Hotel-48° Nord (Breitenbach, Frankreich, 2020, siehe Seite 322) von Reiulf Ramstad oder der Paradinha-Komplex in Alvarenga (Portugal, 2021, siehe Seite 430) von Samuel Gonçalves (SUMMARY). Auch wenn diese Minilodges nicht alle Merkmale eines „echten" Hauses aufweisen, so sind sie doch

Ausdruck des Trends zu kleinen individuellen Erlebnisunterkünften.

Architektenhäuser gibt es natürlich überall auf der Welt, aber die Dynamik kleiner Wohnhäuser scheint momentan in der zeitgenössischen Architektur allgegenwärtig. Wie lassen sich die Fragen des modernen Komforts auf kleinstem Raum lösen? Wie können die Menschen sich in immer kleineren Wohnungen wohlfühlen, die ihnen aufgrund wachsender Bevölkerungszahlen nur noch zur Verfügung stehen? So wie Tadao Ando mit seinem Sumiyoshi Row House zum einflussreichen und letztlich weltberühmten Architekten avancierte, so sind wohl auch viele der jüngeren Architekten, die in einem Buch wie diesem vorgestellt werden, die „Stars" von morgen. Geformt im Schmelztiegel der Kleinheit sind sie bereit zu beweisen, dass die notwendigen Talente eines echten Architekten nichts mit der Größe eines Projekts zu tun haben. Jene, die bislang kleine Häuser für belanglose Anekdoten in einer Welt voller Wolkenkratzer und 3000-Quadratmeter-Villen gehalten haben, seien hiermit eingeladen, sich den in diesem Band versammelten Entwürfen zu widmen. Und wer weiß: Vielleicht packt sie dann auch die Lust, mit ihren Händen an Tadao Andos glatten und soliden Betonwänden entlangzufahren und jene Solidität und Beständigkeit zu spüren, die auch viel größeren Gebäuden zu eigen ist.

Wie klein soll mein Haus sein?

Heute lautet die Frage nicht mehr „Wie groß soll mein Haus sein?", sondern vielmehr „Wie klein soll mein Haus sein?" Globale Ereignisse wie Klimakatastrophen und sicherlich auch die Umweltverschmutzung, die den Temperaturanstieg vorantreibt und zu einem nicht unerheblichen Teil durch die Bauindustrie verursacht wird, lösen Verhaltensänderungen in nahezu planetarischem Ausmaß aus. Die sogenannte und vor allem in den USA stark etablierte Tiny-House-Bewegung wird weitgehend von dem Wunsch angetrieben, die Erde zu schonen und sich einer ungewissen Zukunft anzupassen. Der Bevölkerungsanstieg, insbesondere in den Städten, erzwingt auch eine Kompromisslosigkeit, die für Japaner seit jeher an der Tagesordnung ist: Leben auf engem Raum, Leben mit der potenziellen Instabilität der Erde. Unter diesen Umständen scheinen sehr große Häuser, die Generationen überdauern, der Vergangenheit anzugehören. Sicherlich, Ausnahmen

Gustavo Penna, Sustainable House, Ouro Branco, Minas Gerais, Brazil, 2019.

Following pages: *ORTRAUM, Kynttilä, Savonlinna, Finland, 2020.*

wird es immer geben. Die Reichen werden nur ungern auf das pompöse Image verzichten, das mit einem ausgedehnten Anwesen einhergeht. Auch sind die Kosten für ein winziges Haus in Tokio nicht zu vernachlässigen, denn die Grundstücksknappheit treibt die Preise in verblüffende Höhen. Am anderen Ende der Einkommensskala präsentiert sich die Vorstellung, überhaupt jemals ein Haus zu besitzen, als unmöglicher Traum. Bei den hier vorgestellten Wohnstätten handelt es sich um Einzelhäuser, die fast alle für vier Personen oder weniger konzipiert sind.

Weniger ist immer noch mehr

Die Frage, wie wenig wir eigentlich brauchen, ist nicht neu. Sie stand Pate für Le Corbusiers Cabanon-Entwurf und für viele andere Bemühungen, den Lebensraum effektiv an die (minimalen) menschlichen Bedürfnisse anzupassen. Das heute als Kunstwerk geltende Cabanon ist auch ein Echo der frühesten Behausungen, Hütten oder Leichtbauten, die nur mit jenem Material gebaut wurden, das eben gerade zur Verfügung stand. So wie es Paläste und Herrenhäuser seit Hunderten oder gar Tausenden von Jahren schon gibt, existieren auch die kleinsten Wohnstätten seit Anbeginn der Zeit, auch wenn ihre Spuren oft im Laufe der Zeit verweht wurden. Die Architekten der hier vorgestellten Häuser sind vielleicht nicht immer die bekanntesten ihrer Generation, aber sicher ist, dass sie sich nicht vor dem gedrückt haben, was als ihre grundlegende „Pflicht" gelten muss: Wege zu finden, kleine Häuser komfortabel und im besten Fall ästhetisch ansprechend und innovativ zu gestalten. Um für uns mit weniger ein Mehr zu schaffen. Das Diktum „Weniger ist mehr“ (Ludwig Mies van der Rohe, 1947) bezog sich vor allem auf das Ornament bzw. dessen Fehlen in der modernen Architektur, doch lässt sich der Satz auch ohne Weiteres auf die gegenwärtigen Herausforderungen in der Architektur anwenden. Zu viel Architektur ist zu teuer, zu schmutzig und zu unmodern. „Weniger ist mehr“, liefert auch heute noch die Lösung, aber aus anderen Gründen und auf anderer Ebene als der ornamentalen. Die Annahme sei gewagt, dass gerade die Architekten, die mit ihren winzigen Häusern erfolgreich neue Perspektiven schaffen, heute zu den wohl wichtigsten Vertretern ihres Berufs gehören. Die gleichen Überlegungen lassen sich auf größere, aber schlichte Bauten mit kleinem Budget anwenden, doch werden Privathäuser häufiger gebaut als größere Strukturen. Mit einem erfinderischen Architekten und einem willigen Bauherrn kann ein kleines Haus neue Horizonte für die Zukunft eröffnen. Die Kultur des (übermäßigen) Konsums verbrennt sich selbst und ihre Ausweitung stößt schon jetzt auf grundlegende Hindernisse. Diese gesellschaftliche und sogar wissenschaftliche Tatsache wird den weltweiten Trend zu kleinen Häusern weiter vorantreiben, denn ihre Vorteile sind umfassend und unbestreitbar.

Die einzige Lösung

Ohne Überheblichkeit oder übertriebene Gewissheit lässt sich behaupten, dass dieses Buch im Grunde von der Zukunft der Architektur handelt und, gestatten Sie mir die Kühnheit, auch von der Zukunft der Menschheit. Lernen Sie, in einem kleineren Haus zu leben, lernen Sie, weniger Ressourcen zu verbrauchen und mit dem zufrieden zu sein, was vorhanden ist. Der einstige Traum vom industrialisierten monotonen Raum symbolisiert durch durchgehende Raster und angedeutet in Corbusiers Dom-Ino-Haus. Diese Idee war auch von politischer Dimension, nämlich von einer Dimension der Gleichheit. Aber um reine Politik geht es bei den Vorteilen kleiner Häuser schon lange nicht mehr. Es geht schlichtweg darum, was heute und in Zukunft möglich ist. Offensichtlich gehören die in diesem Buch vorgestellten Häuser keiner bestimmten Stilrichtung an, im Gegenteil. Hier finden sich so viele Stile wie Projekte. Mode oder Stil sind kleinen Häusern egal. Sie werden von stärkeren, grundlegenden Kräften erschaffen. Ressourcen gehen zur Neige, während die (meisten) Bevölkerungen wachsen. Abgesehen von Krieg und Hungersnot besteht die einzige mögliche Antwort auf diese Situation darin, kleiner und bescheidener zu sein. Die Architekten der hier präsentierten Häuser beweisen uns erfolgreich, dass „klein“ gewiss nicht hässlich oder ungemütlich heißt, sondern ein anhaltender Anreiz für Kreativität sein kann. Antoine de Saint-Exupérys kleiner Prinz bittet den Erzähler, ihm ein Schaf zu zeichnen ... *Dessine-moi un mouton* ... In diesem Sinne: Bitten Sie Ihren Architekten, Ihnen ein kleines Haus zu zeichnen. *Dessine-moi une petite maison* ... Zum Wohle der Erde und ihrer Bewohner mag das kleine Haus nicht die ultimative Lösung sein, aber es ist ein Schritt in die richtige Richtung.

1 *https://www.census.gov/construction/chars/highlights.html abgerufen am 26. Mai 2022.*
2 *https://www.statista.com/statistics/1255411/japan-average-size-dwellings-by-prefecture/ abgerufen am 26. Mai 2022.*
3 *https://www.housebeautiful.com/uk/lifestyle/property/a35405209/average-house-price-england-square-foot-yes-homebuyers/ abgerufen am 26. Mai 2022.*
4 *http://eileengray-etoiledemer-lecorbusier.org/le-cabanon/ abgerufen am 26. Mai 2022.*

Philip Jodidio

DESSINE-MOI UNE PETITE MAISON

Qu'est-ce qu'une petite maison, et quel est son intérêt ? La taille des habitations individuelles varie selon les pays, pour des raisons culturelles et économiques, ou pour d'autres facteurs tels que les terrains disponibles. Une comparaison statistique suffit pour se rendre compte dans quels pays les petites maisons publiées ici entrent dans les catégories « moyennes » : les États-Unis, le Japon et l'Angleterre. La taille moyenne d'une maison individuelle complète aux États-Unis en 2020 était de 210 m² [1]. Malgré une base statistique différente, elle peut être comparée à une étude semblable de la surface au sol moyenne par logement au Japon en 2018, qui a obtenu les chiffres de 65,9 m² à Tokyo et 86,9 m² à Kyoto[2]. De même, à partir d'une base elle aussi légèrement différente, la recherche a montré que la taille moyenne d'une propriété en Angleterre est de 68 m² [3].

Une tendance moderne

Pour la sélection présentée ici, « petit » a été défini comme disposant d'une surface intérieure au sol de moins de 100 m². Si l'une ou l'autre des maisons publiées ici dépasse cette limite, d'autres présentent la taille incroyablement minuscule de 7 m². On trouve un certain nombre de projets japonais dans les pages qui suivent, ce qui n'est pas un hasard – la tendance dans le pays est depuis longtemps aux petites maisons du fait de l'urbanisation très dense, et sans doute aussi parce que les Japonais ont l'habitude de vivre dans des espaces probablement considérés comme trop petits dans d'autres pays, de l'Australie aux États-Unis. Les architectes japonais ont, par conséquent, adopté depuis de nombreuses années une approche innovante en matière de petites maisons. La maison mitoyenne à Sumiyoshi (maison Azuma, Osaka, 1976) de Tadao Ando, aujourd'hui presque légendaire, présente une surface au sol de seulement 34 m² sur une parcelle de 57 m². Elle a pourtant fait l'objet de milliers de publications. Sa présence de béton coulé sur place est adoucie par une surprenante cour centrale qui oblige les habitants à sortir pour rejoindre leurs chambres. Cependant, l'air et la lumière qui entrent ainsi donnent vie à la maison et y font pleinement entrer la « nature », malgré la congestion urbaine à Osaka.
Deux autres petites maisons japonaises particulièrement remarquables méritent l'attention. La première est la maison Love2 (Tokyo, 2019, voir page 198) de Takeshi Hosaka, qui ne pèse pas plus dans la balance que 19 petits m². L'architecte s'est appuyé sur des récits de la période Edo où des familles de quatre personnes vivaient dans de minuscules *nagayas* (9,6 m²) pour son concept de maison minuscule, et il cite aussi comme source le Cabanon de Le Corbusier. L'ensemble comprend un système ingénieux de sept « murs courts » qui divisent la maison en trois espaces destinés à accueillir la cuisine, la salle à manger et la chambre. Une fenêtre sur la rue peut être ouverte pour favoriser la

discussion avec les passants. « La rue devant la maison a un parterre de fleurs dont nous profitons comme si c'était notre jardin. Dans cette maison, nous sentons que la ville est toute proche. » Cette extension astucieuse dans l'espace public qui tire profit d'un parterre côté rue fait paraître plus généreuses les dimensions de la toute petite maison. La Toolbox House ou Maison boîte à outils de 90 m² (Miyakojima-ku, Osaka, 2021, voir page 460) construite par Yoshihiro Yamamoto est un autre projet japonais très intelligent. Les différentes fonctions domestiques y sont divisées en une partie est et une partie ouest. Construite en feuille d'acier galvanisé, contreplaqué, carrelage, chêne et cèdre du Japon pour le sol, mortier, tatamis et liège, elle témoigne d'une grande rigueur, tant sur le plan économique que sur celui de l'exploitation de l'espace. Enfin, une troisième maison japonaise mérite d'être citée ici, celle de Studio NOA à Nobeyama (Nagano, 2017) dont l'espace au sol ne compte que 38 m², mais dont un étage entier est occupé par une « salle d'observation » où un télescope permet d'observer le ciel nocturne par une coupole en acier inoxydable.

Small is Beautiful

Bien sûr, une maison isole du monde extérieur ses habitants, auxquels elle procure confort et protection. Se pourrait-il qu'une petite maison, même dans un milieu urbain, rapproche ses habitants de la nature? La résidence personnelle emblématique de Toyo Ito, Silver Hut (Nakano-ku, Tokyo, 1984), est enveloppée d'aluminium perforé mais est par ailleurs très largement fermée à la confusion de l'environnement urbain, à l'exception du toit ouvert qui crée un lien avec la nature malgré la présence envahissante de la ville. La surface au sol est de 138 m², soit plutôt grande pour les limites fixées ici, mais elle constitue un bon exemple de maison de taille modeste qui incarne l'idée du contact direct avec la nature. L'économiste E. F. Schumacher a fait école en 1973 avec son livre *Small is Beautiful : Une société à la mesure de l'homme.* Ce titre et l'ouvrage lui-même pourraient bien fournir une explication de la faveur dont jouissent les petites maisons – c'est parce qu'elles sont pour l'essentiel conçues « à la mesure de l'homme » qu'elles sont populaires, elles ne sont pas surdimensionnées pour donner trop d'importance à certains individus. Le texte de Schumacher rejette l'idée

Norgeshus, The Bolder, Stavanger-Lysefjord, Norway, 2020.

du « bigger is better », un *leitmotiv* fréquent en architecture. Une grande maison témoigne sans doute de l'importance de son propriétaire, mais est-ce vraiment toujours le cas ? Et ces manifestations d'egos financiers ou architecturaux ont-elles encore lieu d'être ? Il est définitivement temps de partager, de penser à réduire notre consommation d'espace au même titre que toutes les autres ressources qui seront bientôt épuisées sur terre.

Déserts préfabriqués

Les contraintes imposées par les petites maisons donnent souvent des résultats très intéressants en ce qui concerne l'architecture : les espaces multi-usages, et plus généralement le fait de tirer le maximum du minimum, sont de puissants moteurs d'exploration et de découverte pour beaucoup d'architectes. Sans compter un autre effet secondaire de la construction à petite échelle, le petit nombre d'architectes de renom qui s'y lancent. Tadao Ando n'était pas encore célèbre en 1976 et seules quelques-unes des personnalités présentées ici sortent du lot par l'importance de leurs agences, la composition de leur portefeuille de réalisations – comme Bjarke Ingels (BIG). L'Américain Tom Kundig d'Olson Kundig est l'une de ces agences vedettes et nous avons pris la liberté de traiter l'un de ses projets plus anciens, la cabane des îles Gulf de 18 m² (îles Gulf, Colombie-Britannique, Canada, 2008, voir page 284). Le projet de BIG, lui, est intitulé Klein A45 (nord de l'État de New York, 2018, voir page 118) et constitue une tentative de préfabriquer une petite maison (17 m²) de luxe.

Barry Connor, Skylark Cabin, Twizel, New Zealand, 2020.

La préfabrication est, de fait, une technique assez courante dans la conception et la construction des petites maisons, peut-être en raison du coût des éléments sur mesure produits à l'échelle individuelle. Fran Silvestre, surtout connu pour ses sublimes (et immenses) villas blanches en Espagne, a innové lui aussi avec ses maisons NIU – des habitations préfabriquées dont la taille varie de 70 à 160 m² (voir par exemple NIU N70, Valence, Espagne, 2021, page 380). Silvestre apporte ici la preuve que la pureté éthérée qui caractérise ses vastes demeures peut être traduite efficacement dans des formats plus petits.
Une autre structure préfabriquée a déjà connu plusieurs adaptations, la Minimod Curucaca (Santa Catarina, Brésil, 2017, voir page 242) par les architectes de MAPA. Construite en bois d'œuvre lamellé croisé (CLT) et métal ondulé, la petite maison de 70 m² est durable à presque tous les égards. Construction raffinée, elle peut être installée à peu près n'importe où et utilisée sur le mode PnP *(plug-and-play)* sans nécessiter de préparation excessive. Le bois CLT, créé et fabriqué numériquement, est aujourd'hui assez courant dans la construction, mais profite particulièrement aux petites maisons auxquelles un design plus complexe apporte toujours plus de confort et une meilleure compatibilité environnementale. Kynttilä (Savonlinna, Finlande, 2020, voir page 292) par ORTRAUM, qui ne mesure que 16 m², a fait le choix du CLT pour la structure, mais aussi pour la porte d'entrée et le mobilier intérieur : les machines assistées par ordinateur donnent désormais plus largement accès à des formes en bois originales et ouvragées avec soin qu'un menuisier qualifié mettrait des semaines à réaliser.

Todd Saunders, qui a construit en Norvège et à Terre-Neuve, s'est lancé activement sur la voie des petites maisons préfabriquées et écoresponsables. Sa micro-maison XS de 17 m² (2021), dont un prototype a été construit à Bergen, en Norvège, est conçue pour être fabriquée en usine sous forme de douze éléments et acheminée sur place. Elle se compose d'une cuisine et salle d'eau derrière un lit. La récupération de l'eau de pluie, des panneaux solaires et des toilettes à compost lui permettent de fonctionner entièrement hors réseau. L'architecte explique que le système peut servir à assembler de plus grandes habitations, de 50 à 100 m².
Les Scandinaves entretiennent une grande tradition de petites maisons, souvent sous forme de retraites pour le week-end, à laquelle Saunders fait référence avec ce type de projet.

Une météorite et du minerai de fer

La Meteorite (Kontiolahti, Finlande, 2020, voir page 404) d'Ateljé Sotamaa a recours à des panneaux préfabriqués en CLT et présente par ailleurs une forme extrêmement inhabituelle. Les murs épais permettent d'utiliser la couche d'air en guise d'isolation. La maison, expliquent les architectes, « est isolée par l'air et utilise la ventilation naturelle ». Ici comme dans de nombreux autres cas, les questions d'environnement ont gagné le devant de la scène. « Durabilité » est désormais le maître-mot, alors qu'il y a quelques années encore, les architectes n'auraient sans doute prêté aucune attention aux pollutions multiples que même une toute petite construction peut potentiellement générer. L'architecte brésilien de renom Gustavo Penna a été jusqu'à collaborer avec une grande compagnie minière afin de trouver une manière d'utiliser les restes de minerai de fer et d'autres déchets miniers dans le bâtiment. Sa Casa Sustentável, Maison durable de 45 m² (Ouro Branco, Minas Gerais, Brésil, 2019, voir page 298) a également recours au chauffage solaire, aux biodigesteurs, aux composts et à la récupération de l'eau de pluie pour mettre en avant une approche écologique qui n'est généralement pas associée aux compagnies minières. On pourrait dire que cela montre à quel point le mouvement est général. S'il est sans doute plus facile de construire une petite structure durable qu'un immense bâtiment, le fait même que la question soit aussi posée pour les petites maisons est positif en soi et portera

certainement ses fruits si un nombre suffisant d'habitations appliquent les méthodes connues pour réduire leur empreinte carbone.
Du fait des budgets relativement faibles, les petites maisons présentent un autre avantage, celui de permettre un niveau d'expérimentation et d'innovation supérieur par rapport à leurs « grandes sœurs ». La Maison en contreplaqué de 24 mm d'Alphaville (Kyoto, Japon, 2020, voir page 46) fait ainsi l'expérience dans 43 m² d'un espace non différencié et pourtant en partie divisé. Le bâtiment, où le contreplaqué est le matériau le plus visible, peut servir de domicile, de lieu de travail, ou même de galerie. À l'aide d'une approche de la « nature » typiquement japonaise, les architectes font entrer la lumière et le vent à l'intérieur, alors que la maison se trouve dans un quartier densément peuplé de Kyoto.

La vie dans les bois

La cabane des îles Gulf de Kundig incarne une catégorie fondamentalement différente de petites maisons : celle des retraites, refuges ou cabanes dans les bois dont la petite taille s'explique par un souci de commodité (et parfois de budget), et non par la densité urbaine. Le célèbre architecte australien Sean Godsell a notamment imaginé sa Shack in the Rocks (Cabane dans les rochers, Victoria, Australie, 2021, voir page 182) à partir d'inspirations étonnamment diverses. Il s'est tourné vers les granges locales pour la forme de son abri de 32 m², mais aussi vers la maison de campagne Yamakawa de Riken Yamamoto (Yatsugatake, Japon, 1977) pour la manière dont la toiture unique abrite à la fois les espaces intérieurs et l'espace extérieur.
Les deux projets évoquent le désir de passer du temps, et peut-être même de vivre, dans un endroit désert.
La littérature ne manque pas d'exemples de ce choix qui peuvent être ramenés à *Walden ou la vie dans les bois* de Henry David Thoreau (1854). La cabane que le poète et philosophe américain bâtit près de Concord, dans le Massachusetts, en 1845, et dans laquelle il vécut quatorze mois symbolise à bien des égards les raisons pour lesquelles des hommes et des femmes se réfugient dans de minuscules logements, loin du stress et de la pollution des villes. L'idée du retour à la nature est aujourd'hui plus répandue que jamais, depuis que ce qui reste comme endroits déserts est gravement menacé par l'urbanisation ou les

Sean Godsell, Shack in the Rocks, Victoria, Australia, 2021.

substances que la vie « moderne » répand dans l'air et dans les eaux. En effet, lorsque l'excès et le « luxe » deviennent les forces motrices des sociétés, le besoin de revenir à un minimum absolu, de vivre à l'opposé du soleil levant ou d'entendre chaque jour le bruit de la nature augmente. Cela ne veut pas dire que les toutes petites maisons ou les refuges n'offrent aucun confort – en fait, la plupart de celles présentées ici possèdent bel et bien tous les agréments de la « civilisation ». Selon les mots de Thoreau : « Je gagnai les bois parce que je voulais vivre suivant mûre réflexion, n'affronter que les actes essentiels de la vie, et voir si je ne pourrais apprendre ce qu'elle avait à enseigner, non pas, quand je viendrais à mourir, découvrir que je n'avais pas vécu. Je ne voulais pas vivre ce qui n'était pas la vie, la vie est si chère ; pas plus que je ne voulais pratiquer la résignation, s'il n'était tout à fait nécessaire. Ce qu'il me fallait, c'était vivre abondamment, sucer toute la moelle de la vie, vivre assez résolument, assez en Spartiate, pour mettre en déroute tout ce qui n'était pas la vie, couper un large andain et tondre ras, acculer la vie dans un coin, la réduire à sa plus simple expression [...] » Son ode à la vie dans la nature pourrait résonner encore plus aujourd'hui dans nombre de pays que dans l'Amérique du XIXe siècle.

L'art dans les interstices

Beaucoup de petites maisons entrent davantage dans la catégorie des œuvres d'art que dans celle de l'architecture pure. C'est le cas de la maison Keret de Jakub Szczęsny (Varsovie, 2012, voir page 438). Elle ne mesure que 12 m², mais c'est aussi sa largeur maximale de 133 cm qui la

baumraum, Dark Room, Ruinen, The Netherlands, 2020.

rend remarquable. Elle est littéralement coincée dans une fente entre deux immeubles à Varsovie. Elle porte le nom d'un auteur israélien (Etgar Keret) et cette présence inattendue en Pologne est aussi une évocation poignante de la Seconde Guerre mondiale. Le modèle réduit de la maison Keret a été le premier projet architectural polonais à entrer dans la collection permanente du Museum of Modern Art (New York, 2013).
La Casa parásito, Maison parasite d'El Sindicato (Quito, Équateur, 2019, voir page 168) ne fait elle aussi que 12 m², mais elle est placée sur le toit d'une autre maison. Les architectes expliquent que « s'il est possible de réaliser ce type de projet en zone rurale ou urbaine sans autre construction, l'idéal est d'utiliser les toits sous-exploités d'immeubles en ville aux structures solides – ce qui permet aussi de se raccorder aux réseaux existants d'eau, d'électricité et de traitement des déchets. Nous contribuons ainsi à la densification de la ville à une toute petite échelle pour un investissement et des ressources réduits au minimum, ainsi qu'à la préservation du patrimoine architectural ». Si une petite maison en milieu urbain contribue, certes, à la « densification », elle permet aussi à ceux qui n'ont pas les moyens de construire plus grand de se loger. La petite maison devient ici un instrument de militantisme social nourri par l'inventivité des architectes.

Mad Max se déconnecte

Tous ceux que l'avenir écologique intéresse plus particulièrement peuvent s'aventurer encore plus loin dans le désert, jusqu'au point où l'approvisionnement en électricité et l'eau courante cessent d'être assurés et où il est possible d'opter résolument pour le « hors réseau ». L'Australie, ses immenses territoires et son esprit indépendant, est l'une des régions par excellence où la vie hors réseau est très prisée. Le projet bien nommé Off-Grid FZ (montagnes Bleues, Sydney, 2020, voir page 64) en est un exemple, une maison de 94 m² conçue par Simon Anderson (Anderson Architecture). Faite pour l'essentiel de béton, fibrociment et « volets coupe-feu coulissants, rabattables et roulants », elle est classée FZ pour « fire zone » ou « zone de feu ». On pourrait, sans rire, y voir une préparation au Meilleur des mondes de *Mad Max*. Le projet de Permanent Camping Two (Camping permanent deux, Berry, Nouvelle-Galles-du-Sud, 2020, voir page 136) de Casey Brown, non moins protégé, exhibe une tour de deux étages revêtue de cuivre qui résiste aux vents soufflant en tempête et aux incendies du bush. En plus de cette protection, l'ensemble est aussi hors réseau et dispose de panneaux photovoltaïques pour la lumière et l'électricité. La construction présente incontestablement un aspect fortifié lorsqu'elle est entièrement fermée, mais elle offre aussi à ses propriétaires une splendide vue sur la mer et un sentiment de sécurité face à tous les dangers, même les plus dystopiques.

Reprendre le passé

La rénovation de constructions existantes, notamment de petites granges ou d'autres bâtiments agricoles, est aussi une source d'inspiration pour de nombreux architectes. Le Genevois Charles Pictet a, par exemple, relevé le défi de transformer une cabane à outils près de sa maison en un logis complet avec un espace de travail, un lit et une cuisine. Son atelier et logement dans un abri de jardin (Genève, 2021, voir page 306) mesurent 24 m² (plus un poulailler de 5 m²). L'architecte n'a pas fondamentalement modifié l'aspect extérieur du bâtiment existant, mais il en a rendu l'intérieur clair et moderne, et on comprend que d'autres architectes lui emboîtent déjà le pas sur cette voie. Pictet a imaginé ici ce qu'on pourrait appeler un refuge s'il n'était pas à 5 m de sa maison, non loin du centre de Genève. Sans doute se sent-il bien dans un petit espace, peut-être même mieux que dans sa grande maison ?
Parmi les autres exemples de reconversion, on peut citer le travail des architectes espagnols

mar plus ask, les maisons de l'Olive (Majorque, Espagne, 2019, voir page 250). L'une des petites structures était aussi une cabane à outils, tandis que l'autre est une nouvelle construction. En leur donnant les couleurs rose et violet, leurs créateurs ont donné naissance à une retraite pleine de poésie pour des « architectes, artistes et écrivains ». Ils ont su ici imposer une cohérence à cette association très esthétique de l'ancien et du nouveau. Une autre maison de taille relativement réduite, de l'autre côté de l'océan, est elle aussi divisée en deux : les Pabellones Cosmos, les pavillons Cosmos (Valle de Bravo, Mexique, 2019, voir page 340) par Claudia Rodríguez et Rozana Montiel sont composés d'une structure « commune » et d'une « privée », construites sur un terrain boisé. Le pavillon commun est, logiquement, plus ouvert mais les deux bâtiments donnent l'impression d'avoir été construits à partir de bâtiments existants, avec par exemple des murs de pierre qui pourraient avoir été réutilisés dans la partie privée. Ce n'est cependant qu'une impression, celle d'être chez soi dans ce décor de verdure que tout un monde sépare des soucis de la vie en ville.

Deux projets chinois publiés ici ouvrent un dialogue actif avec leurs voisinages. Hutong 02 (Nanluoguxiang, Pékin, 2015, voir page 124) par B.L.U.E. Architecture Studio est une reconversion de deux minuscules « maisons » (3,6 et 2,8 m^2) dans un quartier résidentiel ancien et très dense de la capitale chinoise. Des éléments particuliers comme la table à rallonges permettent aux habitants d'étendre la salle à manger à la cour voisine. La rénovation de la maison Mengsheng à Guangzhou (2018) par la grande agence URBANUS est plus ambitieuse avec 96 m^2. Il s'agissait de remettre en état une construction à trois étages en briques et béton de 1985. Les architectes ont coupé dans les plaques de sol et ajouté des lucarnes pour faire entrer la lumière du jour à l'intérieur, qui était auparavant assez sombre. Ils ont choisi de petites pierres couleur bordeaux pour le mur extérieur afin que la maison reste assortie aux constructions de ce quartier très dense. Dans les deux cas, les architectes ont tenu compte de la configuration spatiale compacte des villes chinoises et ont réussi à rendre plus modernes et confortables de petites (ou toutes petites) maisons.

Le charme des bâtiments en hauteur, néanmoins petits, apparaît lorsque des parcelles urbaines ne disposent que d'une empreinte au sol trop petite pour des constructions plus basses. L'un des exemples intéressants de ce type de nouvelle construction est la Tour de 83 m^2 (Amsterdam, 2021, voir page 130) par l'architecte croato-néerlandaise Lada Hršak. Elle a été bâtie sur un terrain minuscule (32 m^2), l'un des derniers encore disponibles dans le centre historique d'Amsterdam. Chaque étage remplit une fonction distincte et offre une vue définie sur la ville ; ils sont reliés par un escalier en bois très raide. L'architecte surprend ici, comme Sean Godsell en Australie, en citant l'architecture japonaise moderne comme source d'inspiration – la sévère Tour en béton construite à Tokyo par Takamitsu Azuma (1966) est bien connue de nombreux architectes. Hršak explique que « la maison d'Azuma, la "grand-mère" de toutes les maisons de poche de Tokyo, est l'une de nos sources d'inspiration depuis longtemps avec sa maîtrise de l'espace minimal qui produit une richesse spatiale inattendue ».

Un confort extravagant

Si de nombreuses raisons pratiques sont à l'origine de la tendance mondiale aux petites maisons, d'autres profondément ancrées dans l'histoire de l'architecture moderne l'expliquent aussi. Le Cabanon de vacances construit de 1951 à 1952 à Roquebrune-Cap-Martin par Le Corbusier est un exemple évident. L'architecte travaille alors depuis 1948 à un projet de résidences de vacances appelées Roq et Rob. Ces dernières ne seront jamais construites, mais il créera à Roquebrune le seul bâtiment qu'il a jamais réalisé pour son usage personnel, une cabane de seulement 3,66 × 3,66 × 2,26 m. Préfabriqué en Corse, le Cabanon se trouve à proximité de la célèbre maison de son amie Eileen Gray (Villa E-1027, 1924) et jouxte le bar « L'Étoile de Mer » qui appartient au client de Roq et Rob, Thomas Rebutato. Fait de matériaux industriels, le Cabanon en bois d'apparence brute, voire rustique, expérimente la notion inventée en 1943 par Le Corbusier, le Modulor, un système des proportions humaines de référence. En dépit d'une simplicité apparente, il est le fruit d'une réflexion approfondie dont témoigne notamment le mobilier disposé en spirale. En 1954, Le Corbusier achète 1 290 m^2 de terrain à Rebutato, dont celui du Cabanon, et construit en échange cinq « unités de camping » pour son client[4]. L'architecte aimait visiblement

Roquebrune-Cap-Martin et sa cabane, déclarant notamment : « J'ai un château sur la Côte d'Azur, qui a 3,66 m par 3,66 m. C'est pour ma femme, c'est extravagant de confort, de gentillesse. » Certainement un lieu « où une déesse pouvait laisser sa robe traîner ».

En route vers le futur

Il va de soi qu'une petite maison sur un petit terrain, ou alors dans une zone rurale ou déserte, devrait coûter moins qu'une grande. Certaines sont imprégnées de légèreté et d'économie, comme le Cabanon de Le Corbusier, tandis que d'autres sont plus robustes. Beaucoup s'inscrivent aujourd'hui résolument dans les nouvelles tendances à la numérisation de la conception et de la construction. De même, bon nombre des maisons publiées ici témoignent d'un engagement actif en faveur des valeurs actuelles de durabilité et de conscience écologique. Si certains pays, comme le Japon, ont une longue histoire de l'habitat dans des espaces réduits, d'autres, comme les États-Unis, continuent d'afficher une préférence pour les plus vastes demeures. Et ce, alors même que la situation économique et les réalités du réchauffement climatique semblent annoncer un mouvement presque universel vers une réduction des surfaces disponibles par personne. Ce simple fait, ou plutôt cette affirmation logique, est aussi la confirmation absolue de l'importance de trouver comment créer un petit environnement meilleur : les hommes sont trop nombreux sur terre pour permettre à tant de personnes d'occuper autant d'espace. L'heure des comptes a sonné. Il faut mettre plus dans une enveloppe plus petite ; il doit bien y avoir un lieu sain où habiter qui ne vomit pas son poison dans le monde. Ce n'est pas une posture politique de déclarer qu'une petite maison représente l'avenir, c'est un état de fait : les maisons doivent rapetisser au fur et à mesure que les populations augmentent et que les ressources sont menacées par la surconsommation.
Il ne faut pas non plus être particulièrement clairvoyant pour prédire que les petites maisons seront de plus en plus nombreuses à l'avenir. Plusieurs raisons très claires l'expliquent, à commencer, bien sûr, par des coûts plus raisonnables. Elles correspondent aussi, en second lieu, à plusieurs mouvements qui favorisent la diminution de la pollution et de l'empreinte carbone des bâtiments : plus une maison est petite et écoresponsable, plus ses propriétaires (et architectes) peuvent se sentir vertueux. Par ailleurs, l'accroissement de la population dans de nombreux pays crée une pression sur le terrain à bâtir disponible. Après avoir été longtemps le cas à Tokyo, c'est désormais un phénomène plus général. On peut aussi prévoir avec une certitude raisonnable que l'inventivité des architectes contemporains s'exprimera sans doute très fréquemment dans les petites maisons. La capacité à innover est bien plus grande lorsqu'il s'agit de traiter avec un seul client à l'esprit ouvert qu'avec une grande entreprise ou un gouvernement.
Enfin, on peut imaginer que des petites maisons remplaceront à l'avenir des bâtiments existants, agricoles dans les zones rurales et sinon simples, discrètes et bon marché dans les environnements urbains. Qu'il s'agisse de construire sur un toit comme le fait El Sindicato à Quito ou de transformer un abri de jardin comme Charles Pictet dans le Genève urbain, les petits projets sont plus faciles à réaliser et possèdent le potentiel pour donner libre cours à la créativité dont est capable un architecte. Aucun conseil d'administration ou administrateur n'est normalement mis en place pour gérer la construction d'une petite maison, mais un client individuel ne doit même pas forcément être riche pour créer le logis idéal – petit, discret et, avec un bon architecte, innovant.
Les petites maisons publiées ici se sont aussi révélées propices à l'utilisation des dernières techniques en matière de design architectural et de réalisation. Les systèmes informatisés, notamment ceux qui peuvent donner au CLT n'importe quelle forme sur mesure, rendent aujourd'hui la version moderne de la construction en bois idéale pour les petites maisons. Mais le plus étonnant reste – et on peut espérer que ce livre le démontre à son échelle – que la construction de petites maisons est un phénomène international, de la Nouvelle-Zélande à la Californie et retour. Plus proches de leur environnement parfois naturel, plus faciles à obtenir et à construire que les plus grandes, les petites maisons sont aussi une ode au provisoire. En effet une petite maison, surtout si elle a été conçue pour réduire l'impact sur l'environnement, peut facilement être enlevée sans laisser de traces. Par ailleurs, les différents types de préfabrication sont faciles à mettre en œuvre pour les petites maisons ou les « presque maisons » incarnées notamment par les pavillons-chambres d'hôtes de l'hôtel paysager de Breitenbach – 48 ° Nord (Breitenbach,

France, 2020, voir page 322) par Reiulf Ramstad ou le complexe Paradinha créé par Samuel Gonçalves (SUMMARY) à Alvarenga (Portugal, 2021, voir page 430). Ces « cabanes » d'hôtel ne possèdent, certes, pas toutes les caractéristiques d'une vraie maison, mais n'en représentent pas moins une expression de la tendance aux petites structures indépendantes où trouver refuge et bonheur.
On trouve naturellement des maisons d'architectes dans le monde entier, mais les forces auxquelles obéissent les petites maisons semblent l'une des tendances les plus universelles et significatives de l'architecture contemporaine. Mais comment répondre aux exigences actuelles de confort dans la plus petite des enveloppes ? Et comment procurer un sentiment de bien-être dans les maisons de plus en plus réduites que l'accroissement de la population exige ? De même que la maison de ville à Sumiyoshi a fait de Tadao Ando un architecte influent dans le monde entier, beaucoup des architectes plus jeunes qu'on peut trouver dans un livre comme celui qui suit seront sans doute les « stars » de demain, formés à l'épreuve de la petitesse afin de prouver que le talent d'un véritable architecte importe, même lorsque la taille du projet est en apparence insignifiante. Tous ceux qui voyaient les petites maisons comme anecdotiques à l'ère des gratte-ciel et des villas de 3000 m² sont invités à feuilleter ce volume pour voir les solutions qui y sont proposées. Ils sont aussi invités à passer leurs mains sur les murs de béton lisses et solides de Tadao Ando qui a su conférer la robustesse et la permanence de bâtiments bien plus grands à ses premières petites maisons.

La plus petite taille nécessaire

Aujourd'hui la question n'est plus « de quelle taille maximale ai-je besoin pour ma maison ? », mais plutôt : « Quelle est la plus petite taille nécessaire ? » Plusieurs facteurs, parmi lesquels les catastrophes climatiques et la pollution qui tire les températures vers le haut, causés en bonne partie par la construction, sont autant de leviers du changement de comportement à une échelle presque planétaire. Le mouvement des minimaisons, surtout présent aux États-Unis, se nourrit en grande partie du désir de fouler la terre d'un pas léger pour pouvoir évoluer et s'adapter à un avenir incertain.

El Sindicato, Parasitic House, Quito, Ecuador, 2019.

Page 43: *Takeshi Hosaka, Love2 House, Tokyo, Japan, 2019.*

Pages 44/45: *BIG, Klein A45, Upstate New York, USA, 2018.*

L'accroissement de la population, surtout dans les centres urbains, impose aussi désormais la rigueur que les Japonais connaissent depuis longtemps pour vivre dans de petits espaces avec l'instabilité potentielle de la terre elle-même. Dans ces conditions, les immenses maisons appelées à durer plusieurs générations semblent aujourd'hui appartenir au passé. Certes, il y aura toujours des exceptions, les très riches répugnant à abandonner l'image de grandeur qui accompagne une grande maison. De même, le prix à payer pour une maison même minuscule à Tokyo ne devrait pas paraître négligeable – la rareté du terrain tire les prix vers des hauteurs étonnantes. Et à l'autre extrémité de l'échelle des revenus, la seule pensée de posséder, même une maison miniature, reste un rêve impossible à réaliser. Les logements présentés ici sont des maisons individuelles, presque toujours destinées à quatre personnes ou moins.

Less is still more

La question du peu nécessaire n'est pas nouvelle ; c'est elle qui a inspiré le Cabanon de Le Corbusier et de nombreuses autres tentatives d'adapter véritablement l'habitat aux exigences humaines (minimales). Aujourd'hui élevé au rang d'œuvre d'art, le Cabanon fait aussi écho aux premières demeures jamais construites, huttes ou structures légères faites à partir des matériaux disponibles. Si les palais et les manoirs existent depuis des siècles, ou même des millénaires, c'est aussi le cas des plus petites maisons dont les traces ont souvent été balayées par le passage du temps. Les architectes qui ont réalisé les maisons publiées ici ne sont pas toujours les plus connus de leurs générations, mais ils n'ont certainement pas manqué à ce qui doit être considéré comme leurs « devoirs » fondamentaux. Car c'est à l'architecte qu'il revient avant tout de trouver comment rendre les petites maisons confortables et leur conférer une esthétique au mieux attachante et innovante – comment donner plus avec moins. La maxime « Less is more » (Ludwig Mies van der Rohe, 1947) faisait directement référence à l'ornementation, ou à son absence dans l'architecture moderne, mais elle peut aussi être appliquée aux préoccupations très contemporaines de l'architecture. Trop d'architecture coûte trop cher, pollue trop et passe de plus en plus de mode. La solution reste donc « less is more », mais pour d'autres raisons et dans un autre registre que celui de la seule ornementation. On pourrait avancer que ce sont précisément ceux des architectes qui réussissent à ouvrir de nouvelles perspectives avec de toutes petites maisons qui dominent aujourd'hui leur profession. Bien sûr, le même raisonnement peut être appliqué aux bâtiments plus grands qui doivent aussi devenir moins chers et moins spacieux, mais les maisons sont la forme de construction la plus commune : avec un architecte inventif et un client décidé, une petite maison peut ouvrir de nouveaux horizons. La culture de la (sur) consommation se brûle les ailes et se heurte déjà à de hautes barrières qui empêchent la poursuite de son expansion. Ce fait de société, scientifique, va encore contribuer à la tendance mondiale vers les petites maisons ; car ce sont elles qui ont du sens, à tous les niveaux.

La seule solution

On peut dire, sans prétention ni certitude excessive, que ce livre consacré aux petites maisons traite véritablement de l'avenir de l'architecture, et on pourrait même oser dire l'avenir de l'humanité. Il nous apprend à vivre dans une maison moins grande, à utiliser moins de ressources et à nous satisfaire de celles qui sont disponibles. On a connu le rêve d'un espace industrialisé répétitif, symbolisé par les grilles fugitives de la maison Dom-Ino de Le Corbusier. L'idée avait une dimension politique, celle de l'égalité. Mais aujourd'hui, vanter les vertus des petites maisons n'est même plus politique, cela revient simplement à évoquer ce qui est possible et ce qui le sera à l'avenir. L'un des faits qui sautent aux yeux est que les maisons publiées ici n'ont aucun style particulier – au contraire, elles ont presque autant de styles qu'il y a de projets. Mais les petites maisons ne suivent pas un style ou une mode ; elles résultent de forces sous-jacentes supérieures. Les ressources s'épuisent, alors même que (certaines) populations augmentent. Pour éviter guerres et famines, la seule solution consiste à faire plus petit et plus modeste. Les architectes des maisons publiées ici démontrent avec un certain succès que petit n'est en aucun cas synonyme d'affreux ou d'inconfortable – mais peut, au contraire, stimuler sans fin la créativité. Le Petit Prince d'Antoine de Saint-Exupéry demande au narrateur de lui dessiner un mouton... Dessine-moi un mouton... Peut-être pourrait-on demander aux architectes: dessine-moi une petite maison... Pour le bien de la Terre et de ses habitants, elle ne doit pas être la solution ultime, juste un pas dans la bonne direction.

1 *https://www.census.gov/construction/chars/highlights.html consulté le 26 mai 2022.*
2 *https://www.statista.com/statistics/1255411/japan-average-size-dwellings-by-prefecture/ consulté le 26 mai 2022.*
3 *https://www.housebeautiful.com/uk/lifestyle/property/a35405209/average-house-price-england-square-foot-yes-homebuyers/ consulté le 26 mai 2022.*
4 *http://eileengray-etoiledemer-lecorbusier.org/le-cabanon/ consulté le 26 mai 2022.*

ALPHAVILLE

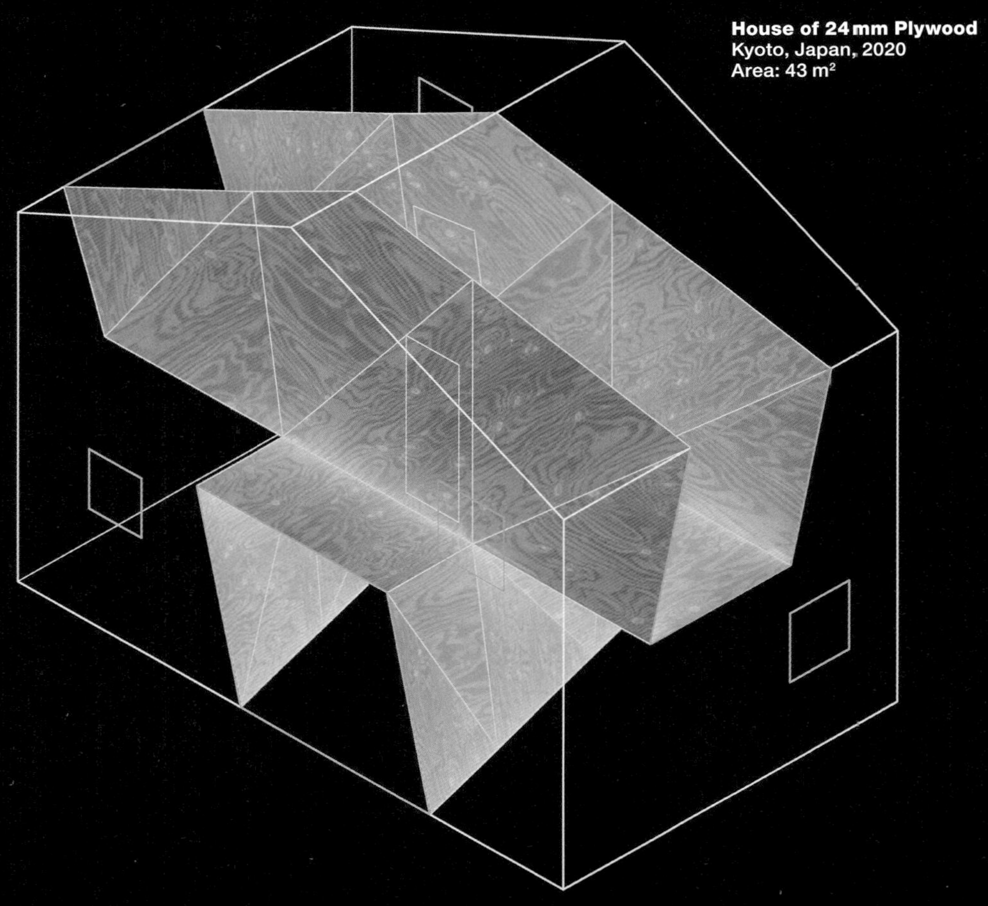

House of 24 mm Plywood
Kyoto, Japan, 2020
Area: 43 m²

Although the exterior form of the house is extremely simple, the diagonal cutout of the door and the asymmetric windows make it stand out in its residential neighborhood.

This single-family two-story house has a total floor area of just 45 square meters, but, as the architects say, it is "gorgeous as compared to a one-room apartment." The size is small even by the standards of dense Japanese urban areas, but Alphaville Architects succeed in creating two areas with "different relationships with the outside world." The first of these penetrates the center of the house and has a cross-like shape. It includes the entrance, a large fish tank, and a place for the family dogs. The second-floor terrace, with windows that allow "the outside environment directly into the house," is also part of this first area. The rest of the house forms the second area and includes atrium-like windows at the four corners of the structure, further enhancing contact with wind, sound, and sun from the exterior. An angled 24-millimeter-thick plywood partition wall, which is thin enough not to completely separate the two areas, marks the interior, which is for the most part clad in plywood. Since the house is too small for differentiated rooms, the architects imagined spaces that can be used indifferently for private or public use, or for working inside. In an unusual twist, the house was conceived to allow the display of drawings by the grandfather of the owner who was a locally well-known artist.

A small area is left outside to park a car on this corner lot. The house looks modest even by Japanese standards, where high land prices and local culture make small houses common.

Trotz seiner Gesamtfläche von nur 45 m² ist das zweigeschossige Einfamilienhaus nach Empfinden der Architekten „im Vergleich zu einer Einzimmerwohnung wahrlich prachtvoll". Alphaville Architects gelang auf dieser selbst für japanische Standards kleinen Fläche eine Aufteilung in zwei Bereiche mit „unterschiedlichem Bezug zur Außenwelt". Der erste, kreuzförmige Bereich durchdringt das Zentrum des Hauses und besteht aus dem Eingang, einem großen Fischbecken und einem Ruheplatz für die Familienhunde. Auch die Terrasse im zweiten Stock mit Fenstern, die „die Außenwelt direkt ins Haus einladen", ist Teil dieser ersten Zone. Der Rest des Hauses bildet den zweiten Bereich mit atriumähnlichen Fenstern an den vier Hausecken, die den Einfluss von Wind, Schall und Sonne spürbarer machen. Eine schräge Trennwand aus Sperrholz ist mit 24 mm so dünn, dass sie im Grunde nicht als echte Trennung der beiden Teile bezeichnet werden kann. Vielmehr wirkt sie als Markierung des Innenraums, der größtenteils ebenfalls mit Sperrholz verkleidet ist. Da das Haus zu klein für Einzelräume ist, wird der vorhandene Raum gleichberechtigt privat, beruflich und gemeinschaftlich genutzt. Kleine Ausstellungsflächenfür die Zeichnungen des Großvaters des Eigentümers, eines regional bekannten Künstlers, verleihen dem Konzept eine weitere interessante Nuance.

The angular cutouts already seen outside continue nto the house, where plywood has been used extensively for walls and ceilings. The diagonal central stairway is visible on the opposite page and in the plan.

La surface au sol totale de cette maison individuelle de deux niveaux compte seulement 45 m², mais les architectes soulignent à quel point c'est « fantastique par rapport à un studio ». C'est petit, même pour les normes des denses zones urbaines du Japon, mais Alphaville Architects a réussi à créer deux espaces aux « rapports au monde extérieur différents ». Le premier, en forme de croix, pénètre au cœur de la maison. Il comprend l'entrée, un vaste aquarium et un espace pour les chiens de la famille. La terrasse du premier étage et ses fenêtres qui laissent « directement entrer l'environnement extérieur dans la maison » fait aussi partie de ce premier espace. Le second espace se compose du reste de la maison et comprend des fenêtres aux quatre coins qui rappellent un atrium favorisant le contact avec le vent, le bruit et le soleil de l'extérieur. Une cloison anguleuse en contreplaqué de 24 mm d'épaisseur, suffisamment fine pour ne pas séparer complètement les deux espaces, marque l'intérieur en grande partie revêtu de contreplaqué. La maison est trop petite pour avoir des pièces distinctes, de sorte que les architectes ont imaginé des espaces qui peuvent servir indifféremment à des usages collectifs ou personnels, ou encore pour travailler à l'intérieur. Fait inattendu, la maison a été conçue pour exposer les dessins réalisés par le grand-père du propriétaire, un artiste local connu.

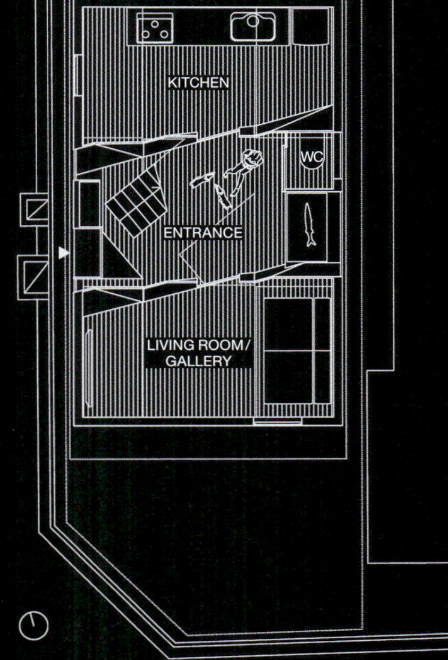
KITCHEN
WC
ENTRANCE
LIVING ROOM/
GALLERY

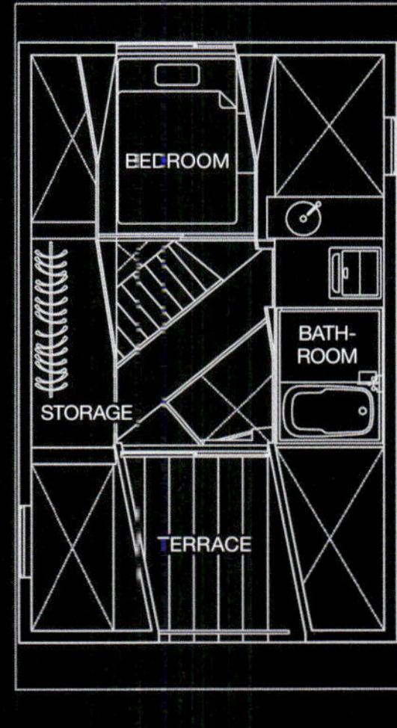
BEDROOM
BATH-
ROOM
STORAGE
TERRACE

CAMERON ANDERSON

Gawthorne's Hut
Mudgee, New South Wales,
Australia, 2020
Area: 40 m²

Collaboration:
Callander Constructions

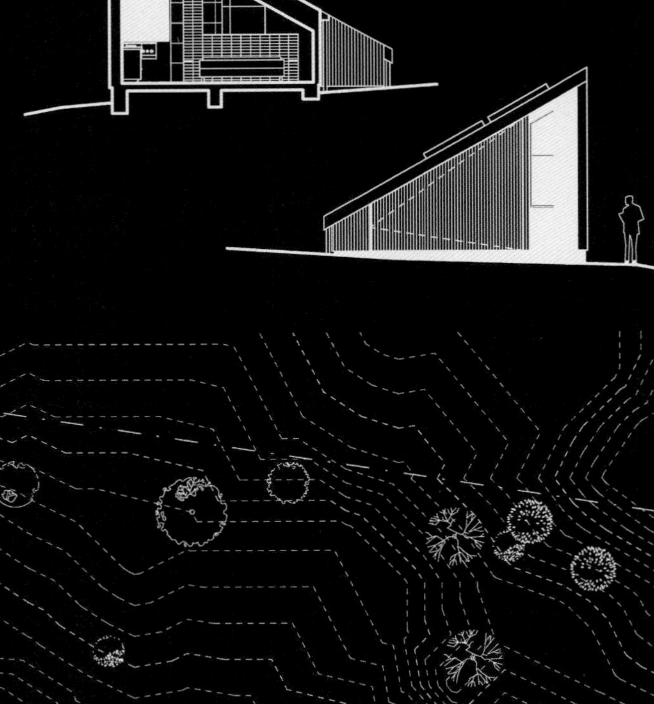

Although the architects refer to "local vernacular," Gawthorne's Hut stands out as a modern form in its natural setting.

The hut stands ten minutes from the center of Mudgee, a town of about 12 000 people located in Central West New South Wales. The architect describes it as a "luxury, two-person, off-grid tourism experience." The galvanized-steel exterior cladding and timber-lined interior are seen to "reference the predominant rural vernacular of hay sheds and outbuildings." A solar array is placed on the roof to provide electricity. An open-floor plan allows only for the enclosed WC. Solar batteries, the electrical board, and a gas hot-water unit were carefully concealed, and the entire project has been given a high rating for its resistance to potential bush fires. The structure relies on 40 000 liters of rainwater storage. The house was built with recycled bricks recovered from the site that are not used in a load-bearing function, galvanized-steel custom-Orb cladding, double-glazed Blackbutt *(Eucalyptus pilularis)* windows and doors, Armourpanel-engineered plywood linings (Blackbutt face), and Blackbutt timber cladding.

The kitchen and dining area is filled with light and views of the countryside. The floor plan shows a bed in the center of the small space.

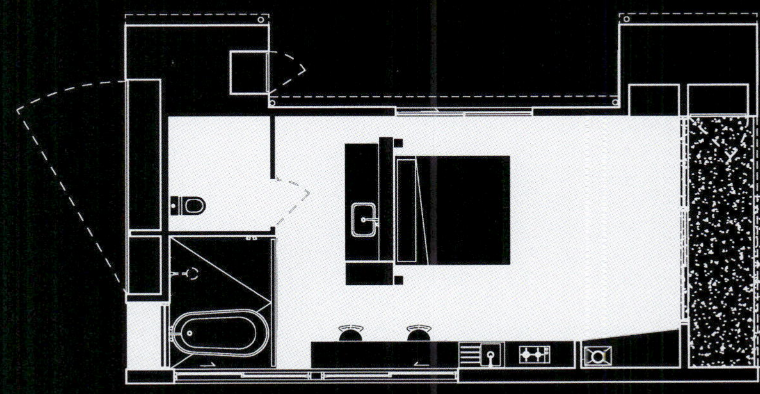

The interior, with its angled ceiling, is basically a single space with the bed near the kitchen and dining area visible near the bed, and bright open views to the exterior all around.

Die Minilodge liegt zehn Minuten vom Zentrum von Mudgee entfernt, einer Stadt mit etwa 12 000 Einwohnern im zentralen Westen von New South Wales. Der Architekt beschreibt sie als „luxuriöses, netzunabhängiges Tourismuserlebnis für zwei Personen". Die Außenverkleidung aus verzinktem Stahl und das mit Holz verkleidete Innere verweisen „auf die vorherrschende ländliche Bauweise mit Heuschuppen und Nebengebäuden". Der offene Grundriss ließ nur einen einzigen geschlossenen Raum – das WC – zu. Eine Solaranlage auf dem Dach erzeugt Strom. Solarbatterien, Elektrik und Gaswarmwasseranlage wurden sorgfältig verborgen. Das gesamte Projekt wurde als besonders widerstandsfähig gegen mögliche Buschbrände eingestuft. Sein Regenwasserspeicher fasst 40 000 Liter. Das Haus wurde aus recycelten, auf dem Grundstück gefundenen Ziegelsteinen errichtet, die keine tragende Funktion haben und von einer maßgeschneiderten Wellblechverkleidung aus verzinktem Stahl umgeben sind. Blackbutt-Holz *(Eucalyptus pilularis)* wurde für die doppelt verglasten Fenster und Türen verwendet sowie für die Verschalung aus Armourpanel-Sperrholz mit Blackbutt-Oberfläche und die innere Wandverkleidung.

The sloped ceiling makes for a very high space on one side. Following spread: *the bathtub is near the main space.*

La petite maison est située à dix minutes du centre de Mudgee, une ville d'environ 12 000 habitants dans le centre-ouest de la Nouvelle-Galles-du-Sud. L'architecte la décrit comme une « aventure touristique de luxe déconnectée pour deux personnes ». Le revêtement extérieur en acier galvanisé et l'intérieur lambrissé sont considérés comme des « références à la nature vernaculaire majoritairement rurale des granges et dépendances ». Des panneaux solaires sur le toit fournissent l'électricité. L'espace ouvert est uniquement fermé autour des toilettes. Des batteries solaires, le panneau électrique et un chauffe-eau à gaz ont été soigneusement dissimulés. Le projet dans son ensemble a été très bien noté pour sa résistance aux éventuels incendies du bush. La structure dispose aussi d'une réserve d'eau de pluie de 40 000 litres. La maison est construite en briques recyclées récupérées sur place pour les parties non porteuses, avec de l'acier galvanisé custom-Orb pour le revêtement ; les fenêtres double vitrage et les portes sont en bois de gommier *(Eucalyptus pilularis)*, les panneaux en contreplaqué Armourpanel (à face en gommier), tandis que le bardage intérieur est aussi en gommier.

thankyou.
MILK
HAND WASH

SIMON ANDERSON

Off-Grid FZ
Blue Mountains, Sydney, Australia, 2020
Area: 94 m^2

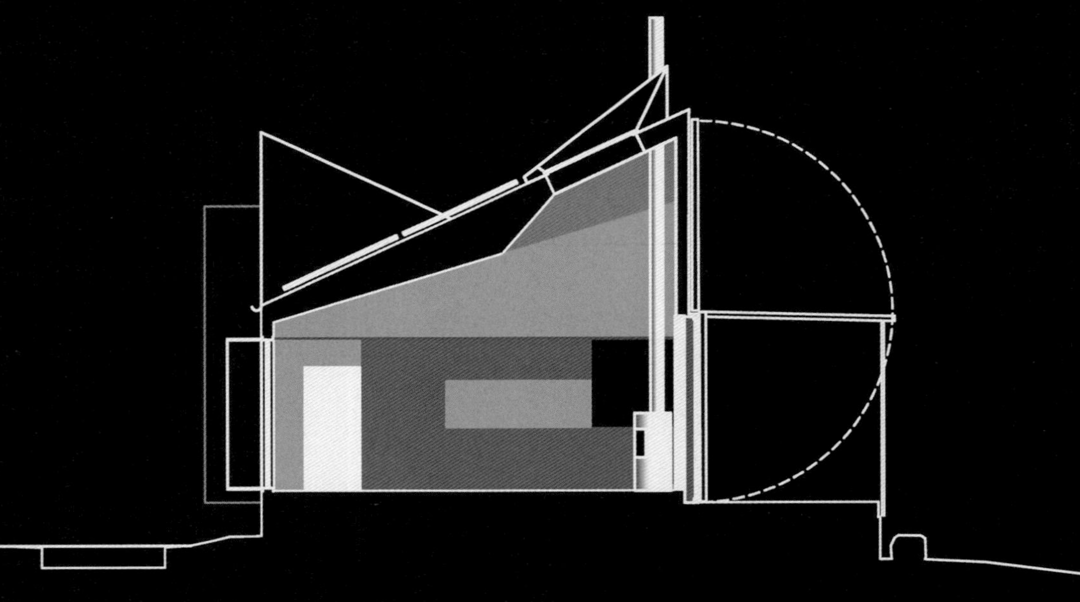

The house can be entirely closed with movable shutters that serve as outdoor canopies when open. The zero-carbon emission design is meant to be able to resist local bush fires.

The house is nestled into its natural setting; very open when in use, it hardly looks as though it can be hermetically sealed.

Made with an insulated concrete floor and walls, fiber cement decking board cladding, a timber-framed Colorbond steel roof, and slide-out, fold-down and roller-down fire shutters, this totally off-grid house was built with a budget of $550 000. It is used by the architect himself and his partner Kim Bell. The letters FZ stand for Flame Zone. It is meant to be a net zero carbon emissions home that is "resilient to future impacts of climate change; able to withstand temperature extremes from subzero to over 40 °C, and even cope with flame zone conditions from bushfires that may impact the home." The living room can be opened completely in the direction of a deck evoking "the feeling of being in a local sandstone cave, with a delicate foundation and overhang providing refuge, while panoramic prospect is afforded." Residents are fully self-sufficient insofar as water and energy needs are concerned.

Dieses komplett netzunabhängige Haus mit gedämmten Betonböden und -wänden, einer Verkleidung aus Faserzementplatten, einem Colorbond-Stahldach in Holzrahmenbauweise und klappbaren Feuerschutzrollläden wurde für ein Budget von 550 000 US-Dollar gebaut. Es wird von dem Architekten selbst und seiner Partnerin Kim Bell genutzt. Die Buchstaben FZ stehen für Flame Zone (Feuerzone). Es ist als Netto-Null-Emissionshaus konzipiert, das „den künftigen Auswirkungen des Klimawandels widersteht. Es soll Temperaturextremen von unter Null bis über 40 °C und sogar FZ-typischen Buschbränden standhalten." Das Wohnzimmer lässt sich zu einer Veranda hin vollständig öffnen und weckt dadurch „den Eindruck, als stände man in einer der nahe gelegenen Sandsteinhöhlen mit filigranem Fundament, schutzbietenden Überhang und Panoramaaussicht". Hinsichtlich Wasser- und Energieversorgung sind die Hausbewohner völlig autark.

Set up on a platform made of stone topped by boards, the house sits above its setting, which will allow it to be removed without a trace if that is ever decided.

The elegant, simple design carries through to the interiors which can, like this living area, be opened to the natural setting almost entirely. A drawing shows the simplicity of the design.

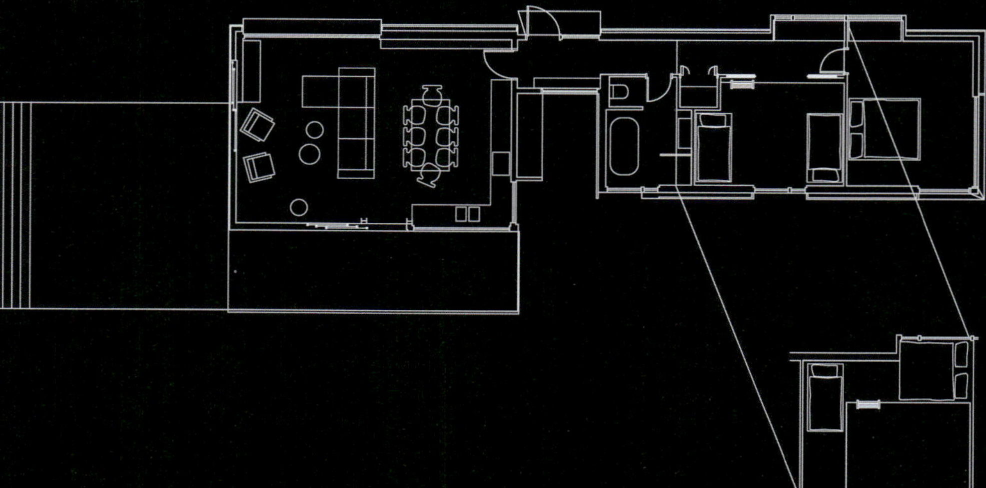

Avec son sol et ses murs en béton isolant, son plancher en fibrociment recouvert de planches, sa toiture en acier Colorbond à charpente en bois d'œuvre et ses volets coupe-feu coulissants, rabattables et roulants, cette maison entièrement hors réseau a été construite avec un budget de 550 000 dollars. Elle est habitée par l'architecte et sa partenaire Kim Bell. Les lettres F et Z de son nom signifient « Flame Zone » ou « zone de feu ». La maison est conçue pour produire zéro émission nette de carbone et « résister aux futurs impacts du changement climatique ; elle peut supporter des températures extrêmes allant de moins de zéro à plus de 40 °C, et même les conditions qui règnent dans la zone de feu des incendies de bush, susceptibles de laisser des traces ». Le salon peut être entièrement ouvert vers une plate-forme en bois pour donner « le sentiment de se trouver dans une grotte de grès locale, avec des fondations raffinées et un surplomb qui forme un abri, tout en offrant une vue panoramique ». Les habitants de la maison sont entièrement autosuffisants en eau et énergie.

Vood furnishings and details and concrete loors blend with the surrounding environment. An outdoor deck allows residents to feel as though they are in nature even as they are protected from its extremes.

ARBOL

House in Akashi
Hyogo, Japan, 2018
Area: 81 m²

Collaboration: Sasahara Corporation (Builder)

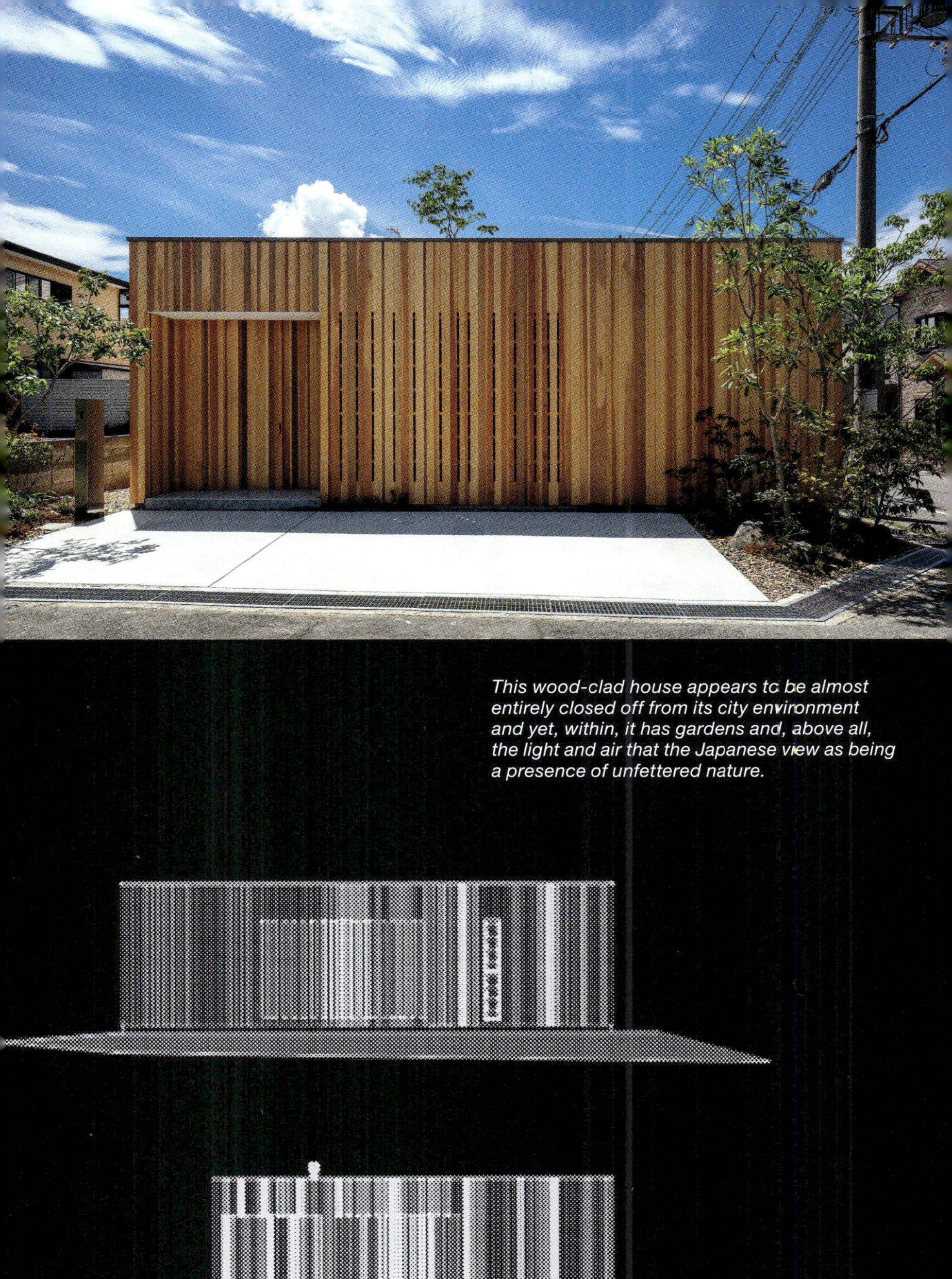

This wood-clad house appears to be almost entirely closed off from its city environment and yet, within, it has gardens and, above all, the light and air that the Japanese view as being a presence of unfettered nature.

Akashi is a city of about 300 000 inhabitants located on the Seto Inland Sea, to the west of Kobe. The house is near the city center but in a quiet residential area. The single-story structure has three courtyards with a "wooden box" that surrounds its vegetable gardens. The site area of the residence is 172 square meters. As is often the case in Japan, the house is isolated from the town environment to insure the privacy of the residents. A traditional earthen-floor family room is at the front, while the middle of the structure is a semi-public living and dining area surrounded by the courtyards. The private (bedroom and laundry) areas are at the back. A number of different woods, including cedar, cypress, and spruce, were used for solid board floors, exterior walls, and furnishings by Mandai Seisakusho. The architect explains: "Through the three gardens, you can touch the plants and soil, enjoy the breeze and the patterns of the sky, and feel the sunlight changing with the seasons and the time of day, without leaving the house. By weaving nature and plants into the fabric of our lives, we hope to create a home that nurtures a rich sensibility through the little things we notice in our daily lives."

The interior of the house opens almost entirely with sliding glass walls to the internal gardens. Wood is nearly omnipresent inside.

Akashi ist eine Stadt mit etwa 300 000 Einwohnern westlich von Kobe am Ufer des Seto-Inlandsees. Das einstöckige Haus in einer ruhigen Wohngegend des Stadtzentrums umschließt drei Höfe und eine „Holzkiste" mit Gemüsegarten. Seine Grundstücksfläche beträgt 172 m². Wie in Japan üblich wurde das Haus von der städtischen Umgebung isoliert, um die Privatsphäre der Bewohner zu gewährleisten. Im vorderen Teil befindet sich ein traditioneller Familienraum mit Lehmboden, während die Hausmitte einen halböffentlichen Wohn- und Essbereich beherbergt, der von den Höfen umgeben ist. Die privaten Bereiche (Schlafzimmer und Waschküche) finden sich auf der Rückseite. Die Böden, Außenwände und das Mobiliar von Mandai Seisakusho sind aus verschiedenen Hölzern gefertigt, darunter Zeder, Fichte und Zypresse. „Dank der drei Gärten sind Pflanzen und Erdreich in unmittelbarer Reichweite", schildert der Architekt. „Ohne das Haus verlassen zu müssen, genießen wir die Brise, beobachten die Himmelsmuster und spüren das Sonnenlicht, das sich mit den Jahres- und Tageszeiten verändert. Indem wir die Natur und Pflanzen in unser Leben einbezogen, wollten wir ein Haus schaffen, das durch die kleinen Dinge des Alltags eine reiche Sensibilität nährt."

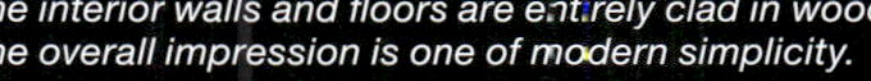

The interior walls and floors are entirely clad in wood. The overall impression is one of modern simplicity.

Akashi est une ville de 300 000 habitants environ au bord de la mer intérieure de Seto, à l'ouest de Kobe. La maison est proche du centre-ville, mais dans un quartier résidentiel calme. De plain-pied, elle se compose de trois cours et d'une « boîte en bois » autour de ses jardins potagers. La surface du site est de 172 m². Comme souvent au Japon, la maison est isolée de son environnement urbain afin de protéger l'intimité de ses habitants. Une salle familiale traditionnelle au sol de terre occupe le devant, tandis que le milieu se compose d'une salle de séjour et salle à manger semi-commune, entourée des cours. Les espaces privés (chambre et buanderie) sont situés à l'arrière. Plusieurs bois différents, parmi lesquels le cèdre, le cyprès et l'épicéa, ont été utilisés pour les planchers massifs, les murs extérieurs et le mobilier créé par Mandai Seisakusho. L'architecte explique que « les trois jardins permettent d'être en contact avec les plantes et le sol, de profiter de la brise et du ciel changeant et de sentir la lumière du soleil différente selon les saisons et l'heure de la journée sans sortir de chez soi. En entremêlan la nature et les plantes au tissu de nos vies, nous espérons créer une maison qui nourrit une riche sensibilité de toutes les petites choses qui nous frappent au quotidien ».

ARANZA DE ARIÑO

Casa Tiny
San Pedro Tututepec, Oaxaca, Mexico, 2016
Area: 36 m²

Large wooden shutters open the high interior of the house to a large cement block, which can serve as a dining or service table.

San Pedro Tututepec is on the southwestern Pacific coast of Mexico located near the resort town of Puerto Escondido. Casa Tiny is set 200 meters from the beach. The house includes a swimming pool with 50 square meters of additional terrace area. It is set along a north-south axis in a heavily wooded area. The architect describes it as a "tribute to Henry David Thoreau and John Burroughs." The house was built with cast in-situ concrete and locally sourced Parota *(Enterolobium cyclocarpum)* wood, which was used for doors, windows, closets, and shelves. The materials for the concrete were also locally sourced. It is intended to be entirely open with a long table uniting exterior and interior. The mezzanine bedroom is open to the rest of the house. The plan of the residence calls for the possibility of creating another terrace, a new bedroom for guests, and possibly... a pizza oven.

San Pedro Tututepec liegt an der südwestlichen Pazifikküste Mexikos, in der Nähe des Ferienortes Puerto Escondido. Casa Tiny liegt 200 m vom Strand entfernt und verfügt über einen Swimmingpool mit 50 m² zusätzlicher Terrassenfläche. Sie schmiegt sich an eine Nord-Süd-Achse in einem stark bewaldeten Gebiet. Die Architektin beschreibt das Häuschen als eine „Hommage an Henry David Thoreau und John Burroughs". Es wurde aus Ortbeton und dem Holz der heimischen Guanacaste *(Enterolobium cyclocarpum)* gebaut, das für Türen, Fenster, Schränke und Regale verwendet wurde. Die Materialien für den Beton stammen ebenfalls aus der Region. Das Haus ist bewusst offen gestaltet, mit einem langen Tisch, der Außen- und Innenbereich miteinander verbindet. Das Schlafzimmer im Hochparterre öffnet sich zum Rest des Hauses. Der Bauplan lässt künftige An- und Einbauten, wie beispielsweise eine weitere Terrasse, ein Gästezimmer oder gar

A swimming pool visible in the axonometric cutaway drawing (previous spread) *and the photo above gives some contrast to the otherwise rather rigorous design of the concrete house.*

San Pedro Tututepec est situé sur la côte pacifique sud-ouest du Mexique, près de la petite ville balnéaire de Puerto Escondido. Casa Tiny est à 200 m de la plage. La maison possède une piscine et 50 m² de surface supplémentaire en terrasse. Elle est construite sur un axe nord-sud dans une zone densément boisée. L'architecte la définit comme un « hommage à Henry David Thoreau et John Burroughs ». Elle est en béton coulé sur place et bois de guanacaste *(Enterolobium cyclocarpum)* d'origine locale pour les portes, les fenêtres, les placards et les rayonnages. Les matériaux qui ont servi à faire le béton sont aussi d'origine locale. L'objectif est une maison entièrement ouverte avec une longue table pour réunir l'extérieur et l'intérieur. Le lit sur la mezzanine est ouvert sur le reste de la maison. Le plan de l'ensemble laisse la possibilité de créer une autre terrasse, une autre chambre pour les invités, ou même, éventuellement… un four à pizza.

Concrete is exposed both outside and inside the house. Foldable wooden shutters allow the bedroom to be in direct contact with the exterior. The drawing shows the main wooden façade and swimming pool to its left.

ARTE-1

6 Tsubo House
Shibuya, Tokyo, Japan, 2020
Area: 57 m^2

Collaboration: Hideaki Hamada (Structural Design),
Kowske Ohno (Decorative Art Crafts),
Yoko Ando (Textiles)

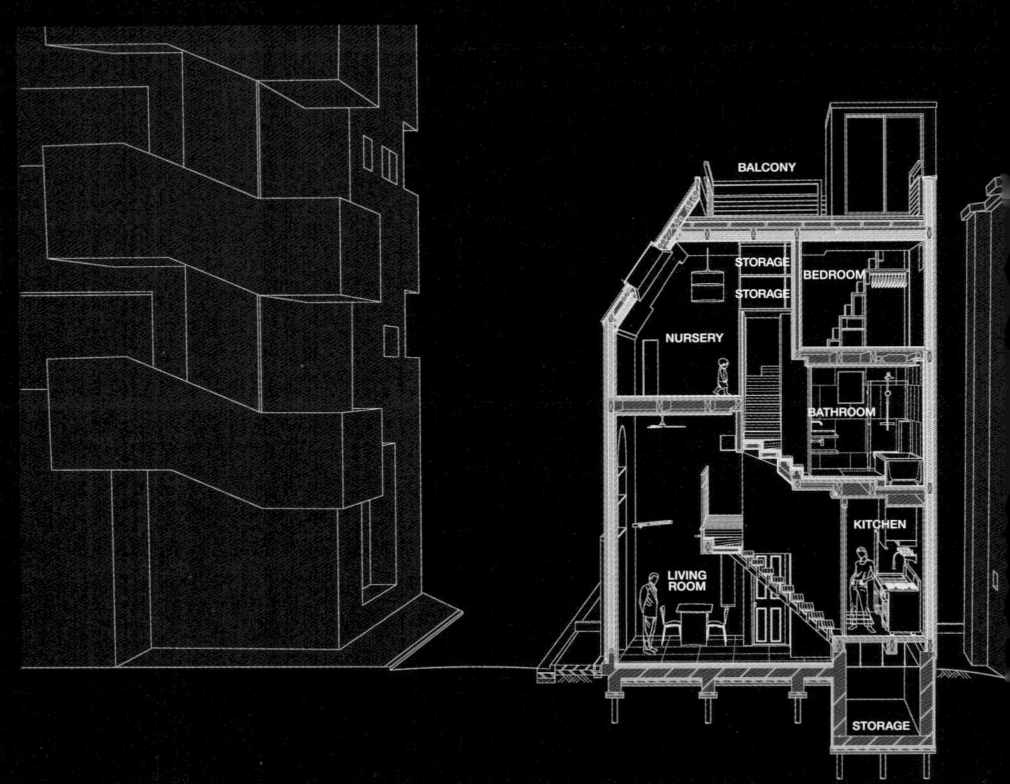

The house has a large, rounded window and a glazed entrance door. It is difficult to imagine that the interior measures 29 square meters.

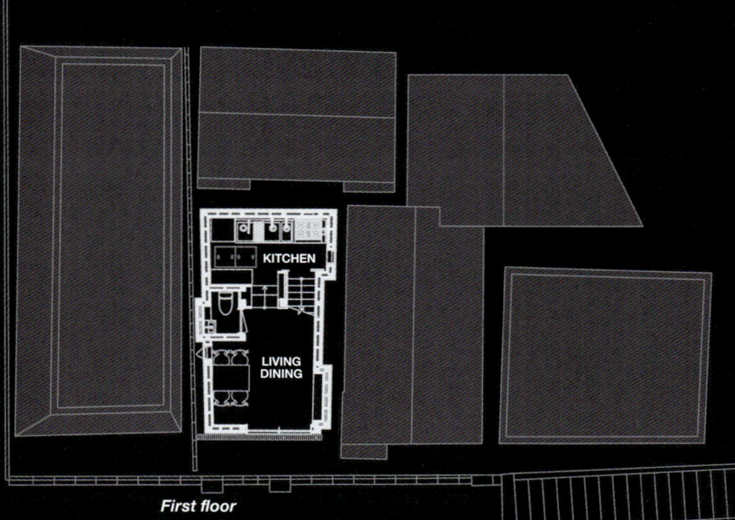

First floor

The compact kitchen is on the ground floor.

This very small house was built on a site that measures just 29 square meters. It has three floors and reaches a maximum height of 9.8 meters. The main exterior finish is metal siding. Inside there are wooden and ceramic tile floors with AEP (Aluminide Electrophoretic Process) coating for the walls. As it is in a dense central Tokyo area, the building had to adhere to strict fireproofing regulations, thus a metal cladding was added to a more traditional wooden structure. The living room and kitchen are connected to an alley by a large opening. Wood was used for the structure because it was less expensive than steel. The open living room atrium, which is connected to the alley, has a height of five meters. The rooms are not partitioned but textiles and horizontal shutters provide privacy. The stairs and handrails in black steel, as well as the very large arched window above the entrance doors, contrast with the more uniform exterior cladding. A *tsubo* is a Japanese measurement of area and is equivalent to 3.3 square meters. The name of the house thus refers to an area of about 20 square meters—corresponding roughly to the 21-square-meter footprint of the structure.

Dieses winzige Gebäude wurde auf einem Grundstück von nur 29 m² errichtet. Mit drei Stockwerken ragt es maximal 9,8 m in die Höhe. Seine Außenverkleidung besteht hauptsächlich aus Metall, sein Inneres birgt Fußböden aus Holz und Keramikfliesen sowie eine AEP-Wandbeschichtung (Aluminide Electrophoretic Process). Aufgrund seiner Lage in einem dicht besiedelten Gebiet im Zentrum Tokios waren strenge Brandschutzvorschriften einzuhalten, weshalb der eher traditionellen Holzstruktur eine Metallverkleidung hinzugefügt wurde. Wohnzimmer und Küche blicken durch eine große Öffnung auf eine Gasse hinaus. Für die Konstruktion wurde Holz verwendet, das preiswerter war als Stahl. Das zur Gasse hinausblickende Wohnzimmeratrium ist 5 m hoch.

The second-floor bathroom participates in the rigorous aesthetic of the house interior—projecting an almost industrial image in the kitchen on the left page.

Die Räume sind zwar nicht unterteilt, doch sorgen Textilien und horizontale Fensterläden für Privatsphäre. Treppen und Handläufe aus schwarzem Stahl sowie das großzügige Bogenfenster über den Eingangstüren kontrastieren mit der monoton gehaltenen Außenverkleidung. Da ein *tsubo* ein japanisches Flächenmaß von etwa 3,3 m² ist, bezieht sich der Name des Häuschens auf eine Fläche von etwa 20 m², was wiederum in etwa seiner Grundfläche von 21 m² entspricht.

Cette toute petite maison a été construite sur un terrain de seulement 29 m². Elle a trois niveaux pour une hauteur maximale de 9,8 m. Les finitions extérieures consistent pour l'essentiel en un bardage métallique. À l'intérieur, les sols sont en bois et en carreaux de céramique, avec des murs à revêtement AEP (Aluminide Electrophoretic Process ou procédé d'aluminiage par électrophorèse) sur les murs. Comme la maison est située dans un quartier central dense de Tokyo, elle devait respecter des règles d'ignifugation très strictes, d'où le revêtement métallique ajouté à la structure en bois plus traditionnelle. Le salon et la cuisine donnent sur une allée par de larges ouvertures. La structure est en bois en raison de son coût inférieur à celui de l'acier. Le salon et son atrium ouvert, qui communique aussi avec l'allée, sont hauts de 5 m. Les pièces ne sont pas cloisonnées, mais des tissus et des volets horizontaux procurent une certaine intimité. L'escalier et les rampes en acier noir, ainsi que l'immense fenêtre cintrée au-dessus de la porte d'entrée, contrastent avec le revêtement extérieur plus uniforme. Le *tsubo* est une mesure de surface japonaise qui équivaut à 3,3 m². Le nom de la maison évoque donc une surface d'environ 20 m² qui correspond à peu près aux 21 m² de son empreinte au sol.

BAUMRAUM

Dark Room
Ruinen, The Netherlands, 2020
Area: 16 m²

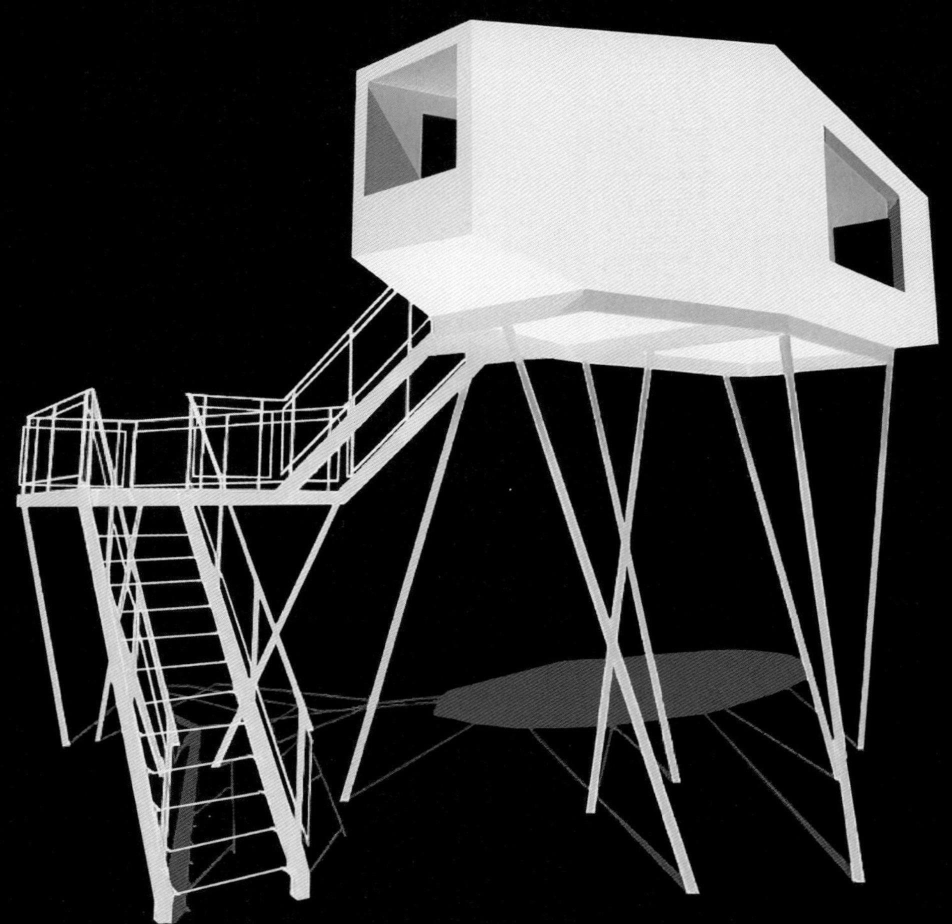

ndreas Wenning and baumraum are known for heir tree houses—usually made more with wood han with black stainless steel, which is the case ere—a modern aerie to view the trees.

ndreas Wenning designed this "black room n sloping supports" using prefabricated comonents on a meadowland site in Ruinen, in ortheastern Holland. The interior has a bed rea with angled, built-in oiled oak furniture, a asin, and sofa. The lower terrace of the Dark Room is set 2.8 meters above the ground while he cabin itself is at a height of 4.2 meters. The upporting structure with four inclined supports vas made with galvanized powder-coated steel. further seven supports hold up the cabin itelf. The deck is in FSC certified Sapele wood *Entandrophragma cylindricum)*. The interior area f the house itself is ten square meters, with a urther 5.4 square meters for the terrace. RIMEX SuperMirror black stainless steel was used for he exterior cladding over a wooden frame and nterior surfaces in solid oiled oak. Although the ark Room may not be a full house in the usual sense, it nonetheless fits well with the worldwide movement toward small spaces for sleeping (in this instance) and living.

Dieses „schwarze Zimmer auf schrägen Stützen" aus vorgefertigten Bauteilen befindet sich auf einem Wiesengrundstück in Ruinen im niederländischen Nordosten. Sein Innenraum birgt einen Schlafbereich mit schräg eingebauten Möbeln aus geölter Eiche, ein Waschbecken und ein Sofa. Die untere Terrasse thront 2,8 m über dem Erdboden, die Minilodge selbst ist 4,2 m hoch. Ihr Tragwerk mit vier schrägen Stützen ist aus verzinktem, pulverbeschichtetem Stahl gefertigt. Weitere sieben Stützen halten den Bau selbst aufrecht. Das Deck besteht aus FSC-zertifiziertem Sapeli-Holz *(Entandrophragma cylindricum)*. Die Innenfläche des Hauses beträgt 10 m², die Terrasse misst weitere 5,4 m². Schwarzer RIMEX SuperMirror

The interior of the Dark Room is rather cozy and bright, with large windows and oiled oak furnishings and surfaces. This internal space is in willful contrast to the shiny, metallic exterior.

Edelstahl gestaltet die Außenverkleidung auf einem Holzrahmen, die Innenverkleidung ist aus massiver geölter Eiche. Auch wenn Dark Room kein vollwertiges Haus im üblichen Sinne ist, reiht es sich doch in den globalen Trend zu kleinen Schlaf- (wie in diesem Fall) und Wohnräumen ein.

Andreas Wenning a construit cette « maison noire sur supports inclinés » avec des éléments préfabriqués dans une prairie de Ruinen, dans le nord-est de la Hollande. L'intérieur se compose d'un espace couchage au mobilier d'angle intégré en chêne huilé, d'un lavabo et d'un sofa. La terrasse inférieure est placée à 2,8 m au-dessus du sol, tandis que la cabane elle-même domine à 4,2 m. La structure porteuse, composée de quatre pieds inclinés, est en acier thermolaqué. Sept autres pieux portent la cabane elle-même. La pas- *cylindricum)* certifié FSC. La surface intérieure est de 10 m², auxquels s'ajoutent les 5,4 m² de la terrasse. Le revêtement extérieur est en acier inoxydable noir RIMEX SuperMirror avec une charpente en bois et des surfaces intérieures en chêne massif huilé. Si la Dark Room n'est pas une maison complète au sens propre, elle s'inscrit parfaitement dans le mouvement global vers de petits espaces où dormir (dans cet exemple) et vivre.

TREEHOUSES

ATTILA BÉRES

Cabin Moss
Köszeg, Hungary, 2021
Area: 40 m²

Collaboration: Jusztina Balázs (Architect)
Zoltán Fazekas (Structural Engineer)

This cabin was built for Attila Hideg, who was also the client for the Hideg House and the Niczky Apartment. "Our task was to create a little hideaway space of about 40 square meters without any compromise regarding living comfort; at the same time we respected the natural values of the site at extraordinary levels," says architect Attila Béres. The cabin sits on the edge of an untouched forest landscape. Thin stilts were carefully located to protect the roots of surrounding trees. The architects further explain that "the cross section of the building, two right angles facing each other, creates great visual contacts with the surrounding sloped landscape. It creates possibilities for taller windows and helps to capture the view toward the endless forest landscape." The warm interior has a rough surface that evokes the forest. A conscientious effort was made to keep the environmentally friendly structure as small as possible with no "wasted" space. Electrical power is used for hot water and heating, but consumption was kept low using a carefully designed insulation system. Cables and pipes are invisible.

Diese Lodge ist eine Auftragsarbeit für Attila Hideg, der zuvor bereits Hideg House und Niczky Apartment bauen ließ. „Unsere Aufgabe bestand darin, einen kleinen Rückzugsort von etwa 40 m² zu schaffen, ohne dabei auf Wohnkomfort zu verzichten", so Attila Béres. „Gleichzeitig nahmen wir besondere Rücksicht auf die natürlichen Werte des Ortes." Die dünnen Stelzen der Minilodge am Rande einer unberührten Waldlandschaft wurden sorgfältig platziert, um die Wurzeln der umliegenden Bäume zu schützen. „Der Gebäudequerschnitt", so die Architekten weiter, „zeigt zwei sich gegenüberliegende rechte Winkel, die den intensiven visuellen Kontakt mit der leicht abschüssigen Umgebung fördern. So

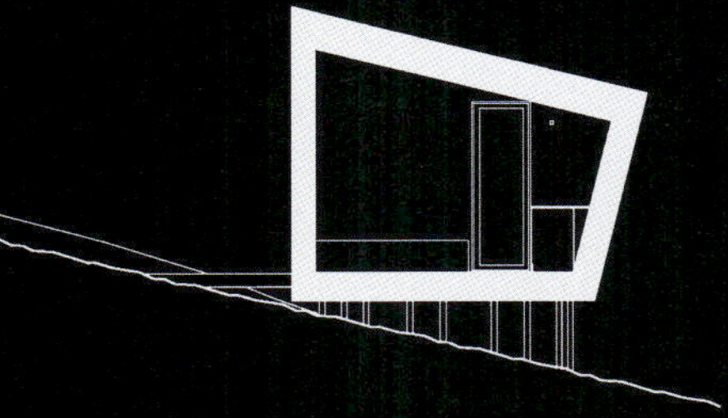

Although its volume seems rather solid, the Cabin Moss has a big, glazed opening near the dining table and sits on a large number of short stilts that lighten its appearance. Opposite: *The interiors use wooden surfaces to recall the neighboring forest.*

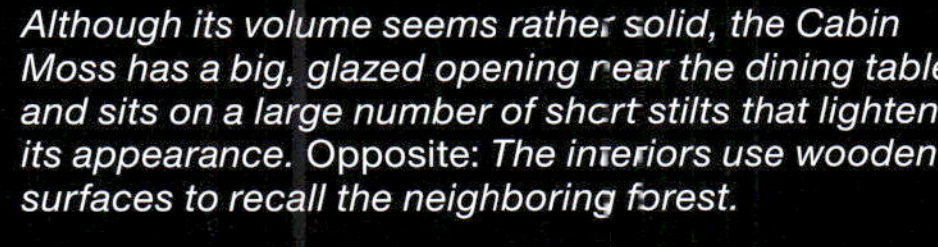

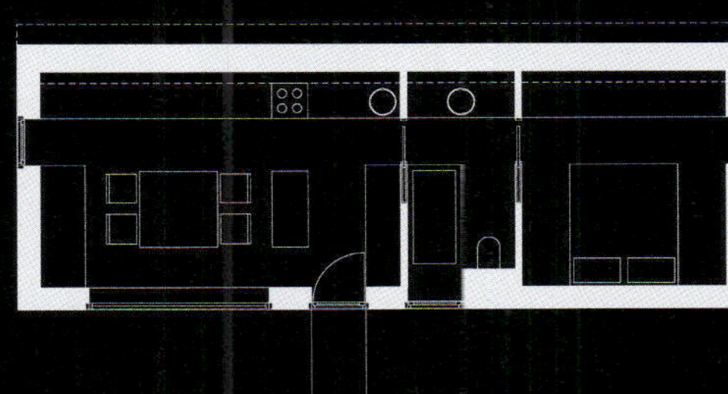

The simplicity of the interiors participates in an impression that the living space is more generous than the 40-square-meter floor area would imply.

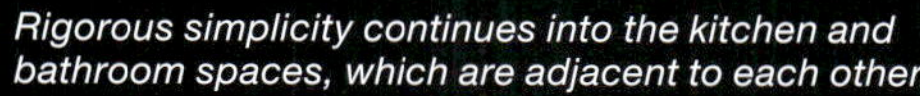

Rigorous simplicity continues into the kitchen and bathroom spaces, which are adjacent to each other.

konnten wir höhere Fenster einplanen und den Blick auf die endlose Waldlandschaft öffnen.“ Die rauen Innenoberflächen erinnern an Wald und schaffen eine warme Atmosphäre. Im bewusst klein gehaltenen umweltfreundlichen Häuschen ist Platzverschwendung ein Fremdwort. Für Warmwasser und Heizung sorgt elektrischer Strom, dessen Verbrauch jedoch dank eines sorgfältig konzipierten Isolationssystems niedrig gehalten wird. Kabel und Rohre bleiben im Verborgenen.

Cette petite maison a été construite pour Attila Hideg, le client de la maison Hideg et de l'appartement Niczky. « Notre mission consistait à créer un petit espace caché 40 m² sans aucun compromis en ce qui concerne le confort, en même temps que nous tenions à respecter la valeur naturelle du site à un point extraordinaire », déclare l'architecte Attila Béres. La maison est située en bordure d'une forêt encore intacte. Les fins pilotis ont été disposés avec soin pour ne pas abîmer les racines des arbres environnants. Les architectes expliquent que « dans sa section transversale, le bâtiment forme deux angles droits qui se font face, ce qui ouvre de superbes contacts visuels avec le paysage environnant en pente, permet des fenêtres plus hautes et met en valeur la vue de la forêt dans son immensité ». La surface brute de l'intérieur évoque la forêt elle aussi. Un effort consciencieux a été fait pour réaliser une structure respectueuse de l'environnement, la plus petite possible, sans espace « gâché ». L'eau chaude et le chauffage sont produits électriquement, mais la consommation reste basse grâce à un système d'isolation conçu avec soin. Les câbles et les conduites sont invisibles.

BIANCHI-FUCILE

House in Los Hornos
La Plata, Argentina, 2018
Area: 100 m^2

Collaboration: Juliana Bertone

The light metal corrugated roof of the house may bring to mind more temporary local structures, but, in this instance, each aspect of the open design is carefully thought out.

Built in the "semi-rural" periphery of La Plata, where large-scale production of fruits and flowers is very present, this small house was conceived as a repetition of seven 2.4 × 6 × 2.9-meter units for a total area of 6 × 16.8 meters. The structure is sheltered by a slightly elevated 12 × 18-meter light corrugated metal roof and has a brick floor laid directly on the earth. The precise location of the house was determined by the presence of existing trees. The living and dining area, together with the kitchen, is near the main entrance. A bathroom area to the left of the entrance leads to the bedroom spaces. The large terrace extends from the façade opposite the entrance of the rectangular structure. This house sits lightly on the earth and manifestly allows a modest consumption of materials and energy.

Dieses kleine Haus in der „halb-ländlichen" Peripherie von La Plata mit ihrem großflächigen Obst- und Blumenanbau wurde aus sieben identischen 2,4 × 6 × 2,9 Meter großen Einheiten mit einer Gesamtfläche von 6 × 16,8 Metern konzipiert. Die Grundstruktur, deren Ziegelboden direkt auf der Erde aufliegt, wird von einem leicht erhöhten 12 × 18 Meter großen Dach aus leichtem Wellblech geschützt. Der genaue Standort des rechteckigen Baukörpers entschied sich nach dem vorhandenen Baumbestand. Wohn- und Essbereich sowie Küche liegen nahe des Haupteingangs, von dem links ein Badezimmer zum Schlafbereich führt. Die großzügige Terrasse grenzt an die Fassade gegenüber des Eingangs. Geradezu leichtfüßig steht das Häuschen auf der Erde und erforderte offensichtlich einen nur bescheidenen Verbrauch von Materialien und Energie.

The roof shelters generous outdoor terraces. Glazing on the opposite side makes it possible to see right through the house.

The rectangular house is built on a rigorous grid pattern as the drawing on the right shows. Interior surfaces in plywood emphasize the direct connection to the forested setting—wooden floors are laid on a simple brick base.

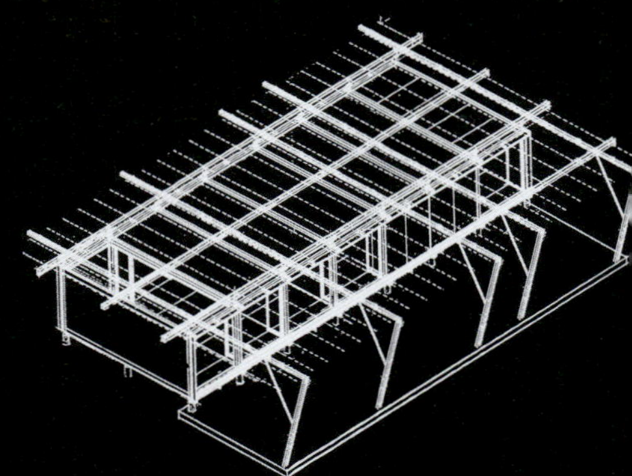

Située dans la périphérie « semi-rurale » de La Plata dominée par la production à grande échelle de fruits et de fleurs, la petite maison est formée de la succession de sept unités de 2,4 × 6 × 2,9 m pour une surface totale de 6 × 16,8 m. Elle est abritée par une toiture légère en métal ondulé légèrement surélevée de 12 × 18 m, tandis que le sol de briques est directement posé sur la terre. L'emplacement précis de la construction a été déterminé par la présence des arbres. L'espace séjour et repas se trouve à côté de l'entrée principale, avec la cuisine. Une salle de bains à gauche de l'entrée mène aux chambres. La vaste terrasse s'étend à partir de la façade qui fait face à l'entrée de la structure rectangulaire. La maison repose légèrement sur le sol et sa consommation d'énergie est visiblement modeste, de même que la quantité de matériaux utilisés.

IG

45
New York, USA, 2018
7 m^2

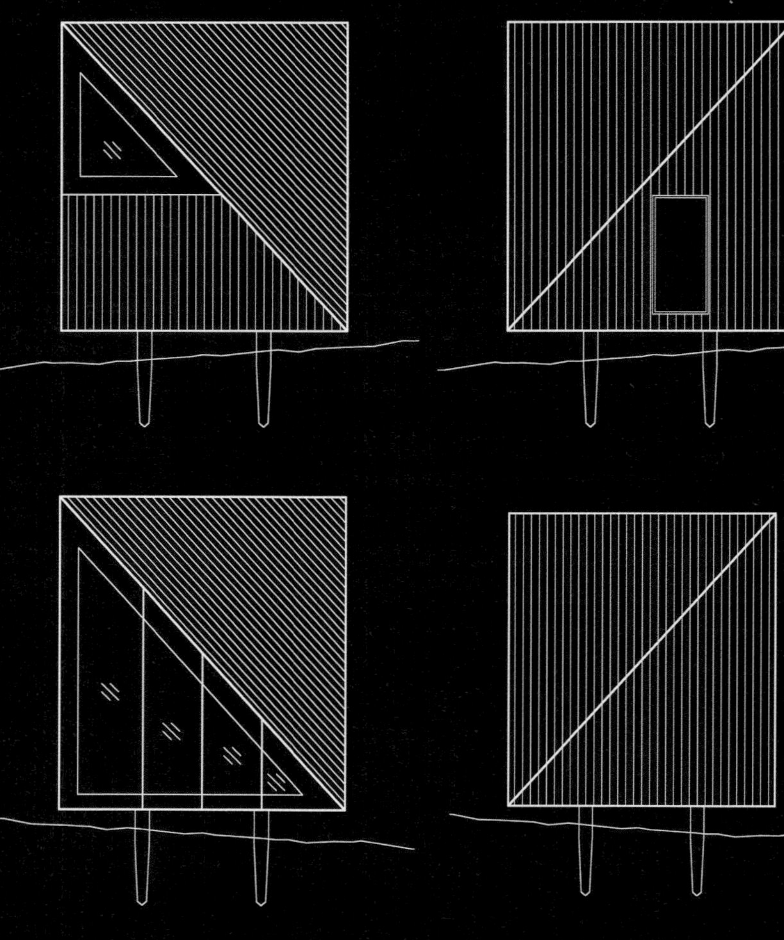

Drawings for the house (previous spread) *show that its plan is a simple square, bisected diagonally by the form of the sloping roof. Its light design makes it well adapted to the forest setting seen here.*

A45 is a prototype that can be "built within 4–6 months in any location, for any purpose". The modular system is completely recyclable. Based on an A-frame structure set on four concrete piers, this design has a twisted roof that allows for a ceiling height reaching four meters in one corner and floor-to-ceiling triangular window made with seven panes. The exposed timber-frame structure is made of solid pine. The interiors are finished with Douglas fir for the floors and natural cork on the walls. A Morsø wood-burning stove, a kitchen designed by Københavns Møbelsnedkeri, handcrafted furniture from Carl Hansen, and a bed with Kvadrat fabric designed by the Søren Rose Studio generate a cozy Scandinavian feeling. The Dane Søren Rose, born in 1972, founded his studio in Copenhagen in 2009 and went on to establish a presence in New York. His subsidiary Klein "specializes in tiny houses designed by the world's leading architects," the first of whom was Bjarke Ingels.

A45 ist ein Prototyp, der „innerhalb von vier bis sechs Monaten an jedem Ort und für jeden Zweck errichtet werden kann". Das modulare System ist vollständig recycelbar. Sein Entwurf basiert auf einer A-Rahmen-Struktur auf vier Betonpfeilern und verfügt über ein gedrehtes Dach, das in einer Ecke eine Deckenhöhe von 4 m ermöglicht, sowie über ein raumhohes dreieckiges Fenster mit sieben Scheiben. Das freiliegende Fachwerk wurde aus massivem Kiefernholz gefertigt. Die Böden der Innenräume sind mit Douglasienholz und die Wände mit Naturkork ausgestattet. Ein Morsø-Holzofen, eine von Københavns Møbelsnedkeri entworfene Küche, handgefertigte Möbel von Carl Hansen und ein vom Søren Rose Studio

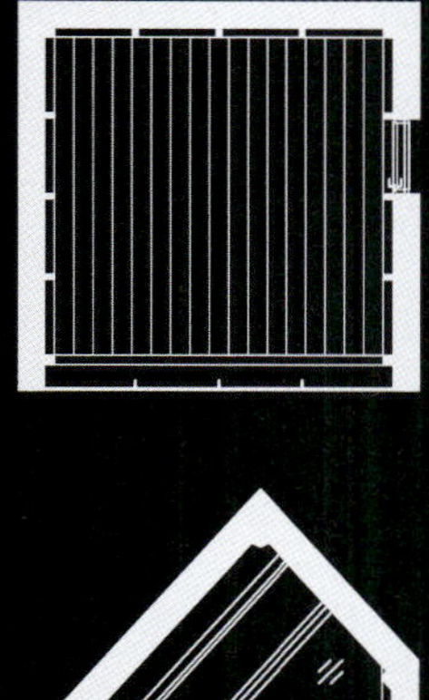

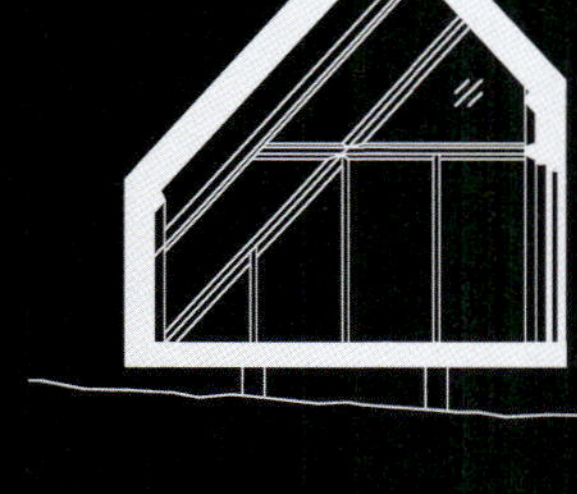

Douglas fir and cork line the interiors. The careful design makes the most of the limited available space, as the kitchen and bathroom areas here demonstrate.

entworfenes Bett mit Kvadrat-Stoff sorgen für eine gemütliche skandinavische Atmosphäre. Der 1972 geborene Däne Søren Rose gründete sein Studio 2009 in Kopenhagen und ist inzwischen auch in New York vertreten. Sein Tochterunternehmen Klein „ist auf kleine Häuser spezialisiert, entworfen von den weltweit führenden Architekten" – mit Bjarke Ingels vorneweg.

A45 est un prototype qui peut être « construit en 4 à 6 mois n'importe où pour n'importe quel usage », modulaire et entièrement recyclable. Basé sur une structure en forme de A posée sur quatre piliers en béton, son toit anguleux offre une hauteur sous plafond de 4 m dans un angle et une fenêtre triangulaire du sol au plafond composée de sept vitres. La structure à charpente apparente en bois d'œuvre est en pin massif. Les finitions intérieures sont en pin Douglas pour les sols et liège naturel pour les murs. Le poêle à bois de Morsø, la cuisine de Københavns Møbelsnedkeri, le mobilier artisanal de Carl Hansen et le linge de lit Kvadrat conçu par le studio Søren Rose donnent à l'ensemble une chaleureuse atmosphère scandinave. Le danois Søren Rose, né en 1972, a ouvert son studio à Copenhague en 2009, avant de s'installer aussi à New York. Sa filiale Klein « est spécialisée dans les minimaisons des plus grands architectes du monde », dont le premier est Bjarke Ingels.

Hutong 02
Nanluoguxiang, Beijing,
China, 2015
Area: 7 m²

Set in the midst of densely populated Beijing, this mini-house design shows that contemporary architecture can be both practical and well adapted to the constraints of a traditional neighborhood.

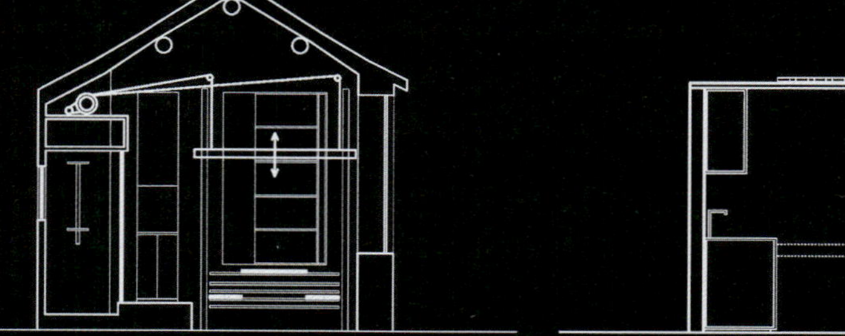

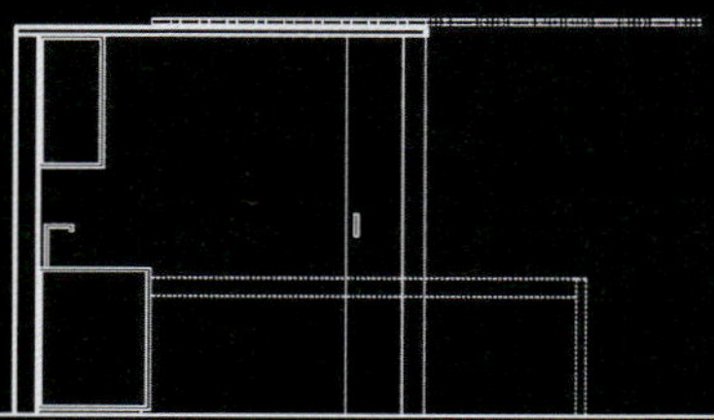

The extreme narrowness of the space is addressed with such features as a bed that is lifted up above the dining table.

While they were working on the Dengshikou Hutong Residence (2016), the architects worked on two tiny houses, with areas of just 3.6 and 2.8 square meters. The kitchen allows for its south-facing wall to open to extend the table into the courtyard, giving enough space to serve eight people. A tabletop and seat can be adjusted to form a bed. Wood panels of five different sizes allow use of the space as a teahouse, shop, or bedroom. The bed can be lifted using a motor connected to steel wires. Nanluoguxiang is an 800-meter-long alley created in the 14th century where the houses are located.

Parallel zu ihrer Arbeit an der Dengshikou Hutong Residence (2016) arbeiteten die Architekten an zwei winzigen Häuschen von nur 3,6 bzw. 2,8 m^2 Grundfläche. In der Küche kann die nach Süden gerichtete Wand geöffnet werden, um den Tisch in den Hof hinaus zu verlängern, sodass er acht Personen Platz bietet. Tischplatte und Sitze können zu einem Bett umfunktioniert

The dining table itself can be unfolded into another bed even as the bed above is lowered by a pulley system, seen in the section drawing (previous spread).

werden. Holzpaneele in fünf verschiedenen Größen ermöglichen die Nutzung des Raums als Teehaus, Laden oder Schlafzimmer. Das Bett kann mit Hilfe von motorbetriebenen Stahlseilen hochgezogen werden. Die Häuschen liegen in Nanluoguxiang, einer 800 m lange Gasse aus dem 14. Jahrhundert.

En même temps que la résidence Dengshikou Hutong (2016), les architectes ont travaillé à deux minuscules maisons aux surfaces respectives de seulement 3,6 et 2,8 m². Le mur sud de la cuisine peut être ouvert pour allonger la table dans la cour et accueillir huit personnes. Le plateau de la table et un siège peuvent être assemblés pour former un lit. Des panneaux de bois de cinq tailles différentes permettent d'utiliser l'espace comme maison de thé, boutique ou chambre à coucher. Le lit monte à l'aide d'un moteur raccordé à un système de câbles en acier. Les maisons se trouvent à Nanluoguxiang, une allée longue de 800 m qui date du XIVe siècle.

BUREAU LADA

Towerhouse
Amsterdam, The Netherlands, 2021
Area: 83 m²

Collaboration: Esther Mecredy, Juliette Gilson, ABT (Consulting Engineers)

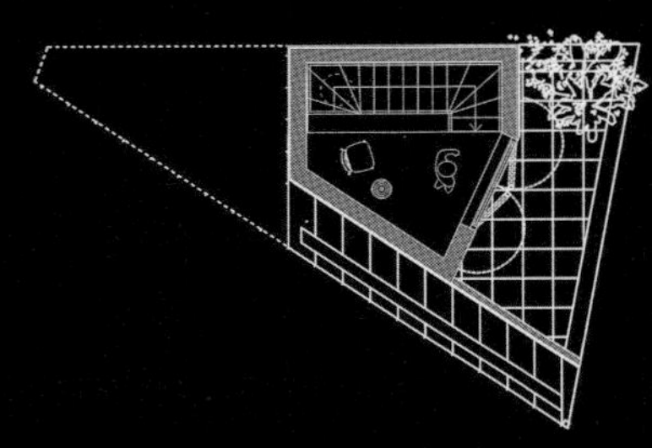

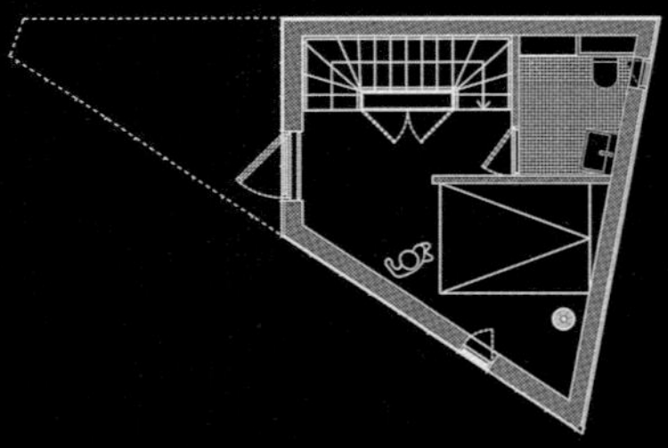

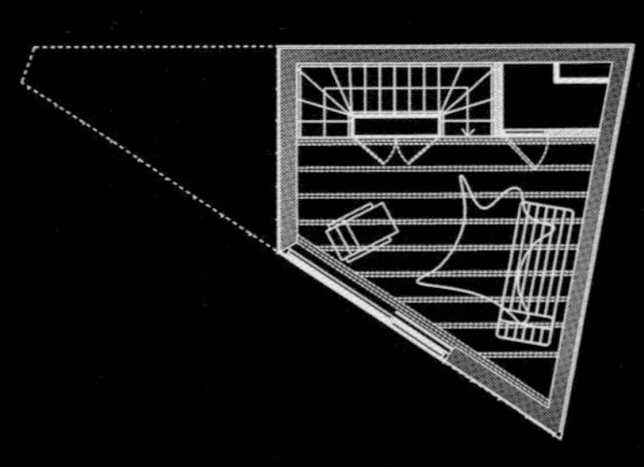

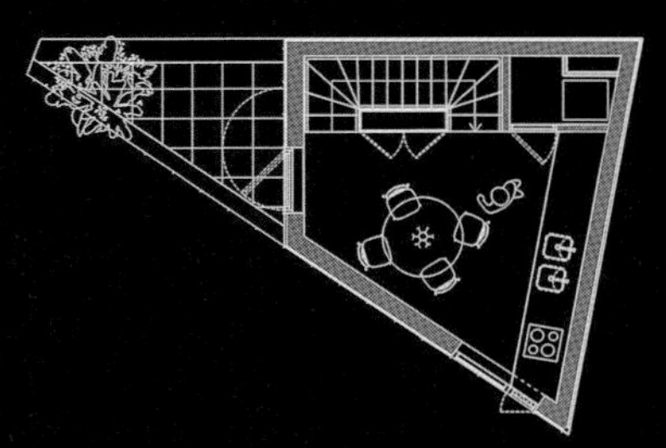

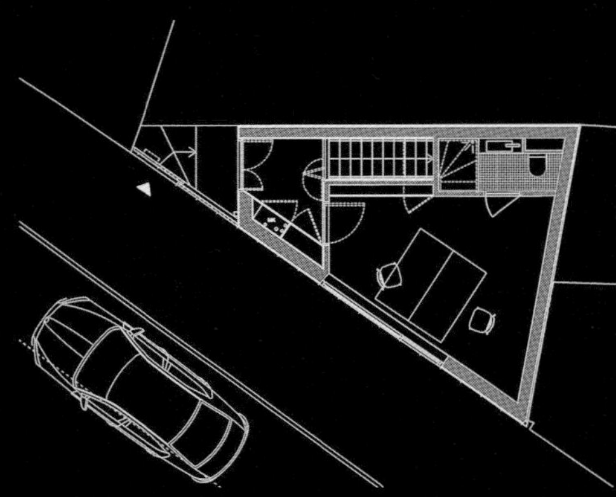

G-220-JZ

The bright interior of the house makes use of every available space, dividing each floor into a specific function. The pre-oxidized zinc façade allows the unusually shaped building to fit well into its historic area.

This five-level home was built on one of the last remaining sites in Amsterdam's historic center, measuring a very small 32 square meters. Each floor has a separate function and a selected city view, with the levels connected by a steep wooden staircase. A fifth-story terrace also offers views over the rooftops in the direction of Amsterdam's IJ. The architects reference the Tower House in Tokyo by Takamitsu Azuma (1966). The architects explain: "The Azuma house, the 'grandmother' of all Tokyo's pocket houses, is a long-time source of inspiration, due to its mastery of minimal space to provide unexpected spatial richness." They do indicate that their use of metal cladding and views to the city make their scheme more "refined and forgiving" than Azuma's concrete block. The Amsterdam building has a prefabricated wood structure, walls, and floors. The façade and roof are both covered in pre-oxidized zinc sheeting. The architects say: "By borrowing from the palette of its surroundings, this house is absorbed by the street-scape, allowing one to see it, and yet not to see it."

Dieses fünfstöckige Haus mit einer Grundfläche von nur 32 m² wurde auf einer der letzten verfügbaren Bauflächen im historischen Zentrum Amsterdams gebaut. Jedes Stockwerk erfüllt eine eigene Funktion und bietet Ausblicke auf die Stadt, wobei eine steile Holztreppe die verschiedenen Ebenen miteinander verbindet. Von einer Terrasse im fünften Stock öffnet sich zudem einen Blick über die Dächer in Richtung des Amsterdamer IJ. Als Inspirationsquelle verweisen die Architekten auf das Tower House in Tokio von Takamitsu Azuma (1966). „Das Azuma-Haus, die ‚Großmutter' aller Tokioter Taschenhäuser, ist schon seit Langem eine Inspirationsquelle", erklären die Architekten, „denn es zaubert aus kleinstem Raum einen unerwarteten räumlichen

Reichtum". Anders als Azumas Betonturm verfügt ihr Tower House über eine Metallverkleidung und bietet seinen Bewohnern einen Ausblick über die Stadt, was ihm einen „kultivierteren und nachsichtigeren" Charakter verleiht. Holzstruktur, Wänden und Böden sind vorgefertigte Elemente, Fassade und Dach sind mit voroxidierten Zinkblechen verkleidet. „Indem es die Farbpalette seiner Umgebung aufgreift, verschmilzt das Haus mit der Straßenlandschaft", schildern die Architekten. „Es oszilliert zwischen Sichtbar- und Unsichtbarsein."

La maison de cinq niveaux a été bâtie sur l'un des derniers terrains restants du centre historique d'Amsterdam et sa taille extrêmement réduite est de 32 m². Chaque niveau remplit une fonction distincte et offre une vue choisie sur la ville. Ils sont reliés par un escalier très raide en bois. Une terrasse au quatrième étage donne aussi sur les toits en direction du lac IJ. Les architectes se réfèrent à la tour construite à Tokyo par Takamitsu Azuma (1966). Ils expliquent notamment que « la maison d'Azuma, la "grand-mère" de toutes les maisons de poche de Tokyo, est l'une de nos sources d'inspiration depuis longtemps avec sa maîtrise de l'espace minimal qui produit une richesse spatiale inattendue ». Ils précisent que leur choix d'un revêtement métallique et des vues sur la ville rend leur concept plus « raffiné et indulgent » que le bloc de béton d'Azuma. L'immeuble d'Amsterdam possède une structure en bois, des murs et des sols préfabriqués. La façade et le toit sont recouverts de feuilles de zinc pré-oxydé. Pour les architectes, « en empruntant dans la palette du voisinage, la maison est absorbée par le paysage de la rue, de sorte qu'on la voit, mais sans la voir ».

.arge windows assure a close contact with he urban environment and bring ample natural ight into the house.

The spiral staircase saves space and unites the different floors in an efficient way.
Below: *elevation and section drawings.*

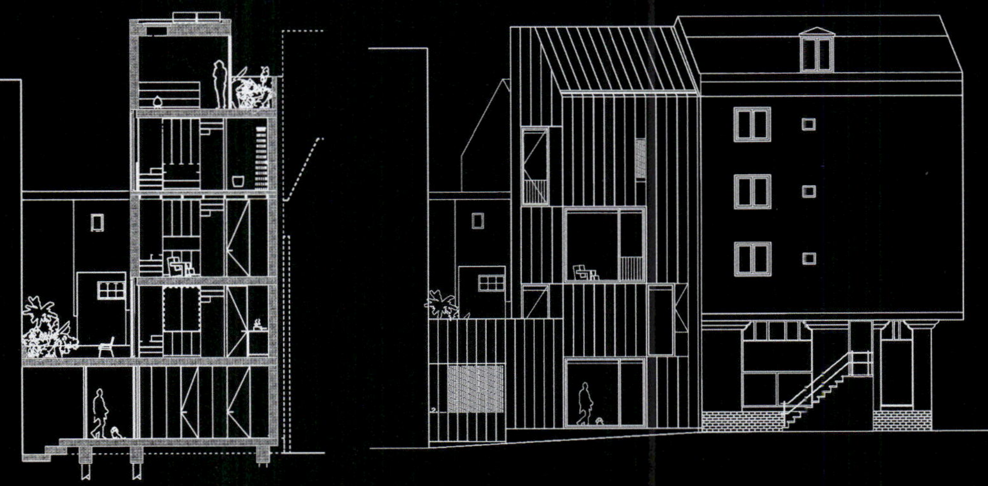

CASEY BROWN

Permanent Camping Two
Berry, New South Wales, Australia, 2020
Area: 16 m²

Collaboration: Antje Mahler (Project Architect), Jeffery Broadfield/ Mark Preston (Master Makers), Pip Smith, Smith and Primer (Builder)

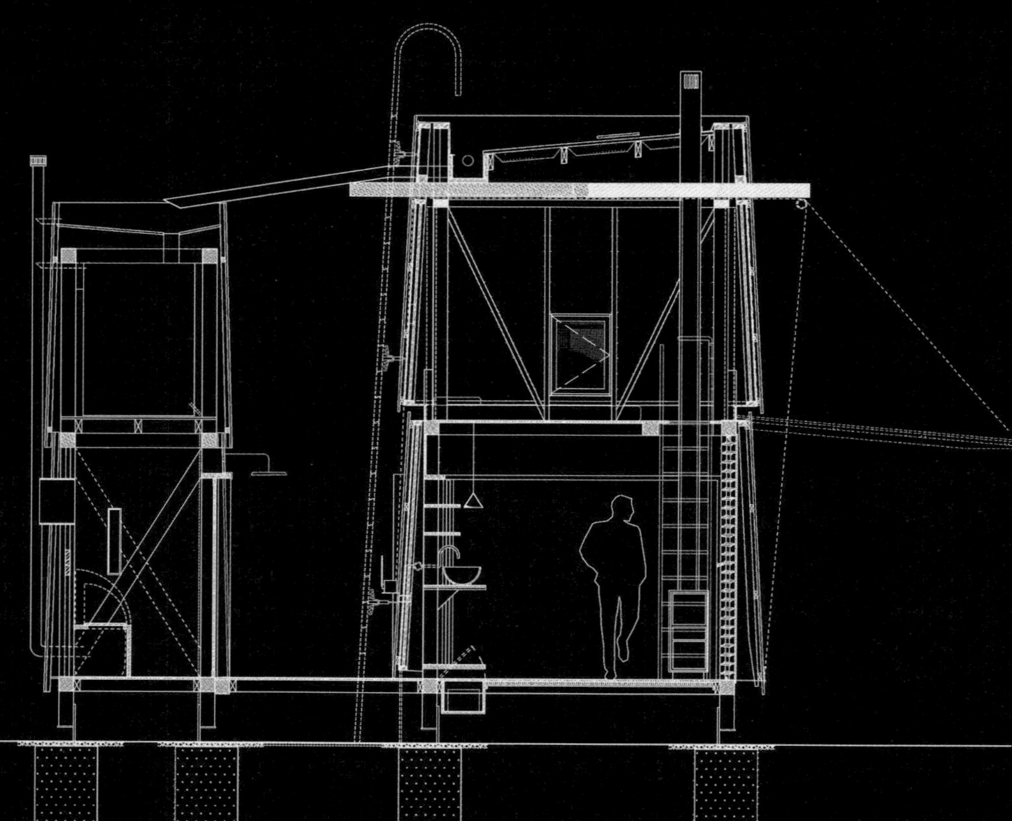

As the name Permanent Camping implies, this house offers a degree of solidity, basic comfort, and protection from the elements in a very open field setting with views that stretch into the distance.

This is a further development of the firm's Permanent Camping House (2007). The site selected overlooks the sea on the southern coast of New South Wales. This version includes a secondary copper-clad tower that houses a composting toilet, shower, and gravity-fed water tank. The two-story tower has an upper-level bedroom and corrugated copper walls that can be raised with winches to provide shade for the 34 square meters of external deck. The copper serves to protect exposed wood structural elements, and when the surfaces are closed, the structure can withstand gale force winds and bushfires. Photovoltaic panels on the roof provide light and power for the house. A wood-burning fireplace and copper kitchen basin are part of the interior fittings, as is an under-floor storage area. The house was built by Jeffery Broadfield using an on-site workshop.

Bei diesem Entwurf handelt es sich um eine Weiterentwicklung des Permanent Camping House (2007), errichtet mit Blick aufs Meer an der Südküste von New South Wales. Dieser Version wurde ein zweiter, mit Kupfer verkleideter Turm hinzugefügt, der eine Komposttoilette, eine Dusche und einen mit Schwerkraft betriebenen Wassertank beherbergt. Die zweistöckige Struktur mit einem Schlafzimmer im oberen Stockwerk hat gewellte Kupferwände, die mit Winden hochgezogen werden können, um der 34 m² großen Außenterrasse Schatten zu spenden. Das Kupfer dient dem Schutz der freiliegenden Holzbauteile und mit geschlossenen Oberflächen kann das Gebäude Windstürmen und Buschfeuern standhalten. Photovoltaikpaneele auf dem Dach liefern Licht und Strom. Ein holzbefeuerter Kamin und ein kupfernes Küchenbecken gehören ebenso zur Einrichtung wie ein im Boden eingelassener Stauraum. Das Haus wurde von Jeffery Broadfield in einer Werkstatt direkt vor Ort errichtet.

The interior of the house, with its generous openings and wood-burning stove, suggests a modernity that is present in the copper-clad exterior as well—approaching a somewhat industrial vocabulary.

Le projet est une extension de la Camping Permanent House (2007) déjà créée par l'agence. Le site surplombe la mer sur la côte sud de la Nouvelle-Galles-du-Sud. Cette deuxième version comprend une tour annexe revêtue de cuivre qui abrite des toilettes à compost, une douche et un réservoir d'eau par gravité. La première tour à deux niveaux possède une chambre au niveau supérieur et des murs en cuivre ondulé qui peuvent être ouverts à l'horizontale au moyen de treuils afin d'ombrager les 34 m^2 de la terrasse. Le cuivre protège les éléments structurels apparents en bois et lorsque tous les côtés sont fermés, la construction résiste aux vents et aux incendies du bush. Les panneaux photovoltaïques sur le toit fournissent lumière et électricité. Les aménagements intérieurs comprennent un poêle à bois et un lavabo en cuivre, ainsi qu'un espace de rangement en sous-sol. La maison a été construite par Jeffery Broadfield dans le cadre d'un atelier sur site.

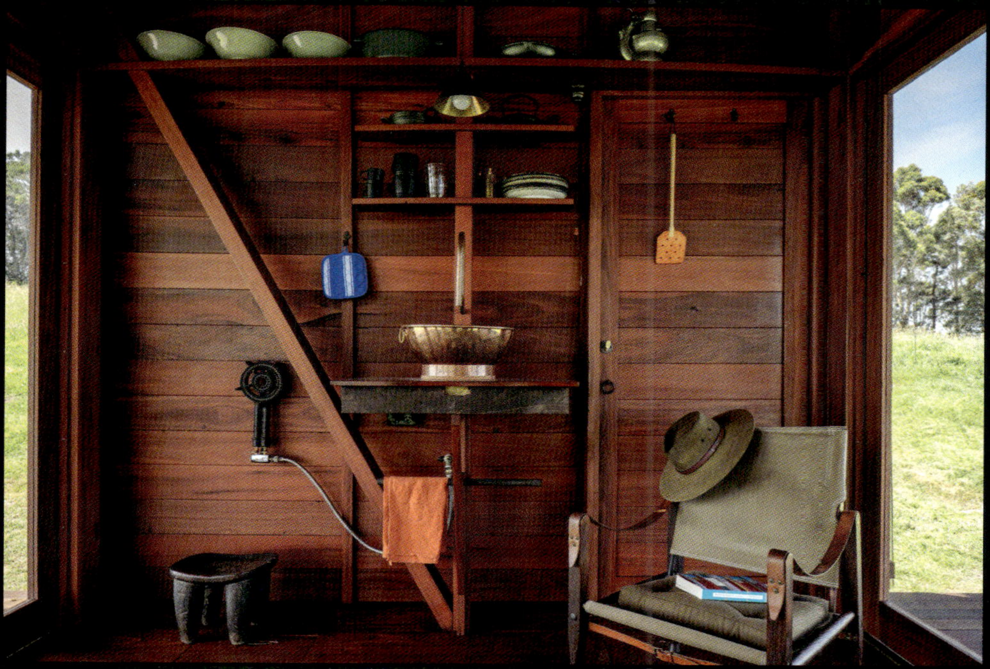

The warm wood interior finishes of the house and details like the copper basin give a carefully crafted feeling to the house despite an element of prefabrication.

First floor

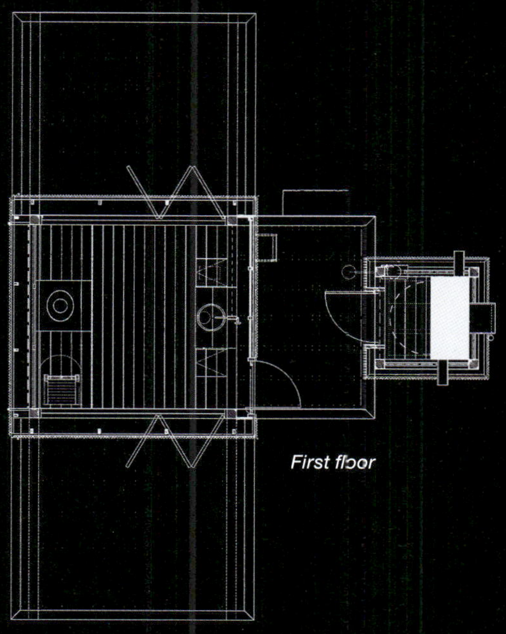

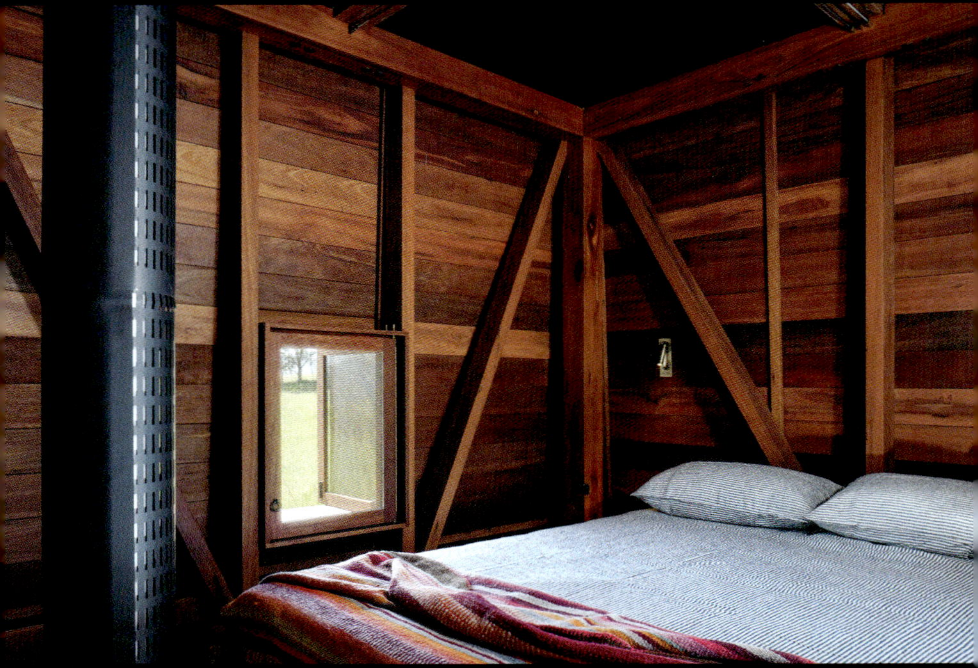

he 3 × 3-meter footprint of the house is seen in the rawings, as well as in the two-story adjacent ›wer finished in corrugated copper that includes toilet and shower.

Second floor

Roof

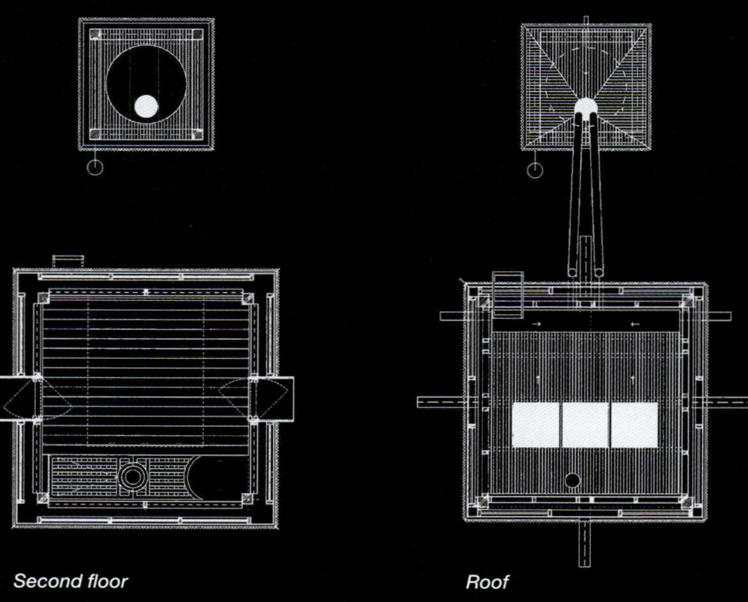

JAIME CHIOCO

Tiny Victories 2.0
Austin, Texas, USA, 2019
Area: 23 m²

Collaboration: Christy Taylor, Benjamin Dimmitt

1739

Despite its tiny size, this house has separate living and sleeping areas; its generous ceiling height also amplifies the impression of space, as seen in the image to the right.

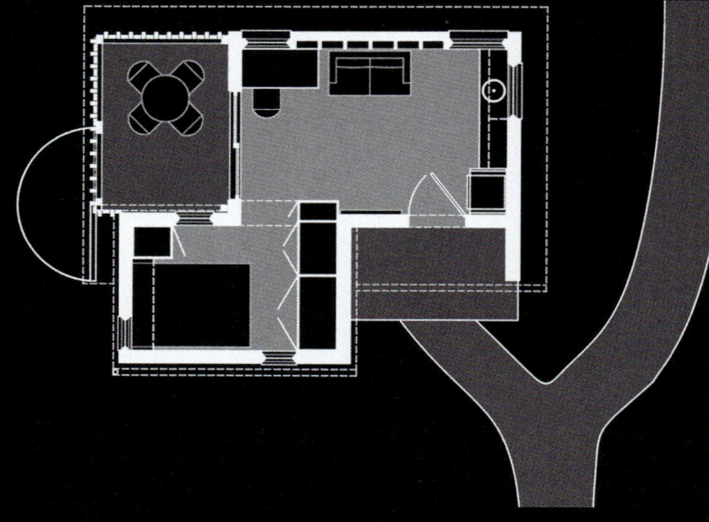

Living and sleeping sections of the house are seen in these images. Wood cabinetry, ceilings, and some walls give warmth to the residence, while natural light makes it agreeable.

Also called Shelia's Home, this small house is located in Community First Village, a neighborhood intended for tiny homes in Austin for people who have been homeless. An outdoor cinema, car garage, and art studios are located in the neighborhood to encourage a sense of community. The Austin Design Voice Committee, organized by the local AIA, worked with five selected architects to design homes in collaboration with a long-time resident of the area, in this case, Shelia. The house has separate living and sleeping areas. Natural light and cross ventilation were priorities. Built for a cost of $20 000 (materials), this house has a further six square meters of screened porch not counted in the floor area. Simple materials—lumber, corrugated metal, stucco, and laminated plywood—were used to keep the budget low. A desk and display shelves for Shelia's art objects are also part of the design, which is meant to be reproduced at least four times as the community project advances.

Dieses Häuschen mit dem Beinamen Shelia's Home liegt im Community First Village, einem Viertel von Austin, in dem vor allem als Obdachlosenunterkünfte dienende Mikrohäuser beheimatet sind. Um das Gemeinschaftsgefühl zu stärken, bietet die Nachbarschaft auch ein Freiluftkino, eine Autowerkstatt und Kunstateliers. Das Austin Design Voice Committee, ins Leben gerufen von der lokalen Zweigstelle des American Institute of Architects, bat fünf Architekten, jeweils gemeinsam mit einem langjährigen Bewohner des Viertels – im vorliegenden Fall Shelia – eine Reihe von Wohnhäusern zu entwerfen. Shelia's Home verfügt über getrennte Wohn- und Schlafbereiche sowie eine 6 m² große, abgeschirmte Veranda, die nicht zur Grundfläche zählt. Natürliches Licht und

Querlüftung zählten zu den Prioritäten des Entwurfs. Die Materialkosten betrugen 20 000 US-Dollar. Um das Budget niedrig zu halten, wurden einfache Materialien wie Holz, Wellblech, Gipsputz und laminiertes Sperrholz verwendet. Auch ein Schreibtisch und Regale für Shelias Kunstobjekte sind vorhanden. Mit Fortschreiten des Gemeinschaftsprojekts soll der Entwurf mindestens noch viermal reproduziert werden.

Aussi appelée Shelia's Home, cette petite maison appartient au Community First Village, un ensemble de minimaisons destinées à d'anciens sans-abri à Austin. Un cinéma en plein air, un garage et des studios d'art y ont aussi été construits pour développer le sentiment communautaire. L'Austin Design Voice Committee mis en place par l'American Institute of Architects (AIA) local a travaillé avec cinq architectes sélectionnés à la conception des maisons, en collaboration avec un habitant de longue date du quartier, ici Shelia. La maison possède des espacesde vie et de couchage séparés. La lumière naturelle et la ventilation transversale étaient des priorités. Construite pour un coût de 20 000 dollars (matériaux), elle dispose, avec le porche protégé des regards, de 6 m² supplémentaires qui ne sont pas comptés dans la surface au sol. Les matériaux sont simples – bois de charpente, métal ondulé, stuc et contreplaqué laminé – pour garantir un petit budget. L'ensemble comprend aussi un bureau et des rayonnages destinés à exposer les objets d'art de Shelia. Il est prévu de le reproduire au moins quatre fois au fur et à mesure de l'avancement du projet communautaire.

BARRY CONNOR

Skylark Cabin
Twizel, New Zealand, 2020
Area: 50 m²

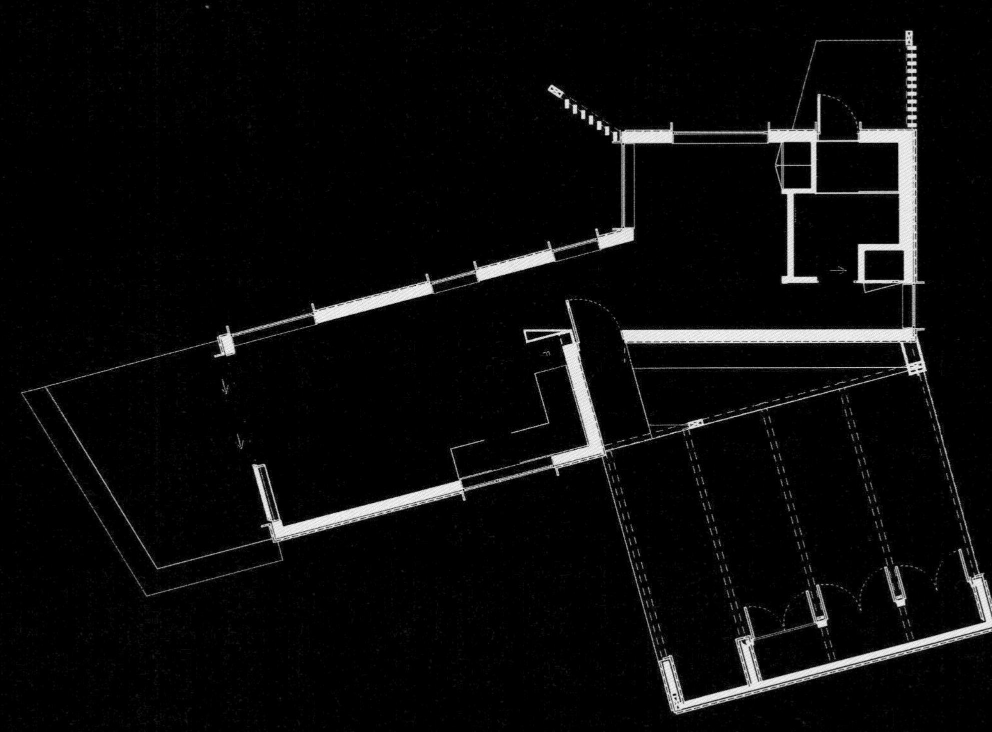

These images make clear the reasons for which the client wanted to be in this location and also why the house is designed with specific views in mind. A wooden deck extends living space into the rocky site.

The client for this cabin wanted a place to retreat to near the Ben Ohau Range. Twizel is in the Canterbury Region of the South Island. It had a population of 1,660 people in 2021. The architect imagined two open-plan spaces, one for the bedroom and bathroom, the other with the kitchen, entrance and living area. The angles of the volumes were calculated to allow specific views when lying in bed, washing the dishes, or having a shower. The circular skylight over the bed, for example, frames views of the Mackenzie Aoraki International Dark Sky Reserve, a 4300-square-kilometer area where light pollution is strictly limited. According to the architect: "The folded form also nods to the distinctive aerial display of the local skylarks with their angular, precise, and purposeful acrobatics." A carport connects directly to the entry porch. A burnt-orange color for the structural elements was used at the request of the client, and the cabin was placed among natural boulders from the site. An exterior rough-sawn larch rainscreen evokes a bird's nest. Light-colored beech plywood is used for the interiors, together with contrasting, black-edged rib detailing.

The kitchen and the living space are connected, and a wood-burning stove provides warmth.

Mit dieser Minilodge wollte sich der Bauherr einen Rückzugsort nahe der Ben Ohau Range schaffen. Twizel liegt in der Region Canterbury auf der Südinsel und zählte im Jahr 2021 1660 Einwohner. Das Häuschen beherbergt zwei offene Bereiche: einen für Schlafzimmer und Bad, den anderen mit Küche, Eingang und Wohnbereich. Die Raumwinkel wurden so berechnet, dass sich von Schlafzimmer, Küche und Bad jeweils eine andere Aussicht bietet. Das kreisrunde Oberlicht über dem Bett beispielsweise gibt den Blick auf das Mackenzie Aoraki International Dark Sky Reserve frei, ein 4300 km² großes Gebiet mit minimaler Lichtverschmutzung. „Die gefaltete Form spielt auch auf den unverwechselbaren Flugstil der heimischen Feldlerche an: kantig, präzise und von zielgerichteter Akrobatik", so der Architekt. Direkt neben der Eingangsveranda liegt ein Carport. Auf Wunsch des Bauherrn sind die Strukturelemente der inmitten natürlicher Felsblöcke platzierten Minilodge in Feuerorange gehalten. Eine Regenschutzwand aus grob gesägtem Lärchenholz erinnert an ein Vogelnest. Für die Innenräume wurde helles Buchensperrholz verwendet, das mit schwarz umrandeten Rippendetails kontrastiert.

A large round opening above the bed provides natural light during the day and allows for stargazing at night.

Le client souhaitait un lieu où se retirer, proche des montagnes de Ben Ohau Range. Twizel est située dans la région de Canterbury, sur l'Île du Sud, sa population était de 1660 habitants en 2021. L'architecte a imaginé deux espaces ouverts, l'un destiné à la chambre et à la salle de bains, l'autre composé de la cuisine, de l'entrée et du séjour. Les angles des volumes ont été calculés pour offrir des vues différentes depuis le lit, pendant la vaisselle ou sous la douche. La lucarne circulaire au-dessus du lit, par exemple, donne sur la réserve internationale de ciel étoilé de Mackenzie Aoraki, une zone de 4300 km² où la pollution lumineuse est strictement limitée. Pour l'architecte: « La forme repliée se rapproche du spectacle aérien particulier des alouettes locales au vol acrobatique saccadé, mais précis et déterminé. » Un auvent pour garer une voiture communique directement avec le porche.

La teinte orange foncé des éléments structurels est une demande du client et la maison a été disposée parmi les rochers naturellement ronds qui parsèment le terrain. Un écran pare-pluie en bois de mélèze grossièrement scié évoque un nid d'oiseau. L'intérieur est en contreplaqué de hêtre teinté clair qui contraste avec les détails aux côtes bordées de noir.

CROXATTO & OPAZO

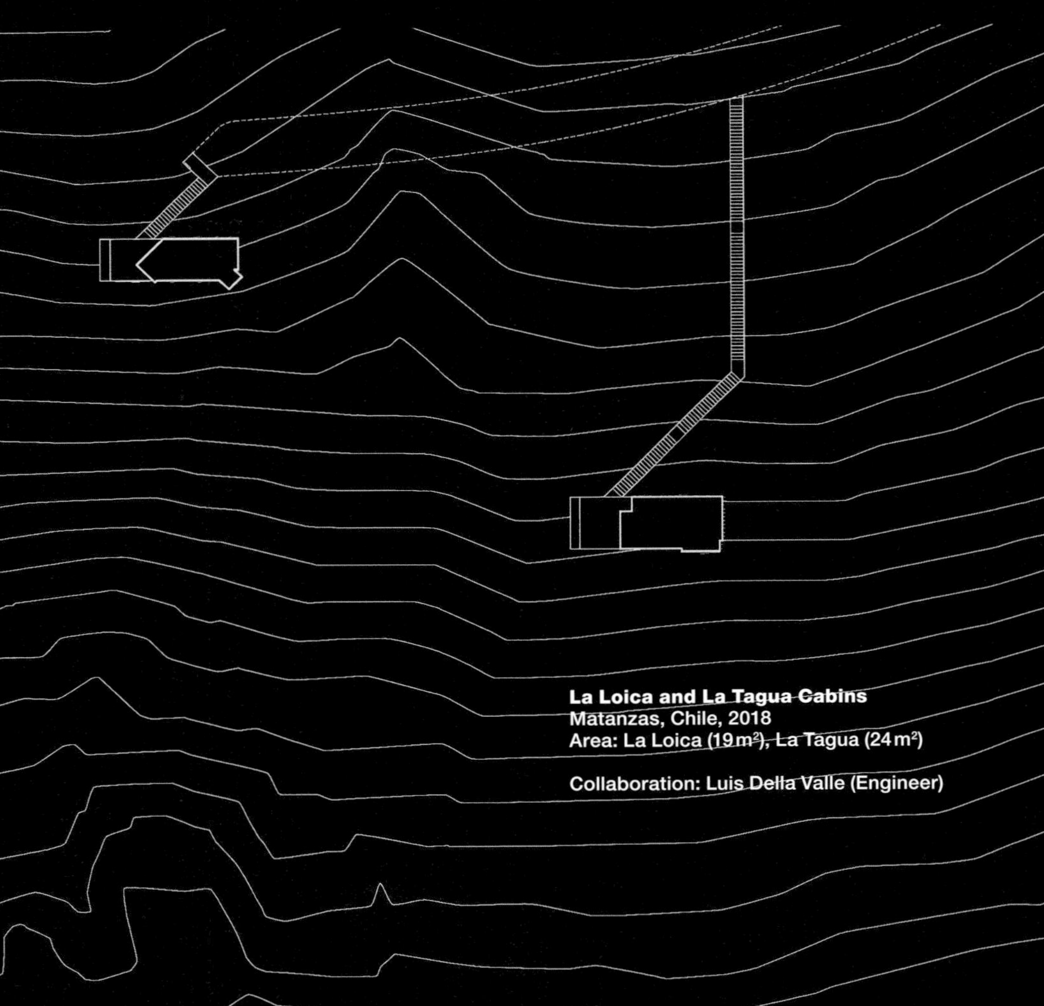

La Loica and La Tagua Cabins
Matanzas, Chile, 2018
Area: La Loica (19 m²), La Tagua (24 m²)

Collaboration: Luis Della Valle (Engineer)

The architects combine rather powerful and unexpected geometric elements with such items as reclaimed wooden railway sleepers treated with oil.

These structures, respectively named after two different local bird species, were built on a steeply sloped site and have kitchen and dining areas that face the Pacific 80 meters below. The upper-level bedrooms are reached by climbing a vertical ladder. The cabins also have north-facing terraces. Matanzas is a wood-producing area, a fact that encouraged the architects to use three varieties of wood. The structure of the cabins employs pressure-impregnated wood (wood that has been immersed in a liquid preservative and placed in a pressure chamber), while the exterior cladding was fashioned from reclaimed oak sleepers treated with oil to improve resistance to weather and humidity. Interiors were finished with pine treated with Osmo coating, which is made of natural vegetable oils and provides protection from sun and dust.

Beide Gebäude, die jeweils nach lokalen Vogelarten benannt sind, stehen auf einem steil abfallenden Gelände. Aus ihren Küchen- und Essbereichen fällt der Blick auf den 80 m tiefer liegenden Pazifik. Die Schlafzimmer im Obergeschoss sind über eine Leiter zu erreichen. Ihre Terrassen sind nach Norden ausgerichtet. Da Matanzas ein Holzanbaugebiet ist, verwendeten die Architekten drei verschiedene Holzsorten. Die Gebäudestruktur besteht aus kesseldruckimprägniertem Holz (Holz, das in einer Druckkammer mit flüssigem Konservierungsmittel behandelt wird), während die wiederverwendeten Eichenschwellen der Außenverkleidung mit Öl behandelt wurden, um ihre Widerstandsfähigkeit gegen Witterung und Feuchtigkeit zu verbessern. Die Innenraumverkleidung ist aus Kiefernholz, das von einer Osmo-Beschichtung aus natürlichen Pflanzenölen gegen Sonne und Staub geschützt wird.

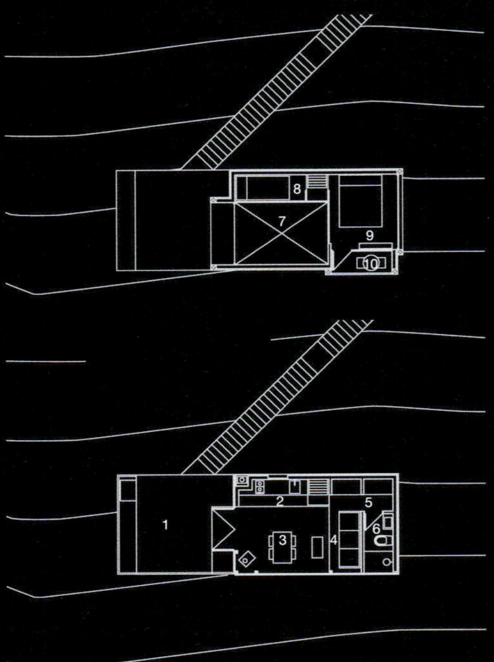

The strong forms of the structures are in keeping with the very rough natural setting; the small size of the cabins and the use of wood make them also appear to be modest.

1 Terrace
2 Kitchen
3 Dining room
4 Living room
5 Closet
6 Bathroom
7 Double height
8 Secondary bedroom
9 Main bedroom
10 Balcony

Les petites maisons, qui portent les noms de deux espèces locales d'oiseaux, ont été construites sur un terrain en pente raide, avec une cuisine et un coin repas face au Pacifique qui s'étend 80 m plus bas. Les chambres de l'étage sont accessibles par une échelle verticale. Les maisons ont aussi des terrasses orientées vers le nord. Matanzas est une région productrice de bois, ce qui a incité les architectes à utiliser trois essences différentes. La structure des constructions est en bois imprégné sous pression (immergé dans un conservateur liquide et placé dans une chambre de pression), tandis que le revêtement extérieur est fait de traverses de chêne récupérées, huilées pour mieux résister aux intempéries et à l'humidité, et que les finitions intérieures sont en pin recouvert d'enduit Osmo, composé d'huiles végétales naturelles, qui protège du soleil et de la poussière.

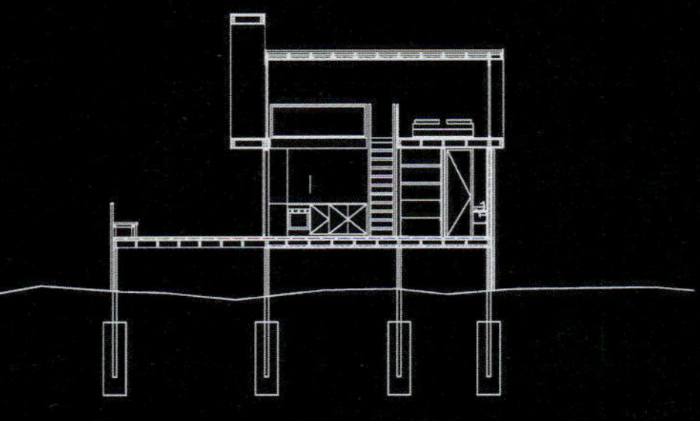

EL SINDICATO

Parasitic House
Quito, Ecuador, 2019
Area: 12 m²

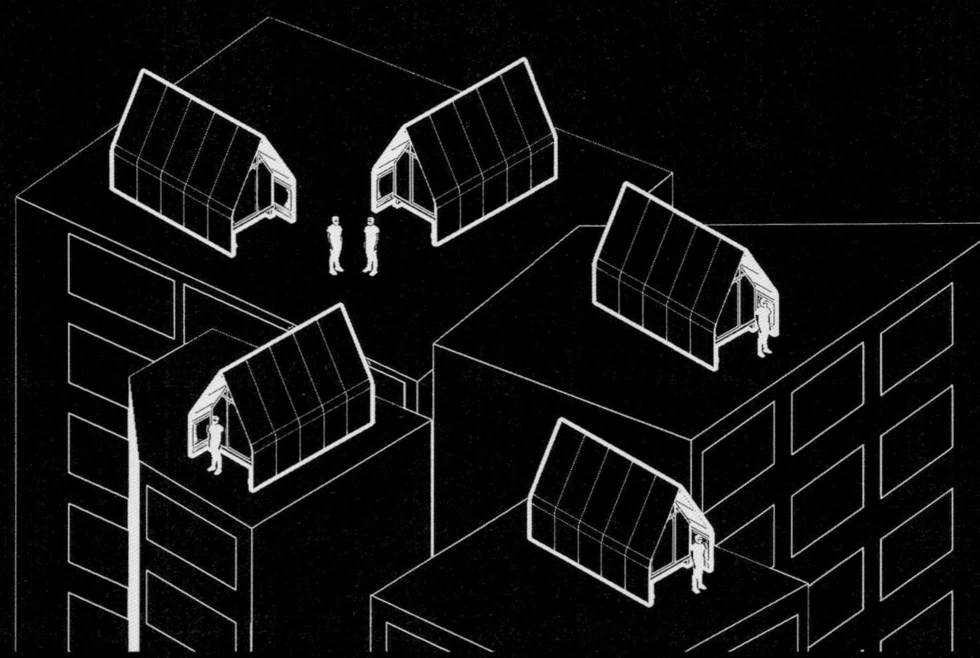

AMERICANO

At just 12 square meters, this "parasitic" house is attached to the roof of an existing building in an effort by the architects to demonstrate the viability of such gestures in attempts to densify cities without creating entirely new buildings.

This tiny house was built on the roof of an existing building in the San Juan neighborhood of Quito. A steel foundation attached the new element to its "host" structure. It includes a bathroom, kitchen, bed, storage, and space for eating, working, and socializing. The A-frame timber house has a rectangular open area on its ground floor, with a kitchen tabletop, bathroom, storage, and pull-down work desk. An elevated platform houses the bed. A large triangular window on the north side provides natural light and views of the city. Steel panels on the eastern and western elevations of the small house protect it from excessive solar gain. The architects declared: "Although it is possible to build this type of project in urban or rural sites without existing buildings, ideally its construction should occur on underused rooftops of urban buildings that are structurally sound—buildings where one can connect to the existing water, waste, and electrical grids. In this way, we contribute to the densification of the city at a very small scale, with a minimum investment and use of resources, as well as contributing to the conservation of architectural heritage."

1 Toilet
2 Shower
3 Sink
4 Storage space
5 Cooking space
6 Living area
7 Bed

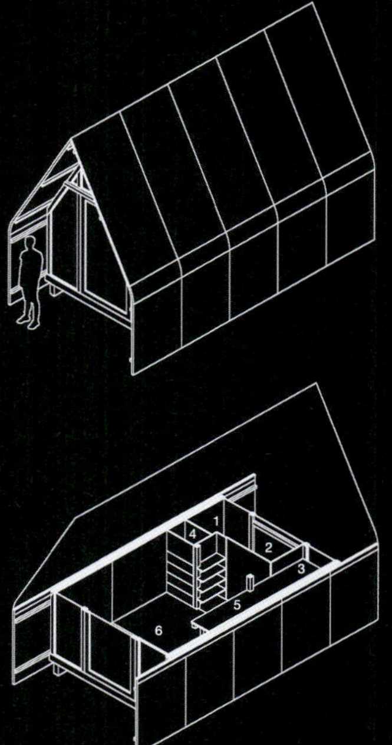

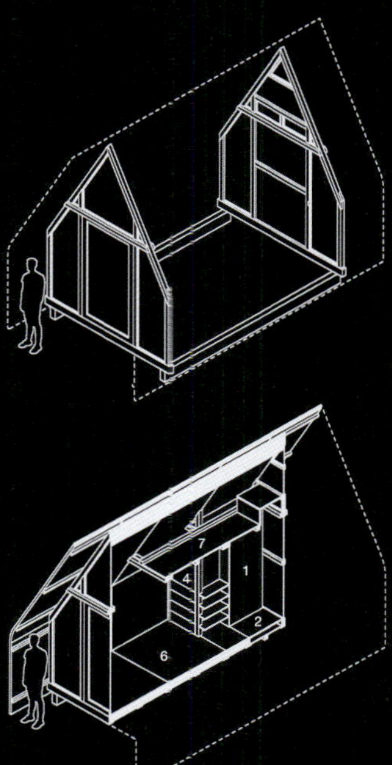

The upper-level bed looks through a north-facing triangular window and sits above the living space on the bottom floor.

Dieses winzige Haus auf dem Dach eines bestehenden Gebäudes im Stadtteil San Juan in Quito klammert sich mittels eines Stahlfundaments an seinen „Wirt“. Es birgt ein Bad, eine Küche, ein Bett, Stauraum und genügend Platz zum Essen, Arbeiten und Beisammensein. Das Erdgeschoss dieses Holzhäuschen in A-Bauweise ist ein rechteckiger offener Bereich mit Küchentisch, Bad, Stauraum und ausziehbarem Arbeitstisch. Das Bett thront auf einer Plattform. Ein großzügiges Dreiecksfenster an der Nordseite sorgt für natürliches Licht und einen Blick über die Stadt. Stahlpaneele an den Ost- und Westfassaden schützen den Bau vor übermäßiger Sonneneinstrahlung. „Es ist zwar möglich, eine solche Struktur in urbanen oder ländlichen Gebieten freistehend zu bauen“, erklären die Architekten, „aber idealerweise sollte es auf ungenutzten Dächern von städtischen, strukturell soliden Gebäuden platziert werden, um deren Wasser-, Abfall- und Strominfrastruktur mitnutzen zu können. Auf diese Weise tragen wir in kleinem Maßstab mit einem Minimum an Investitionen und Ressourcen sowohl zur Verdichtung der Stadt als auch zur Erhaltung des architektonischen Erbes bei.“

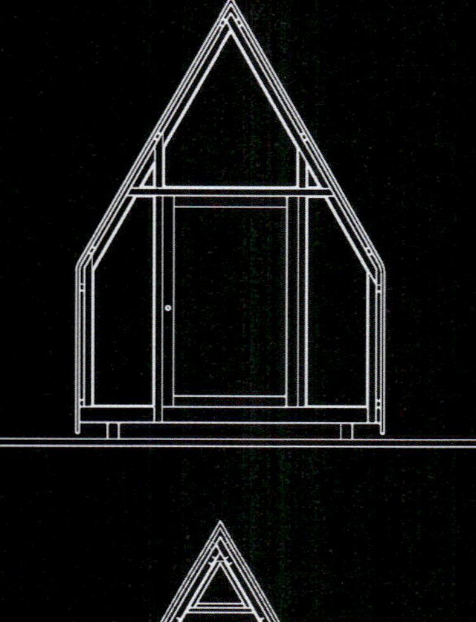

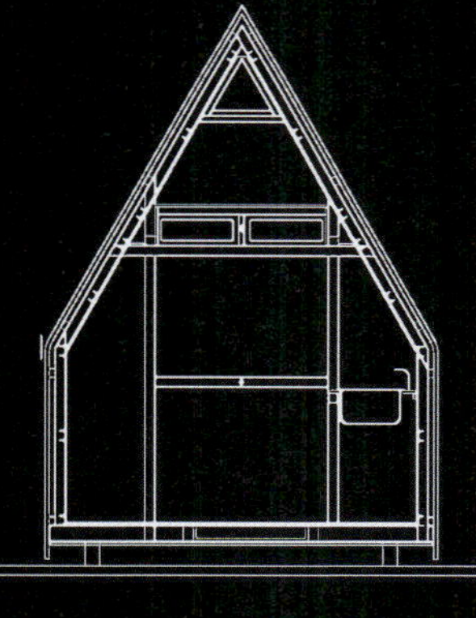

The use of OSB-type panels for interior cladding is economical and durable, as well as being fairly responsible from an ecological point of view.

Cette minuscule maison a été bâtie sur le toit d'un immeuble dans le quartier San Juan de Quito. Elle est fixée à la structure « hôte » par des fondations en acier. Elle comprend une salle de bains, une cuisine, un lit, un rangement et un espace destiné à la vie en commun. Construite en bois d'œuvre, la maison dispose d'un espace rectangulaire ouvert au rez-de-chaussée, équipé d'un plateau de table de cuisine, d'une salle de bains, d'un rangement et d'un bureau rabattable. Le lit est placé sur une plate-forme en hauteur. Une grande fenêtre triangulaire côté nord fait entrer la lumière du jour et offre une vue sur la ville. Les panneaux en acier sur les pentes est et ouest du toit protègent la maison d'un apport solaire excessif. Les architectes expliquent que « s'il est possible de réaliser ce type de projet en zone rurale ou urbaine sans autre construction, l'idéal est d'utiliser les toits sous-exploités d'immeubles en ville aux structures solides – ce qui permet aussi de se raccorder aux réseaux existants d'eau, d'électricité et de traitement des déchets. Nous contribuons ainsi à la densification de la ville à une toute petite échelle pour un investissement et des ressources réduits au minimum, ainsi qu'à la préservation du patrimoine architectural ».

TAKAAKI FUJI + YUKO FUJI

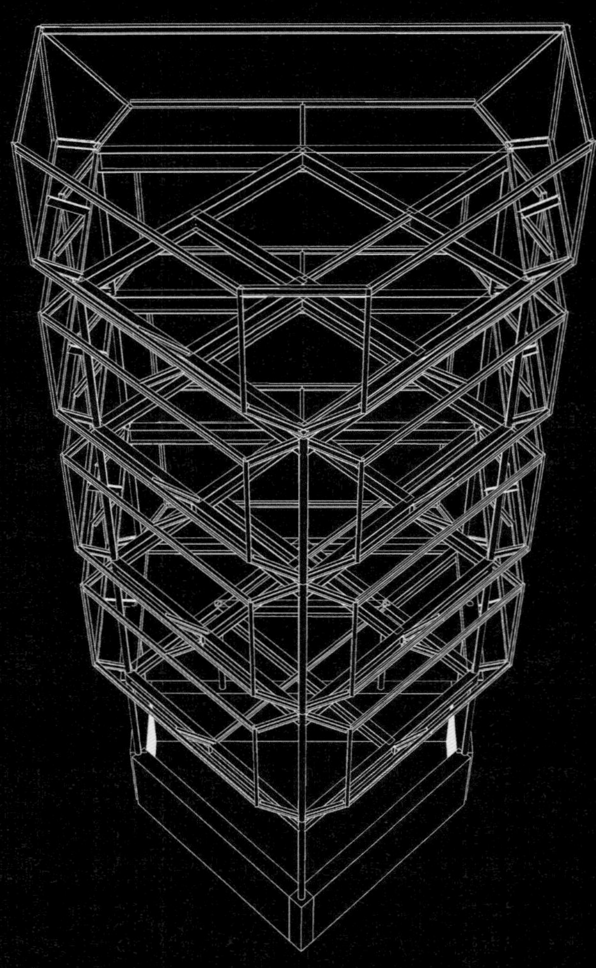

Bay Window Tower Hou
Tokyo, Japan, 2020
Area: 84 m^2

The bay windows that give this house its name are visible in the image above. The house stands out from its typical, densely built, urban Tokyo environment.

This is the residence and office of the architects, located near a train station. They decided to base the structure around the regulated form of a bay window, which must be 50 centimeters deep and located at least 30 centimeters from the floor according to Japanese law. The upper frame of the window is required to rise to the ceiling. They write: "The bay window is treated as a piece of furniture, and by wrapping it around the entire floor and laminating it, a furniture-like boundary is created around the building. Sitting, lying down, washing hands, cooking, bathing, writing, and many other daily activities can be done with the bay windows." In order to avoid too great a proximity with neighboring buildings, they added 45° angles to the corners of their structure. Carbonized cork was used for the exterior walls because it is an environmentally friendly material that does not require the use of chemical substances. It is solidified by the sap exuded by pressing the bark of cork oak. The structure has a steel frame, which allows vertical and seismic forces to be decomposed, with the seismic forces borne entirely by the bay window frames. The cork, interior plastered walls, and Ferrodor paint age well over time. The architects say: "We wanted to create an architecture that would live on as a part of this cityscape."

Dieses Häuschen in Bahnhofsnähe dient den Architekten als Wohnhaus und Büro zugleich. Als Grundstruktur wählten sie eine Erkerform mit 50 Zentimeter Tiefe, die nach geltendem Recht mindestens 30 Zentimeter über dem Boden liegen und deren oberer Fensterrahmen bis zur Decke reichen musste. „Das Erkerfenster gleicht einem Einrichtungsgegenstand", schreiben die Architekten. „Es umgibt den gesamten Boden, *'he architects point out that washing hands can be 'one near windows. Below: a section drawing with he rooftop terrace visible at the top.*

egrenzt so das Gebäude wie ein Möbelstück ınd schafft Raum zum Sitzen, Schlafen, Hän-lewaschen, Kochen, Baden, Schreiben und für iele andere alltägliche Tätigkeiten." Um eine zu große Nähe zu den Nachbarhäusern zu vermei-len, fügten sie den Gebäudeecken 45°-Winkel ıinzu. Der karbonisierte Kork der Außenwände, ein umweltfreundliches Material ohne chemische Substanzen, verfestigt sich durch den Saft, der oeim Pressen der Korkeichenrinde austritt. Der Stahlrahmen der Grundstruktur kann vertikale ınd seismische Kräfte aufnehmen, wobei Letz-ere vollständig von den Rahmen der Erkerfenster ıbsorbiert werden. Der Kork, die verputzten nnenwände und die Ferrodor-Farbe durchlaufen einen ästhetischen Alterungsprozess. „Wir woll-en eine Architektur schaffen, die als Teil des Stadtbildes weiterlebt", so die Architekten

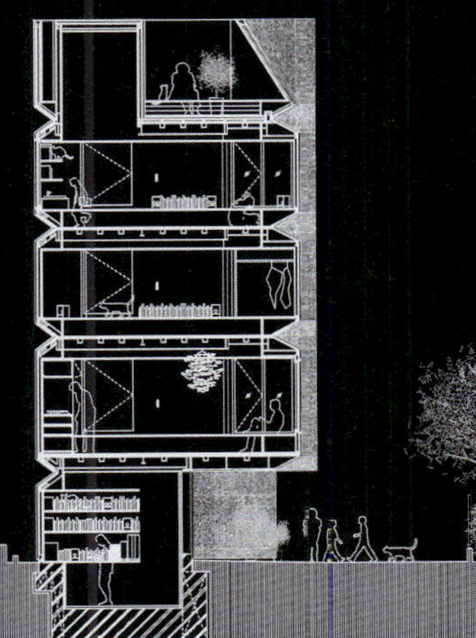

Sparse furnishing is frequent in small Japanese houses: in this instance, the architects say that the windows are viewed like "pieces of furniture."

La maison abrite le domicile et le bureau des architectes, elle est proche d'une gare. Ils ont décidé d'une structure basée sur la forme régulière d'un bow-window dont la profondeur doit être de 50 cm à 30 cm au minimum du sol selon la règlement japonaise. Le cadre supérieur de la fenêtre doit atteindre le plafond. Les architectes expliquent que « le bow-window est considéré comme un élément de mobilier, il est déroulé autour de l'étage et laminé, ce qui en fait comme un meuble séparateur et crée une frontière autour du bâtiment. Dans les bow-windows, on peut s'asseoir, se coucher, se laver les mains, cuisiner, se laver, écrire et se livrer à de nombreuses autres activités de tous les jours ». Pour éviter une trop grande proximité avec les bâtiments voisins, des angles à 45° ont été ajoutés aux coins. Les murs extérieurs sont en liège carbonisé, car c'est un matériau écologique qui n'exige aucun produit chimique. Il est solidifié par la sève exsudée en comprimant l'écorce de chêne-liège. La charpente est en acier, ce qui permet de dissocier les forces verticales et sismiques, ces dernières étant entièrement supportées par les cadres des bow-windows. Le liège, les murs intérieurs talochés et la peinture Ferrodor vieillissent bien, car les architectes affirment avoir « voulu créer une architecture qui subsiste et continue à faire partie du paysage urbain ».

A metal spiral staircase connects the different levels of the house and office, providing an enlivening sculptural and architectural presence to the interiors.

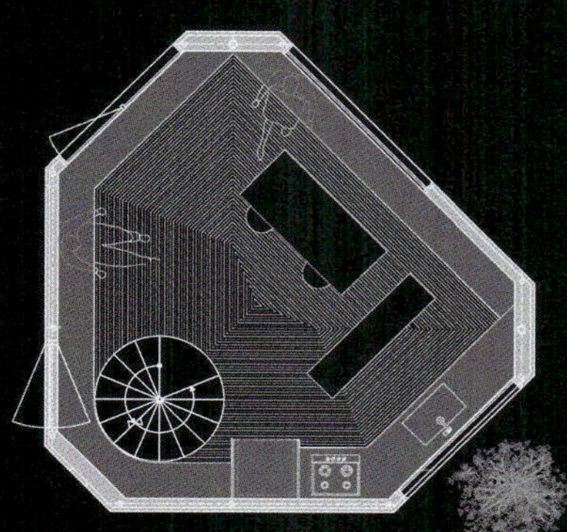

Second floor

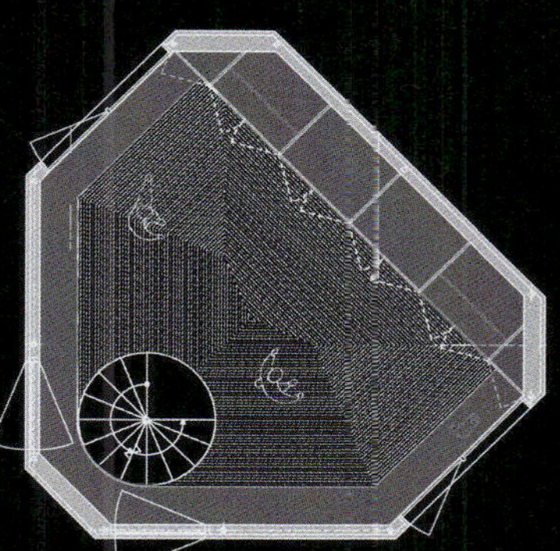

Third floor

Opposite: *the spaces of the house are in part wound around the spiral staircase.* Left: *the rooftop terrace.* Previous spread: *second and third floor plan.* Below: *fourth floor and rooftop plans.*

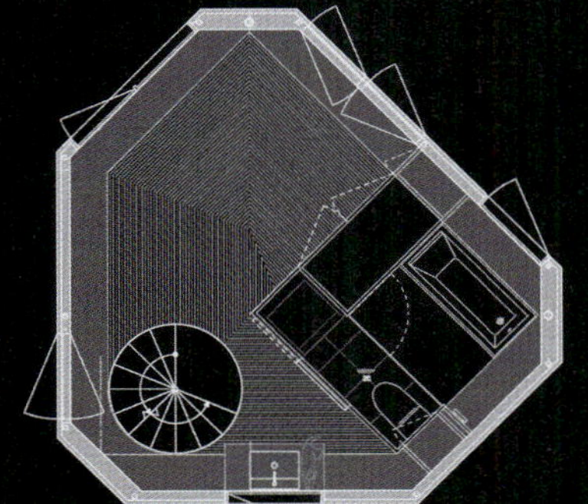

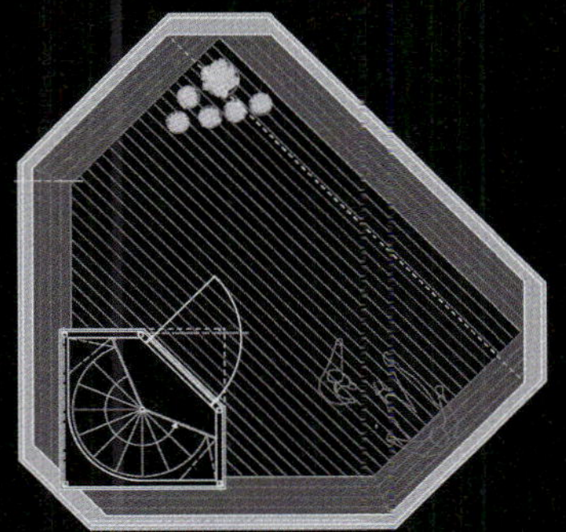

SEAN GODSELL

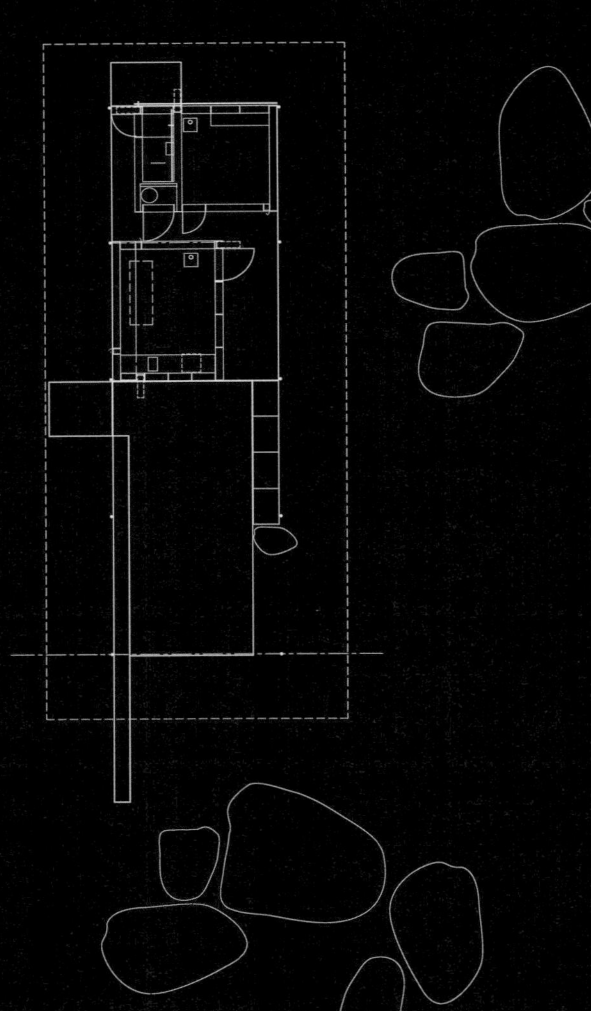

Shack in the Rocks
Victoria, Australia, 2021
Area: 32 m^2

Collaboration: Haley Franklin

An earlier scheme for this small refuge was delayed because of cost. Located one hour's drive west of Melbourne, the Shack in the Rocks is thus the second proposal of Sean Godsell for a different site on the same property. The architect started with what was considered the basics: "A roof parasol that provides some shade and protection from the rain as well as a place to enjoy outdoor activities—cooking, eating, and engaging with and framing the spectacular landscape that exists on this particular site." The final design is an adapted hayshed with translucent roofing. Godsell, in this instance, reveals an unexpected source of inspiration for the project: "Two houses by Riken Yamamoto & Field Shop—Yamakawa Cottage (Yatsugatake, Japan, 1977) and the Ishii House (Kanagawa, Japan, 1978)—disassemble conventional residential programs and then reassemble them in a highly creative way. I remember being intrigued by these projects as a young architect. In the case of the Yamakawa Cottage the functional program is distributed in an ordered and logical way across a single level timber platform. This highly poetic scattering of spaces is controlled by a large shallow gable roof which shelters not only the rooms but the outdoor or 'other' space in the building. This 'other' space is intriguing to me, and I certainly had the Yamakawa Cottage in mind when I designed this shack in the rocks."

Sean Godsell, winner of the 2022 Australian Institute of Architects Gold Medal, has imbued this small structure with a recognizably crisp and light design.

Ein früherer Entwurf dieser Minilodge wurde aus Kostengründen auf Eis gelegt. Shack in the Rocks, eine Autostunde westlich von Melbourne gelegen, ist der zweite Vorschlag von Sean Godsell für einen anderen Standort auf demselben Grundstück. Die zentralen Ausgangspunkte für den Architekten waren „ein Sonnenschirm auf dem Dach, der etwas Schatten und Schutz vor dem Regen bietet und einen Ort für Outdoor-Aktivitäten: kochen, essen und sich der spektakulären Landschaft hingeben". Für den finalen Entwurf des umgebauten Heuschobers mit lichtdurchlässigem Dach verweist Godsell auf eine unerwartete Inspirationsquelle: „Zwei Häuser von Riken Yamamoto & Field Shop – Yamakawa Cottage (Yatsugatake, Japan, 1977) und Ishii House (Kanagawa, Japan, 1978) – demontieren konventionelle Wohnprogramme, die auf höchst kreative Weise wieder zusammengesetzt wurden. Ich erinnere mich, wie sehr mich damals diese Projekte faszinierten. Die geordneten Funktionen sind im Yamakawa Cottage logisch über eine einstöckige Holzplattform verteilt. Diese höchst poetische Raumaufteilung wird durch ein großes, flaches Giebeldach kontrolliert, das nicht nur das Innere, sondern auch den Außenbereich und die ‚anderen Bereiche schützt. Diese ‚anderen Bereiche faszinieren mich, und ich hatte sicherlich das Yamakawa Cottage im Kopf, als ich Shack in the Rocks entwarf."

Interiors confirm the choice of rather industrial materials for the Shack in the Rocks, which can be perceived from the exterior. Large-scale glazing seems to bring the rocks concerned inside.

Un premier projet de cet abri a dû être reporté pour des raisons de coût. Situé à une heure de voiture à l'ouest de Melbourne, Shack in the Rocks est donc la deuxième proposition de Sean Godsell pour un emplacement différent sur la même propriété. L'architecte a commencé par ce qu'il considère comme la base : « Un toit parasol qui ombrage et protège de la pluie, tout en offrant un espace pour des activités extérieures et en fournissant un cadre au paysage extraordinaire de ce site exceptionnel. » Le concept consiste en une grange aménagée à toiture translucide. Godsell révèle ici une source d'inspiration inattendue : « Deux maisons de Riken Yamamoto & Field Shop – la maison de campagne Yamakawa (Yatsugatake, Japon, 1977) et la maison Ishii (Kanagawa, Japon, 1978) – qui démontent les programmes résidentiels conventionnels et les réassemblent avec une extrême créativité. Je me souviens avoir été intrigué par ces projets lorsque j'étais un jeune architecte. Dans la maison Yamakawa, les espaces fonctionnels sont répartis selon un plan ordonné et logique sur une plate-forme en bois à un niveau. Cette dispersion extrêmement poétique des espaces est sous le contrôle d'un vaste toit à pignon creux qui n'abrite pas uniquement les différentes pièces de la maison, mais aussi l'espace extérieur ou "autre". Cet "autre" espace m'intrigue et j'avais Yamakawa en tête lorsque j'ai imaginé cette "cabane dans les rochers". »

H&P

AgriNesture
Quang Ninh, Vietnam, 2018
Area: 75 m²

The house forms a two-story cube made of reinforced concrete clad in brick. It is quite simple but obviously modern.

This house, intended to help promote agriculture in its region, was imagined like a nest made from a "cube of earth cut out from a field." The two-story reinforced-concrete structure can be expanded to include another (third) level. Here, brick cladding is present both outside and inside the house, with some exposed concrete elements, such as the floors, ceilings, and some walls. The architects explain: "Users will directly participate in the process of building the house, and they will actively divide the spaces subject to their own needs. In addition, they are also the ones to produce the cover materials appropriate with their local conditions. In this sense, the building process will help create jobs and shape homes that promote agricultural development and bring about ecological balance as well as economic stability for the population in vulnerable areas."

Das Haus, das Landwirtschaft in der Region attraktiver machen soll, gleicht einem Nest, das aus einem "aus dem Feld herausgeschnittenen Erdwürfel" besteht. Die zweigeschossige Stahlbetonstruktur lässt die Aufstockung um eine weitere (dritte) Ebene zu. Sie ist sowohl außen als auch innen mit Ziegeln verkleidet und verfügt über diverse Sichtbetonelemente, wie Böden, Decken und einige Wände. „Die Bewohner nehmen unmittelbar am Bauprozess teil und definieren die Räume nach ihren eigenen Bedürfnissen", erklären die Architekten. „Darüber hinaus sind sie für die Beschaffung der geeigneten Deckmaterialien aus lokaler Produktion zuständig. Insofern trägt der Bauprozess dazu bei, Arbeitsplätze zu schaffen und Häuser zu gestalten, die die landwirtschaftliche Entwicklung, ein ökologisches Gleichgewicht und wirtschaftliche Stabilität für die Bewohner gefährdeter Gebiete fördern."

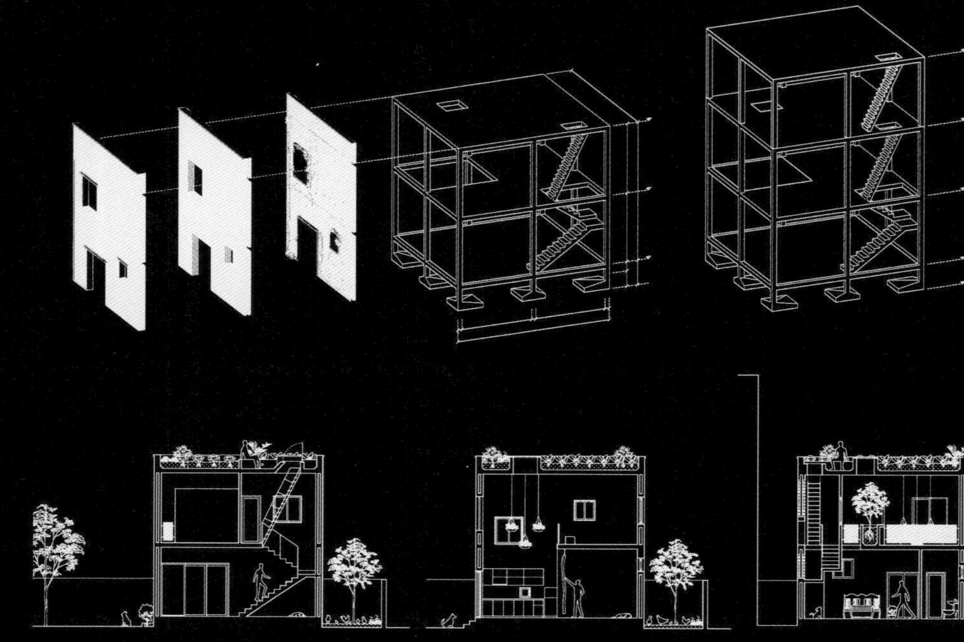

Interior surfaces are in concrete, brick, and wood for such elements as the kitchen cabinets. Hanging green plants add an unexpected presence to the high living space.

La maison, construite dans le but de contribuer à la promotion de l'agriculture dans la région, a été conçue comme un nid fait d'un « cube de terre découpé dans un champ ». La structure à deux niveaux en béton armé peut être agrandie pour comprendre un troisième niveau. Le parement en briques est présent à la fois à l'extérieur et à l'intérieur et complète d'autres éléments en béton apparent tels que les sols, les plafonds et certains murs. Les architectes expliquent que « les utilisateurs sont appelés à participer directement au processus de construction et à diviser activement les espaces correspondant à leurs besoins propres. De même, ce sont eux qui produiront les matériaux de couverture adaptés aux conditions sur place. Ainsi, le processus de construction contribuera à créer des emplois et des maisons qui encouragent le développement agricole et apportent un équilibre écologique et une stabilité économique aux populations des zones vulnérables ».

DAEWOO

TAKESHI HOSAKA

Love2 House
Tokyo, Japan, 2019
Area: 19 m²

Collaboration: Kenji Nawa
(Structural Engineer)

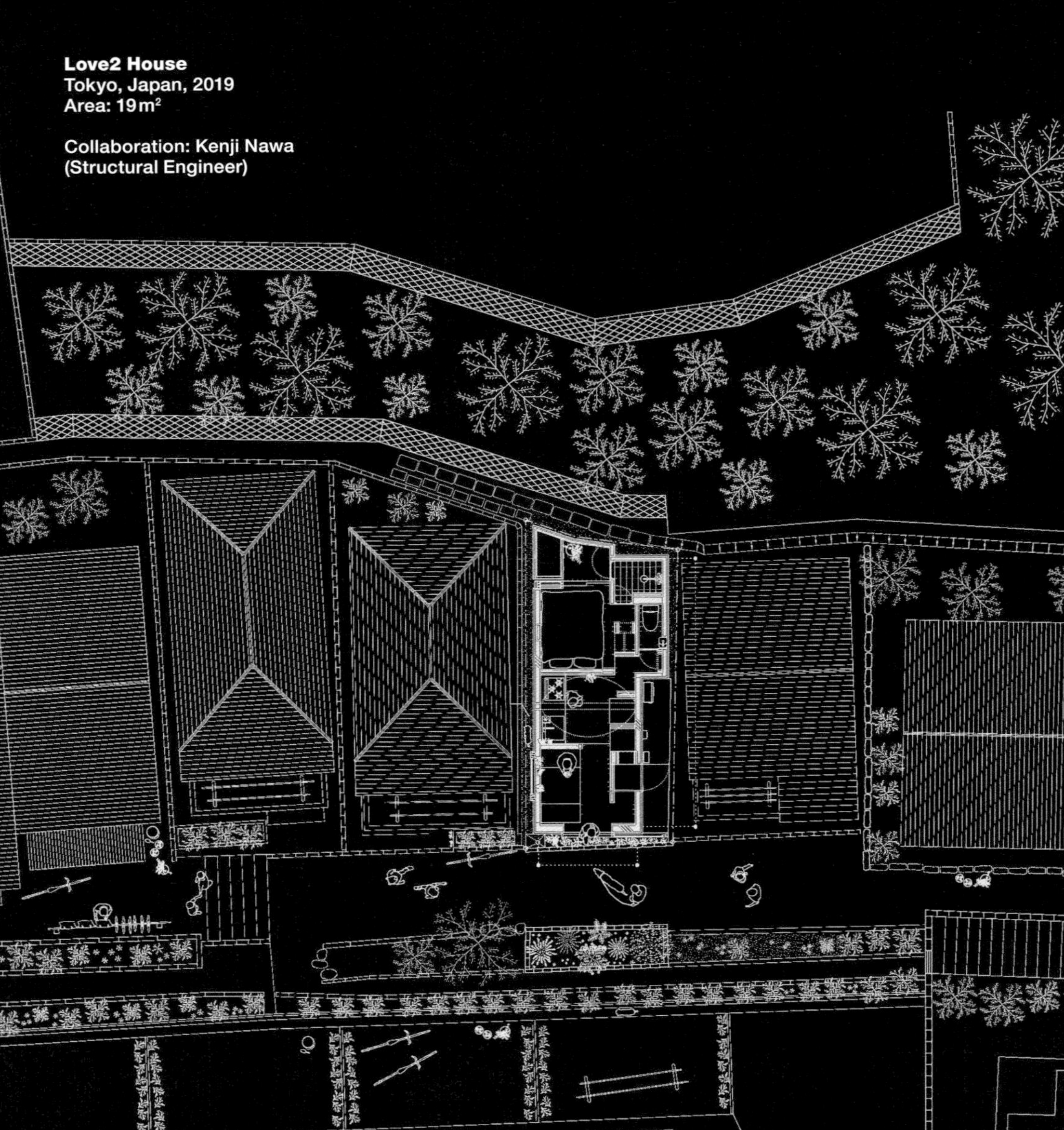

The angled roof of the house allows for these very high and bright interior spaces—almost making the 19 square meters of living space seem ample.

The architect began teaching at Waseda University in Tokyo when he lived in Yokohama. He decided that commuting took too long, so he imagined having a second residence in the capital. His wife evoked Edo-period stories she had read about families of four who lived in a so-called *nagaya*, a 9.6-square-meter apartment. This was the origin of this 19-square-meter house, although Le Corbusier's 16.8-square-meter Cabanon also came to mind, he says. The original home of the architect and his wife is called the Love House (Yokohama, 2005), whence the name Love2 or Love Love for this project. He conceived two curved rooftops to bring light into the house all year round. Seven "short walls" separate the house into three areas for the kitchen, dining area, and bedroom. A window facing the street can be opened to encourage discussion with passersby. "The front street has a flower bed, so we enjoy it as our garden. In this house we feel that the town is very close."

Der Architekt begann seine Lehrtätigkeit an der Tokioter Waseda-Universität, als er noch in Yokohama lebte. Da das Pendeln zu viel Zeit beanspruchte, plante er einen zweiten Wohnsitz in der Hauptstadt. Seine Frau erzählte ihm Geschichten aus der Edo-Zeit, die sie über vierköpfige Familien gelesen hatte. Diese lebten in sogenannten *nagaya*, 9,6 m² großen Wohnungen. Neben den *nagaya* inspirierte den Architekten auch Le Corbusiers 16,8 m² großes Cabanon. Das ursprüngliche Haus des Architekten und seiner Frau heißt Love House (Yokohama, 2005), daher auch der Name Love2 oder Love Love für dieses 19 m² große Folgeprojekt. Zwei gebogene Dächer laden das ganze Jahr über Licht ins Innere ein. Sieben „kurze Wände" trennen das Haus in drei

An open outdoor shower is reached directly from the bedroom space. The concrete surfaces of the house are warmed by the presence of wood window and door frames, as well as some green plants and, of course, sunlight.

Bereiche für Küche, Ess- und Schlafbereich. Ein Fenster kann zur Straße hin geöffnet werden, um Gespräche mit Passanten zu ermöglichen. „Das Blumenbeet an der Straßenfront nutzen wir auch als Garten. In diesem Haus spüren wir die Nähe der Stadt."

L'architecte a commencé à enseigner à l'université Waseda de Tokyo lorsqu'il vivait à Yokohama. Les trajets lui prenaient trop de temps et il a voulu un deuxième domicile dans la capitale. Sa femme a par ailleurs évoqué des récits de la période Edo où quatre personnes vivaient dans un *nagaya*, un appartement de 9,6 m^2. C'est le point de départ de cette maison de 19 m^2, même si son créateur affirme aussi avoir pensé au Cabanon de Le Corbusier de 16,8 m^2. La première demeure de l'architecte et de sa femme porte le nom de maison Love (Yokohama, 2005), d'où celui de Love2 ou Love Love qu'il a donné à celle-ci. Il a imaginé deux toits incurvés pour faire entrer la lumière toute l'année. Sept « murs courts » séparent l'intérieur en trois espaces destinés à servir de cuisine, de salle à manger et de chambre. Une fenêtre sur la rue peut être ouverte pour favoriser la discussion avec les passants. « La rue devant la maison a un parterre de fleurs dont nous profitons comme si c'était notre jardin. Dans cette maison, nous sentons que la ville est toute proche. »

i29

Tiny Holiday Home
Vinkeveen, The Netherlands, 2019
Area: 75 m^2

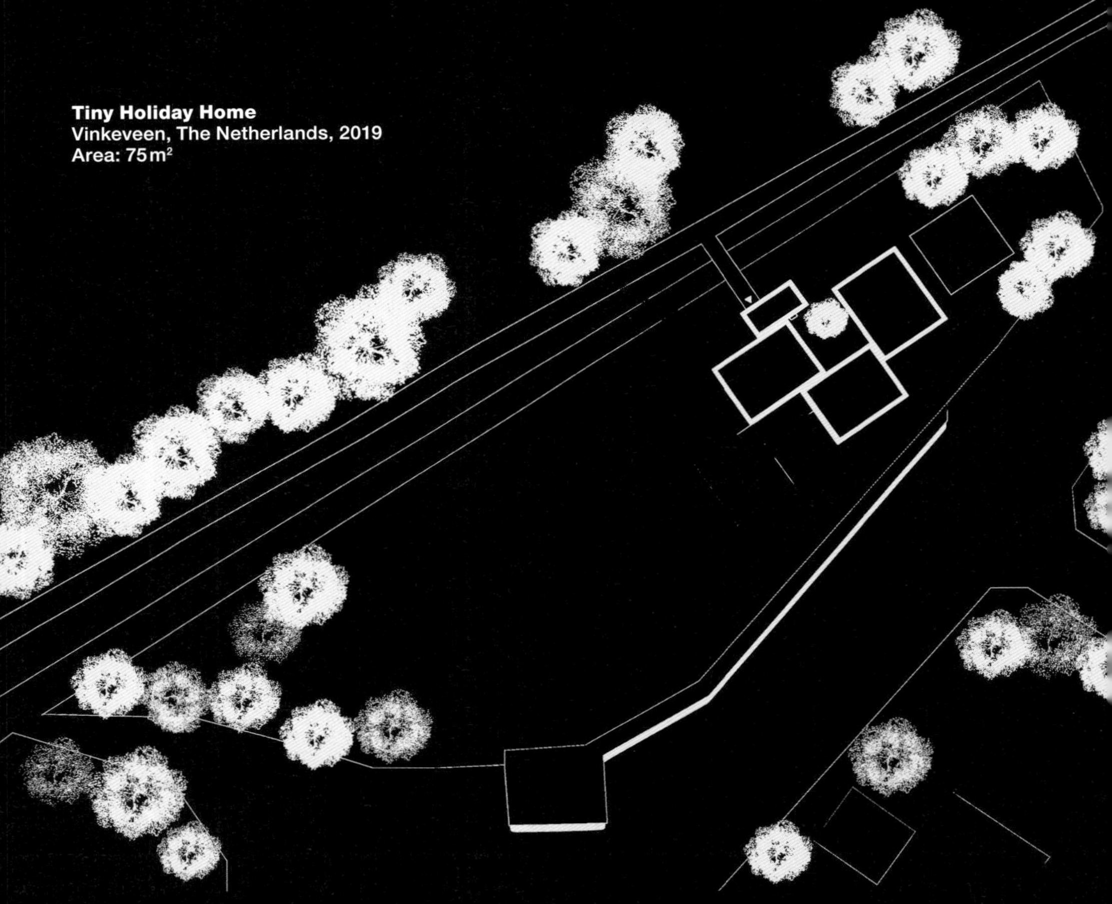

The rough pine used for the exteriors is painted black, giving a strong modern presence to the rectangular elements of the residence.

Intended for a family of four, and including a living room, a kitchen/dining area, a patio, three bedrooms, one bathroom and two toilets, this design was created "from the inside out". Located near a lake, the house is positioned to enhance views and sun orientation. The plan is divided into four pavilion-like rectangular blocks. With a footprint of just 55 square meters, the house has an upper-level bedroom. The furniture and integrated cabinets were custom-designed. The architects explain: "We made use of simple materials like natural oak wooden panels—or stained black to combine with the rough pinewood façade—and a continuous polished concrete floor."

Das für eine vierköpfige Familie entworfene Haus mit Wohnzimmer, Küche, Essbereich, Terrasse, drei Schlafzimmern, einem Badezimmer und zwei Toiletten wurde „von innen nach außen" entwickelt. Unweit eines Sees gelegen profitiert es von besten Ausblicken und günstigem Sonneneinfall. Der Grundriss weist vier pavillonartige rechteckige Blöcke auf. Das Obergeschoss des 55 m² großen Baus beherbergt ein Schlafzimmer. Möbel und Einbauschränke sind Einzelanfertigungen. „Wir verwendeten einfache Materialien", erklären die Architekten, „wie zum Beispiel einen durchgehenden polierten Betonboden, eine Verkleidung aus Natureichenholz oder schwarz gebeizte Eiche, die zur rauen Kiefernholzfassade passt."

Destiné à une famille de quatre personnes et composé d'un salon, d'une cuisine/salle à manger, d'un patio, de trois chambres, d'une salle de bains et de deux toilettes, l'ensemble a été conçu « de l'intérieur vers l'extérieur ». Proche d'un lac, la maison est disposée de manière à optimiser la vue et l'orientation par rapport au soleil. Elle est divisée en quatre blocs rectangulaires de type pavillon. Elle occupe une empreinte au sol de seulement 55 m² mais possède une chambre à l'étage. Le mobilier et les placards intégrés ont été créés sur mesure. Les architectes expliquent qu'ils ont « utilisé des matériaux simples comme des panneaux de chêne naturels – ou teints en noir pour s'associer à la façade de pin brut – et un sol d'un seul tenant en béton poli ».

The continuity of the interior surfaces including the concrete floor, together with the simple furnishings chosen, gives a feeling of serenity that helps to generate an impression of a space larger than it really is.

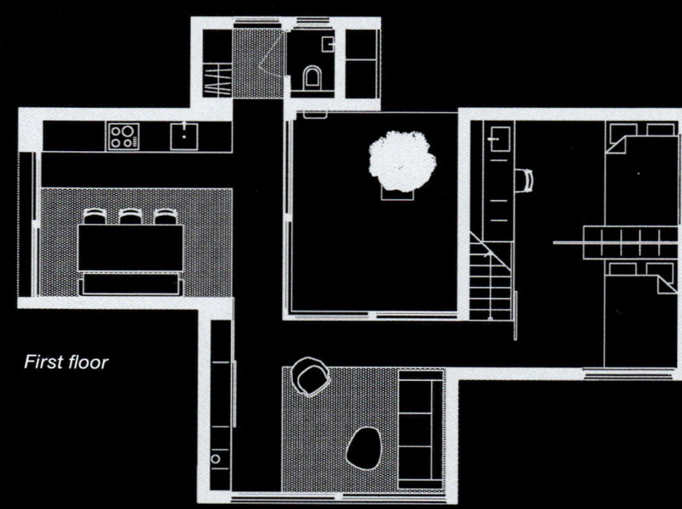

First floor

or.
d
nd light.

PAULO AND BERNARDO JACOBSEN

MPJ Cabin
Rio de Janeiro, Brazil, 2020
Area: 52 m²

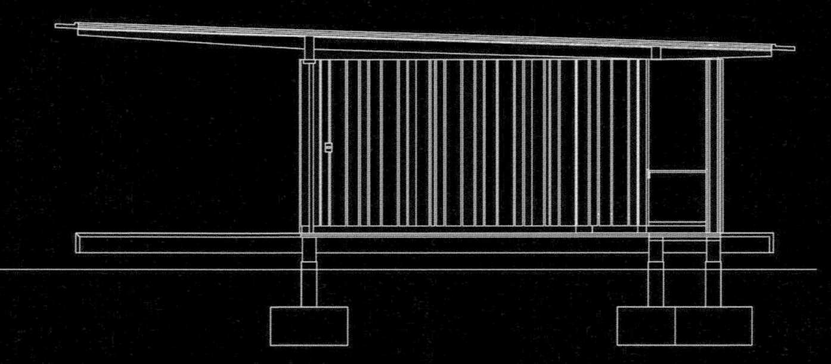

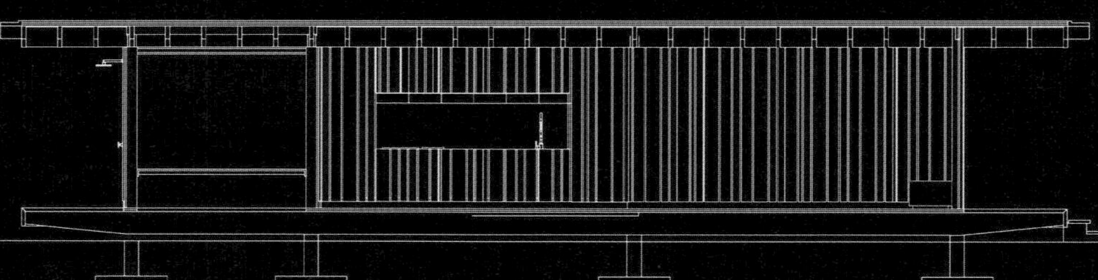

The extended wooden deck of the house brings it right up to the edge of the artificial lake on which it is built. The floor plan reveals the rectangular simplicity of the design.

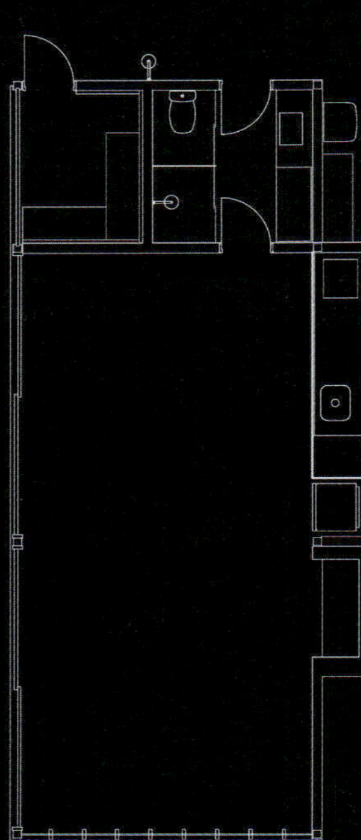

A sliding glass wall allows the interior living space to communicate entirely with the outdoor deck; wood flooring inside accentuates this continuity.

Built in just 30 days at the edge of an artificial lake, this cabin was conceived to allow a couple to isolate themselves at the beginning of the Covid-19 pandemic. A bicycle rack at the back of the house and a pier connected to the external balcony allow small boats to dock nearby. A fiber-optic Internet connection was installed to allow the couple to work remotely. The house sits above the ground to avoid humidity and the intrusion of local jaguars, snakes, spiders, and insects. The floating structure was designed in laminated eucalyptus by the engineer Hélio Olga. A septic tank and solar panels nearby assure the autonomy of the residence, and a vegetable garden provides food. The cabin is equipped with large sliding frames with automatic blackout glass, allowing a generous visual connection to the beautiful natural landscape. As the architects explain: "Paradoxically, the simplicity of the residence contrasts with technology and sustainability."

Diese in nur 30 Tagen am Rande eines künstlichen Sees erbaute Minilodge diente ursprünglich einem Ehepaar als Isolierungsort zu Beginn der Covid 19 Pandemie. An ihrer Rückseite befindet sich ein Fahrradständer und ein mit dem Balkon verbundener Steg, der kleine Boote zum Anlegen einlädt. Um das Arbeiten von zu Hause zu erleichtern, wurde ein Glasfaser-Internetanschluss installiert. Der Baukörper ist vom Boden abgehoben, um nicht nur das Eindringen der Feuchtigkeit, sondern auch Jaguare, Schlangen, Spinnen und Insekten abzuwehren. Die so schwebende Grundstruktur aus laminiertem Eukalyptusholz folgt einem Entwurf des Ingenieurs Hélio Olga. Eine Klärgrube, Sonnenkollektoren und ein Gemüsegarten machen das Haus autark. Seine

The warm wooden interiors of the house give an impression of comfort despite the relatively isolated and off-grid nature of the structure.

großen Schiebefenster mit automatischer Verdunkelung ermöglichen einen weiten Ausblick auf die schöne Naturlandschaft. „Paradoxerweise", so die Architekten, „verbirgt die Einfachheit des Hauses sowohl seine Technologie als auch seine Nachhaltigkeit."

Construite en seulement 30 jours au bord d'un lac artificiel, cette petite maison a été conçue pour permettre à un couple de s'isoler au début de la pandémie de Covid-19. Elle possède un porte- vélos à l'arrière et un ponton relié au balcon qui permet d'amarrer de petits bateaux. Une connexion Internet par fibre optique a été installée pour permettre au couple de travailler à distance. La maison est surélevée pour éviter l'humidité et empêcher l'intrusion de jaguars, serpents, araignées et insectes locaux. La partie flottante en eucalyptus lamellé a été conçue par l'ingénieur Hélio Olga. Une fosse septique et des panneaux solaires à proximité assurent l'autonomie de la maison, tandis qu'un jardin potager fournit de quoi nourrir ses habitants. Elle dispose de vastes panneaux coulissants en verre à opacité commandée pour une vue généreuse sur le superbe paysage naturel. Les architectes expliquent que « paradoxalement, la simplicité de la maison contraste avec la technologie mise en œuvre et la durabilité ».

MACKAY-LYONS SWEETAPPLE

Enough House
Upper Kingsburg, Nova Scotia, Canada, 2015
Area: 65 m²

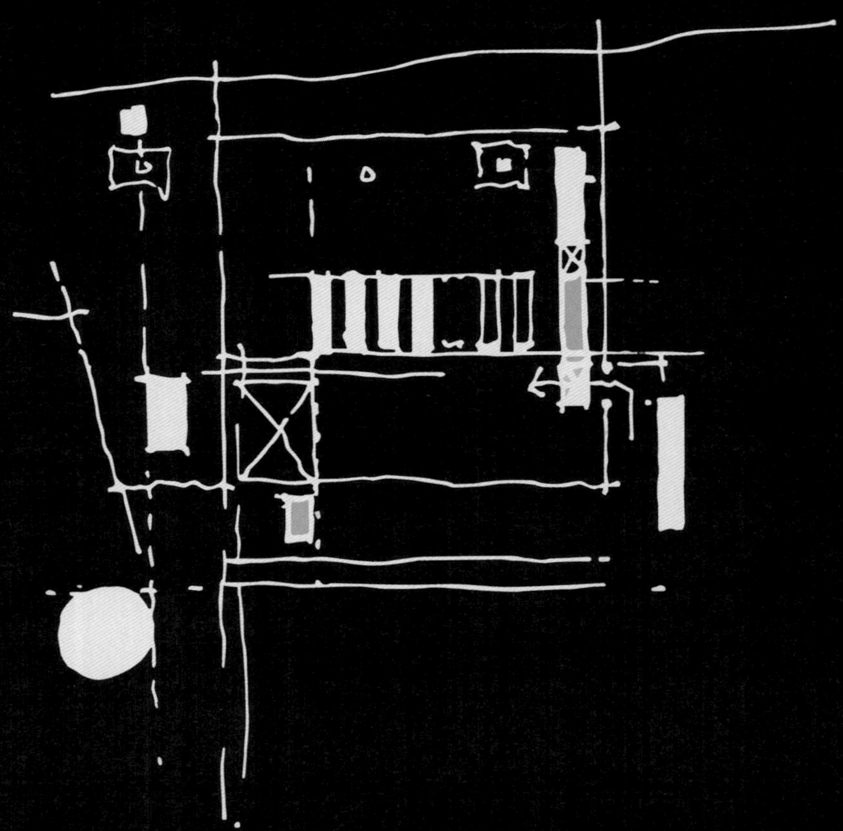

This house is "a flexible prototype that is intended to be replicated and customized to specific sites." Built as a one-bedroom residence, it can be configured with two bedrooms for example. It was originally used as a gatehouse on the architects' Shobac Campus and Ghost Architectural Laboratory (2019) and as accommodation for an intern architect. It has a traditional gabled roof form in relation to neighboring structures. The house has a generous 7.3-meter-wide corner window. Supporting concrete fins "extend into the landscape forming an entry dooryard and a fire court, stitching the cabin into its immediate context." Again, the architects explain: "Enough House is more a verb than a noun, like an unstable molecule. It is an active agent that engages with its situation. This modernist, kinetic quality is due to its consistent use of the dynamic principle of pinwheeling composition, in terms of site plan, plan, section, and elevation, which is found throughout the body of work of the firm."

Konzipiert als „flexibler Prototyp, der sich an verschiedenste Standorte anpassen kann", sieht das Wohnhaus zunächst nur ein Schlafzimmer vor, lässt sich aber auch mit zwei Schlafzimmern konfigurieren. Es diente ursprünglich als Pförtnerhaus des Shobac Campus und des Ghost Architectural Laboratory (2019) sowie als Praktikantenunterkunft. Mit seinem traditionellen Satteldach passt es sich seiner Umgebung an, die durch das großzügige, 7,3 m breite Eckfenster ganz nah heranrückt. Die stützenden Betonrippen „ragen in die Landschaft hinein und bilden einen Vorhof mit Feuerplatz, der die Struktur in ihrer unmittelbaren Umgebung verankert", schildern die Architekten. „Enough House ist mehr Verb als Substantiv, ein instabiles Molekül.

The inside of the house contrasts with the rusted metal exterior, emphasizing the wooden surfaces. Stair railing and the wood-burning stove have the same black color as the window frames. Natural light fills the house.

Es geht aktiv auf Situationen ein. Wir erzielen diesen modernistischen, kinetischen Charakter bewusst, indem wir bei unseren Arbeiten das dynamische Windradprinzip in Bezug auf Lageplan, Grundriss, Schnitt und Aufriss konsequent anwenden."

La maison est « un prototype flexible destiné à être reproduit et adapté à des sites spécifiques ». Construite sous la forme d'un logement à chambre unique, elle peut aussi être configurée avec, par exemple, deux chambres. Elle a d'abord servi de loge de gardien sur le campus Shobac et le Ghost Architectural Laboratory construit par les architectes (2019) et de logement pour un architecte interne. Son toit à pignon traditionnel fait écho aux constructions voisines. Elle possède une vaste fenêtre d'angle large de 7,3 m. Les plaques de béton qui la portent « se prolongent pour former une arrière-cour et un parvis, qui inscrivent la petite maison dans son contexte direct ». Les architectes expliquent encore :« Enough House est plus un verbe qu'un nom, telle une molécule instable. C'est un agent actif qui s'inscrit dans la situation. Cette qualité cinétique moderniste ressort de l'utilisation systématique du principe dynamique de la composition en soleil – en termes de plan de situation, de plan, de section et d'élévation – qu'on retrouve dans tout le corpus des travaux de l'agence. »

MAGUIRE + DEVINE

Boathouse
Hobart, Tasmania, Australia, 2021
Area: 60 m²

The house is set on the bank of the River Derwent in Tasmania, with a spotted gum wooden deck extending from sliding glass doors.

Designed in an open V-shape, the Boathouse has a double-height living/dining/kitchen area on the ground floor, as well as a shower room and a bedroom. The height of the living space is fully exploited with upper-level glazing that brings ample natural light into the small structure and gives it an impression of being larger than it is in terms of square meters. Generous views of the River Derwent are contrasted with a more closed design on the entry side. A carport, morning and afternoon decks, and a stone terrace extend from the structure. The upper level has a small storage loft. The Boathouse is clad in standing seam metal and spotted gum *(Corymbia maculata)*, which is also used for the decking. Tasmanian oak *(Eucalyptus delegatensis)* lining and flooring is used above a sandstone sub-floor wall on the slightly sloped site.

Das als offene V-Form konzipierte Boathouse beherbergt im Erdgeschoss einen doppelhohen Wohn-/Ess-/Küchenbereich, eine Dusche und ein Schlafzimmer. Die Höhe des Wohnraums kommt durch die Verglasung des Obergeschosses voll zur Geltung und natürliches Licht durchdringt das kleine Haus bis in die letzten Ecken, sodass es größer wirkt und seine Quadratmeterzahl Lügen zu strafen scheint. Weite Ausblicke auf den Fluss Derwent kontrastieren mit der geschlossenen Gestaltung der Eingangsseite. Ein Carport, eine Morgen-, eine Nachmittagsterrasse sowie eine Steinterrasse schmiegen sich an das Gebäude. Im Obergeschoss befindet sich ein kleiner Speicherboden. Boathouse ist mit Stehfalzmetall und gesprenkeltem Eukalyptus *(Corymbia maculata)* verschalt, der auch für die Terrassendielen verwendet wurde. Die Innenverkleidung ist aus tasmanischer Eiche (Eucalyptus

delegatensis), ebenso der Bodenbelag über dem Unterboden aus Sandstein, der die leichte Neigung des Geländes ausgleicht.

Conçue selon une forme en V ouverte, la maison comporte un espace séjour/repas/cuisine double hauteur au rez-de-chaussée, ainsi qu'une salle de douche et une chambre. La hauteur est entièrement exploitée avec des vitres au niveau supérieur qui font entrer largement la lumière naturelle dans la petite construction pour donner l'impression qu'elle est plus grande. Les vues très dégagées sur la rivière Derwent contrastent avec la conception plus fermée du côté de l'entrée. Un abri de voiture, des pontons pour le matin et l'après-midi et une terrasse en pierre prolongent l'ensemble. L'étage supérieur se compose d'un petit loft de rangement. La maison présente un revêtement métallique à joint debout et en bois de gommier *(Corymbia maculata)* qu'on retrouve dans les pontons. Le chêne de Tasmanie *(Eucalyptus delegatensis)* des sols et lambris est posé au-dessus d'un mur sous plancher en grès sur le site en pente douce.

A spiral staircase, seen in a mirror, gives access to the upper level, while a square window opens from the bed area in the direction of the water.

Opposite: *a similar square window in the kitchen.*

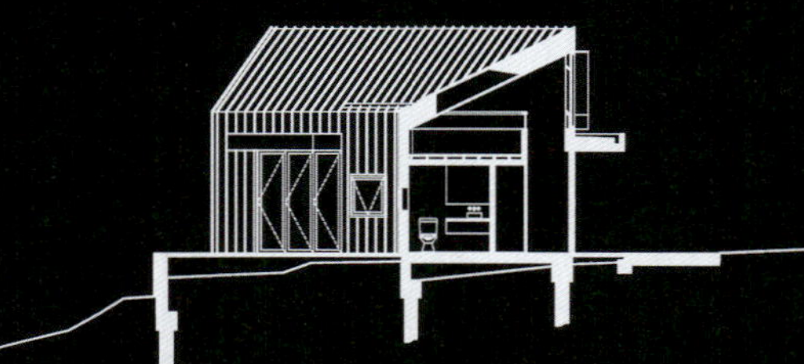

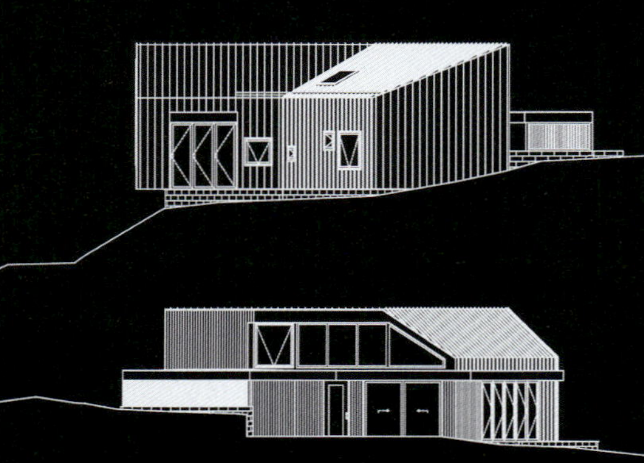

COOK BEAUTIFUL
Miele

MAKERS OF ARCHITECTUR

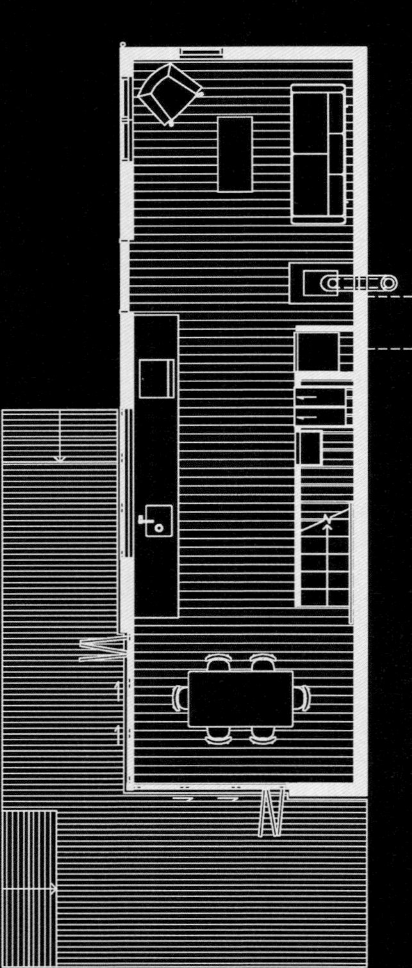

Akaroa Bach
Akaroa, Banks Peninsula
New Zealand, 2018
Area: 81 m²

LEE
CHILD

Vertically applied Douglas fir exterior cladding appears to make the house fit into the surrounding forest. In these pictures taken shortly after construction, the exterior has a natural wood color, which inevitably turns gray with time, humidity, and sunlight.

This *Bach* (a New Zealand term meaning holiday home) is located amidst Manuka bush and rural farmland. It is based on a lengthened version of the Warrander Studio (Governors Bay, 2015), New Zealand's first full CLT (Cross-laminated Timber) home, designed and fabricated using BIM (Building Information Modelling) and CNC (Computer Numerical Control). Large doors near the dining area open to the exterior deck to the northwest. The sloped site dictated a first-floor entrance with a bridge originating at a road above. An open-plan kitchen, dining, and living area is located below, while the two bedrooms, one bunkroom, and a toilet and bathroom are located on the upper level. The building has a New Zealand CLT exposed structure. It is wrapped with timber framing, insulation and clad in fiber cement board with a vertical Douglas fir *(Pseudotsuga menziesii)* rainscreen. CLT is also used for the interiors, where a polycarbonate light shaft stretches through both floors to bring light into the living and bath areas. The Banks Peninsula is on the east coast of South Island, south of Christchurch.

Opposite: *the approach bridge reaching the upper story at the rear of the house.* Above: *full-height corner glazing near the dining area opens to the surrounding terrace.*

Dieser „Bach" (ein neuseeländischer Begriff für „Ferienhaus") befindet sich im Herzen von Manuka-Busch, umgeben von Ackerland. Es ist eine in die Länge gezogene Version von Warrander Studio (Governors Bay, 2015), Neuseelands erstem Brettsperrholzhaus, das mittels Bauwerksdatenmodellierung und computergestützter numerischer Steuerung hergestellt wurde. Große Türen nahe des Essbereichs öffnen sich nach Nordwesten zum Außendeck. Aufgrund der Geländeneigung liegt der Eingang im ersten Stock und ist mit einer Brücke mit der Straße verbunden. Das Untergeschoss ist dem offenen Küchen-, Ess- und Wohnbereich vorbehalten, oben befinden sich zwei Schlafzimmer, ein Etagenbettzimmer sowie Toilette und Bad. Die Grundstruktur ist in typisch neuseeländischer Bauweise aus Brettsperrholz konstruiert mit Holzrahmen, Dämmung und Verkleidung aus Faserzementplatten und vertikalem Regenschutz aus Douglasie *(Pseudotsuga menziesii)*. Im ebenfalls mit Brettsperrholz ausgestatteten Inneren durchdringt ein Lichtschacht aus Polycarbonat beide Stockwerke und erhellt Wohn- wie auch Badezimmer. Die Banks Peninsula liegt an der Ostküste der Südinsel, südlich von Christchurch.

Ce « Bach » (terme néo-zélandais qui désigne une maison de vacances) est situé dans un bush de manuka, sur des terres agricoles rurales. La construction est basée sur une version allongée du studio Warrander (Governors Bay, 2015), la première maison entièrement en bois lamellé croisé (CLT) de Nouvelle-Zélande, conçue et fabriquée par BIM (modélisation des informations de construction) et CNC (commande numérique). De grandes portes près de l'espace destiné aux repas ouvrent sur le ponton au nord-ouest. Le terrain en pente a imposé une entrée au premier étage par une passerelle qui donne sur une route plus haut. L'espace ouvert où se trouvent la cuisine, la salle à manger et le salon occupe le bas, tandis que les deux chambres, un dortoir, les toilettes et la salle de bains sont situés à l'étage. La structure apparente est en bois CLT néo-zélandais. Elle est enveloppée d'une ossature en bois, d'un isolant, et revêtue de panneaux de fibrociment avec un bardage vertical en pin Douglas *(Pseudotsuga menziesii)*. On retrouve le CLT à l'intérieur où un puit de lumière en polycarbonate traverse les deux niveaux pour éclairer le salon et la salle d'eau. La péninsule de Banks est située sur la côte est de l'Île du Sud, au sud de Christchurch.

'he simple, wood-covered interior is filled with light
ı the kitchen and dining space, and above the bunk
eds. Below: the plan shows the upper floor with the
pproach bridge seen extending from the rectangular
olume at the top.

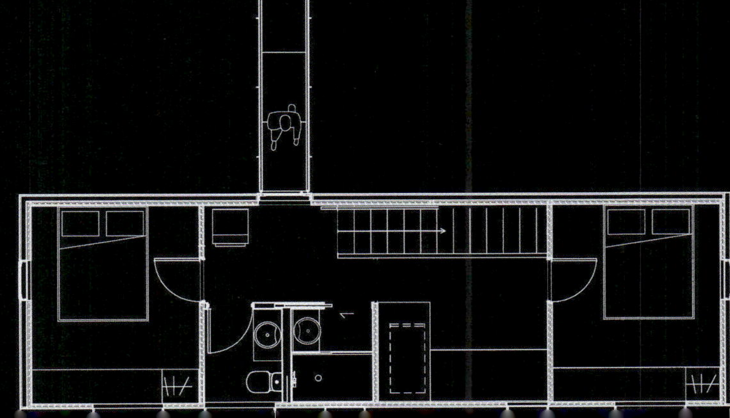

MAPA

Minimod Curucaca
Santa Catarina, Brazil, 2017
Area: 70 m²

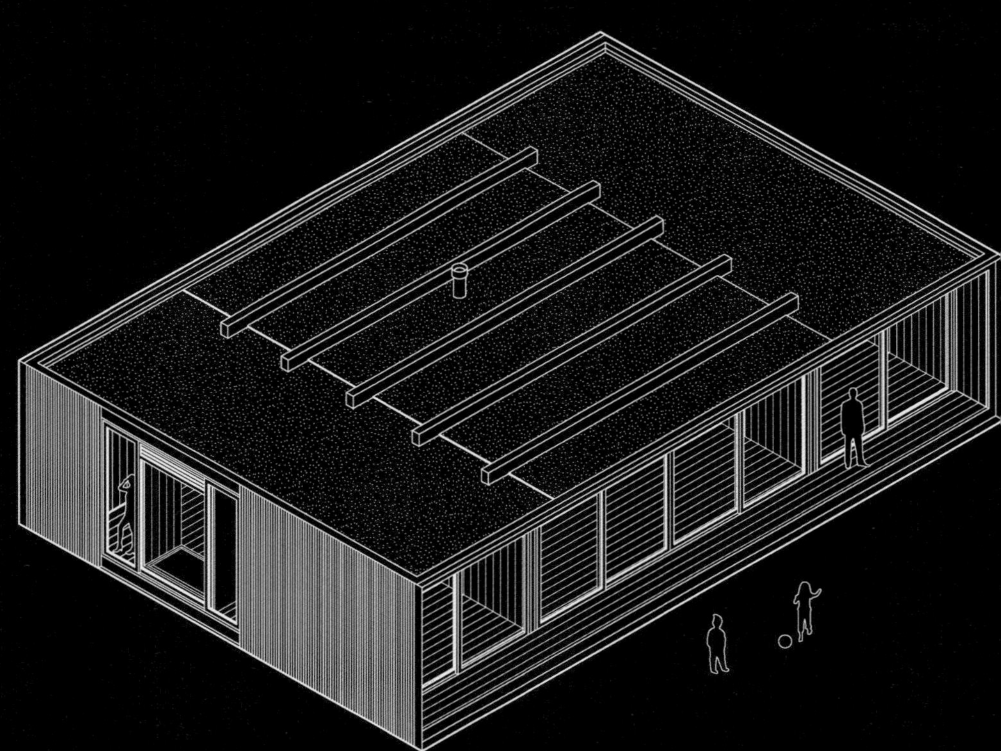

The rectangular house sits lightly on the ground and is entirely surrounded by its green environment—even the roof is green.

Sliding glass doors and an outdoor terrace connect the interior to the outdoors and the forest. Furnishing is simple, as befits the house and its site.

The Minimod designs of MAPA are intended as "primitive retreats with a contemporary reinterpretation." They are prefabricated, compact, and energy efficient. The Curucaca Valley is in the mountains of southern Brazil in the state of Santa Catarina. The architects explain that "Brazil's CLT wood technology combines the efficiency of industrialized products with new technologies focused on sustainability with the sensitivity of natural material par excellence." They compare this design to PnP (plug-and-play) devices or computers that can be used directly, without user intervention. "As such," they say, "the necessary steps to install and enjoy a Minimod must be simple and fast. From the factory to the landscape." This structure was built with cross-laminated timber, black corrugated metal cladding, and glass. It has a green roof and is lifted off the ground on low pilotis. It has two bedrooms with bathrooms at either end and a central living and dining area. Indoors, a wood-burning stove generates heat, and sliding glass walls can be opened to the outdoor deck when weather permits.

„Ein primitiver Rückzugsort in zeitgenössischer Neuinterpretation" soll er sein, der Minimod von MAPA. Das vorfabrizierte, kompakte und energieeffiziente Häuschen steht im Curucaca-Tal in Brasiliens südlichem Bundesstaat Santa Catarina. Laut der Architekten verknüpft „die brasilianische Brettsperrholztechnologie die Effizienz industrialisierter Produkte sowohl mit neuen nachhaltigen Technologien als auch mit der Sensibilität puristischer Naturmaterialien." Das Design gleiche einem Plug-and-Play-Gerät, so die Architekten weiter, oder Computern, die sich selbst aktivieren. „Daher muss ein Minimod von der Fabrik bis zum Aufbau einfach und schnell

A small wood-burning stove provides heat. The entire interior—ceiling, floor, and walls—is clad in wood. Below: section drawings and a floor plan.

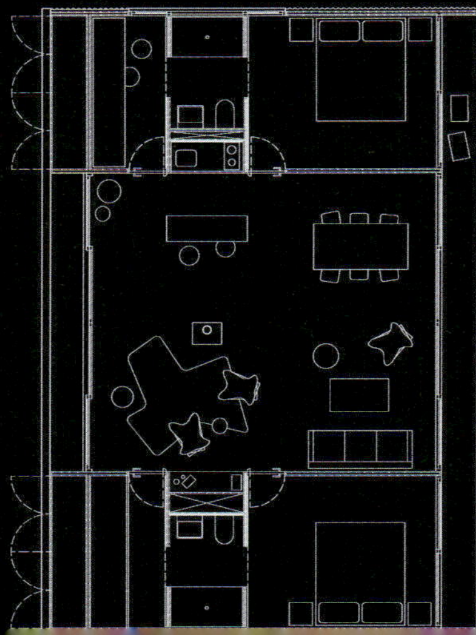

Existing trees on the site were almost entirely preserved—the large opening again connects residents to their environment.

handhabbar sein." Das Dach des aus Brettsperrholz, schwarzer Wellblechverkleidung und Glas errichteten Gebäudes ist begrünt, unten trennen niedrige Pilotis den Bau vom Boden. An seinen beiden Enden liegt je ein Schlafzimmer mit Bad, in der Mitte befindet sich der Wohn- und Essbereich. Ein Holzofen sorgt für Wärme, und wenn das Wetter es zulässt, können die Glasschiebewände zum Außendeck geöffnet werden.

Les concepts Minimod de MAPA sont destinés à servir de « retraites primitives dans une réinterprétation contemporaine ». Ils sont préfabriqués, compacts et écoénergétiques. La vallée de Curucaca se trouve dans les montagnes au sud du Brésil, dans l'État de Santa Catarina. Les architectes expliquent que « la technologie brésilienne du bois CLT associe l'efficacité des produits industrialisés, les nouvelles technologies centrées sur la durabilité et la sensibilité du matériau naturel par excellence ». Ils comparent leur concept aux appareils ou ordinateurs PnP (plug-and-play) qui peuvent être utilisés immédiatement sans intervention de l'utilisateur. « C'est pourquoi, disent-ils encore, les étapes nécessaires pour installer un Minimod et en profiter doivent être simples et rapides. De l'usine au paysage. » La construction est en bois d'œuvre lamellé croisé, avec un revêtement en métal ondulé noir et en verre. Le toit est végétalisé et la structure est surélevée par des pilotis bas. Elle se compose de deux chambres avec salles de bains aux deux extrémités et d'un espace salon et salle à manger central. Un poêle à bois chauffe l'intérieur et des parois vitrées coulissantes peuvent aussi être ouvertes sur le ponton lorsque le temps le permet.

MAR PLUS ASK

Olive Houses
Mallorca, Spain, 2019
Area: 24 m²

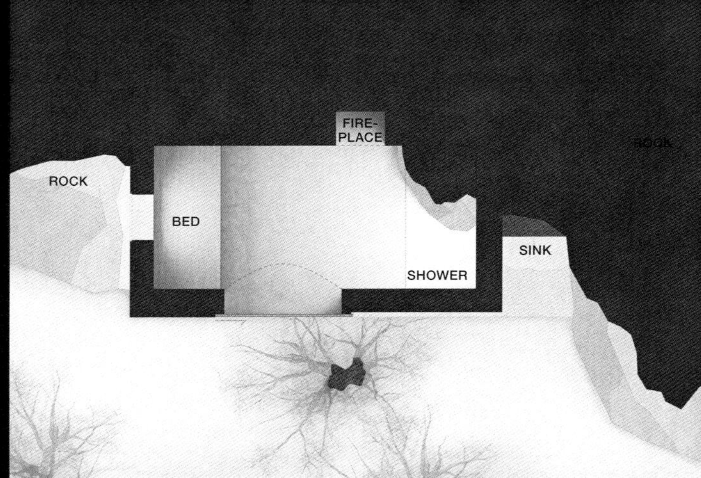

Exterior and interior views of the Purple House, a repurposed toolshed used as living space.

These two small off-grid houses are located about nine meters apart on a six-hectare property near olive trees in the Tramuntana Mountains of Mallorca, a UNESCO World Heritage site with views of the Mediterranean. The Purple House, an existing structure originally used to stock tools, is covered in purple stucco and is intended for cooking and dining. Purple was chosen because it is “the complementary color to the dark side of the olive leaf.” The Purple House also houses a bathroom, two gas burners, a sink, wood-fired oven, table, stools, and a fridge powered by solar panels set behind the house. To complement this existing, renovated building, only one new structure was needed, which is partially housed in an existing terrace so that it can “blend seamlessly into the landscape.” Water for a shower is provided by a natural spring located near the house. A specific pink, “the complimentary shade of the matte lighter side of an olive leaf, was chosen to cover walls, floors, and ceilings...” The second house contains a bed, shower, and fireplace. The architects explain: “The Olive Houses are owned by mar plus ask and are offered as a silent refuge for other architects, artists, and writers around the year.” Ask Anker Aistrup concludes: “The complementary colors create an optical effect that underlines the shape and color of the old olive trees—which is what the project is really about—experiencing the might and beauty of these trees.”

Diese beiden netzunabhängigen Häuschen mit Blick aufs Mittelmeer liegen inmitten eines sechs Hektar großen Olivenhains im mallorquinischen Tramuntana-Gebirge, einem UNESCO-Weltkulturerbe. Für das Purple House wurde ein bestehendes, ursprünglich der Aufbewahrung von Werkzeugen dienendes Gebäude umgebaut. Mit lila Stuck verkleidet beherbergt es einen Koch- und Essbereich. Die Architekten wählten Lila als „Komplementärfarbe zur dunklen Seite des Olivenblatts". Auch ein Bad, zwei Gasbrenner, ein Waschbecken, ein Holzofen, ein Tisch mit Hocker und ein solarzellenbe-triebener Kühlschrank finden darin Platz. Ergänzt wird das Häuschen durch ein neu errichtetes Gebäude, das teilweise in eine bestehende Terrasse integriert wurde, um „sich nahtlos in die Landschaft einzufügen". Eine nahegelegende natürliche Quell liefert Wasser für die Dusche. Die Verkleidung der Wände, Böden und Decken dieses neuen Gebäudes ist in Rosa gehalten als „komplementärer Farbton der matten hellen Seite eines Olivenblatts". Das Häuschen bietet Raum für ein Bett, eine Dusche und einem Kamin. „Mar plus ask stellt die Olive Houses das ganze Jahr über Architekten, Künstlern und Schriftstellern als stille Zuflucht zur Verfügung", so die Architekten und Aistrup fügt hinzu: „Der optische Effekt, der durch die komplementären Farben erzielt wird, betont nicht nur Form und Farbe der alten Olivenbäume, sondern vor allem auch ihre Kraft und Schönheit – und genau darum ging es uns hier im Wesentlichen."

In a different way than the complementary Purple House, the Pink structure is also inserted into the natural, rocky environment, creating architectural spaces around the natural outcroppings.

Ces deux petites maisons hors réseau sont situées à 9 m l'une de l'autre sur une propriété de 6 ha plantée d'oliviers dans les montagnes de Tramuntana, à Majorque, un site classé au patrimoine mondial de l'UNESCO avec vue sur la Méditerranée. La Maison violette, une structure existante qui servait à l'origine de cabane à outils, est recouverte de crépi violet et destinée à la cuisine et aux repas. Le violet a été choisi car c'est « la couleur complémentaire de la face sombre des feuilles d'olivier ». La maison comprend aussi une salle de bains, deux brûleurs à gaz, un évier, un four à bois, une table, des tabourets et un réfrigérateur alimenté en électricité par des panneaux solaires derrière la maison. Pour compléter ce bâtiment existant rénové, il suffisait d'une seule nouvelle construction. L'eau de la douche vient d'une source naturelle à côté de la maison. Un rose spécifique, « la nuance complémentaire de la face mate plus claire des feuilles d'olivier, a été choisie pour les murs, les sols et les plafonds… » La deuxième maison comprend un lit, une douche et une cheminée. Les architectes expliquent que « les maisons de l'Olive sont la propriété de mar plus ask et forment un refuge silencieux offert toute l'année à d'autres architectes, à des artistes et des écrivains .» Aistrup conclut : « les couleurs complémentaireq créent un effet d'optique qui met en valeur la forme et la couleur des vieux oliviers, et c'est le but en soi du projet, faire prendre conscience de la force et de la beauté de ces arbres. »

MARTE.MARTE

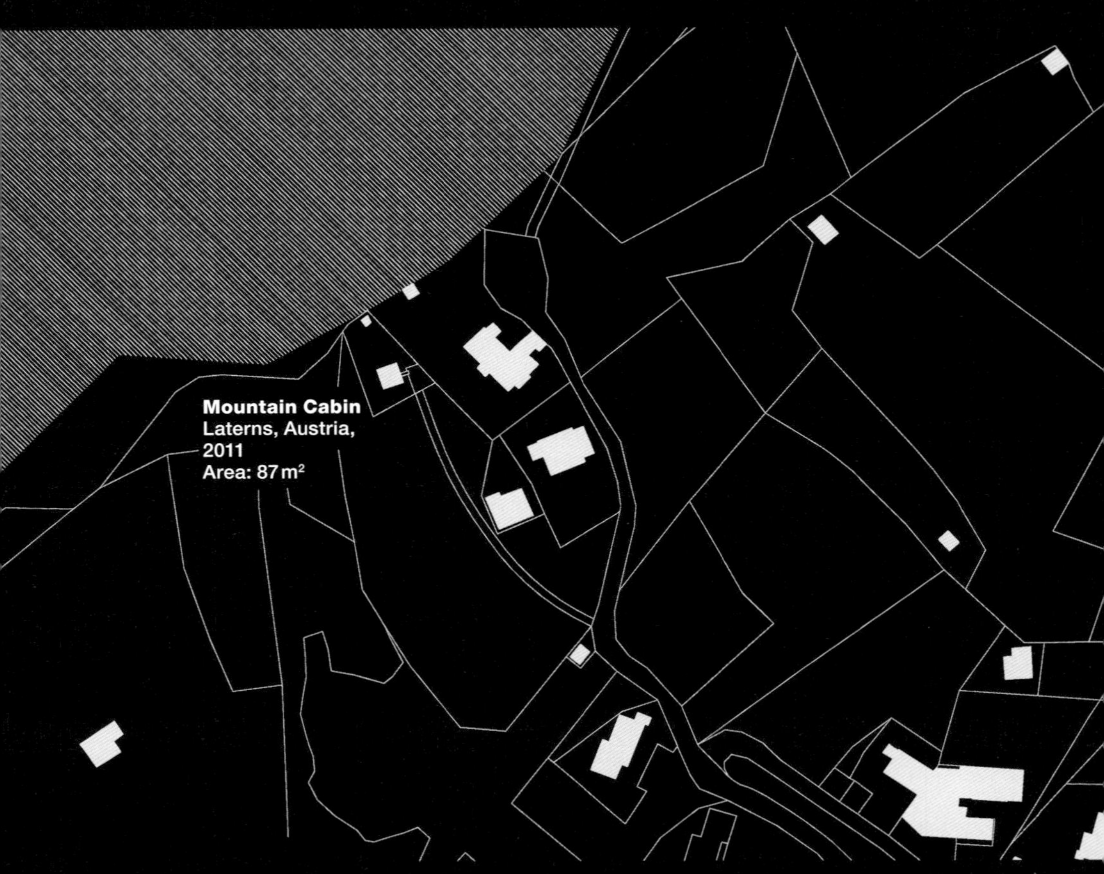

Despite its coloring and its strictly square plan, the house fits into its natural environment like a kind of observation post.

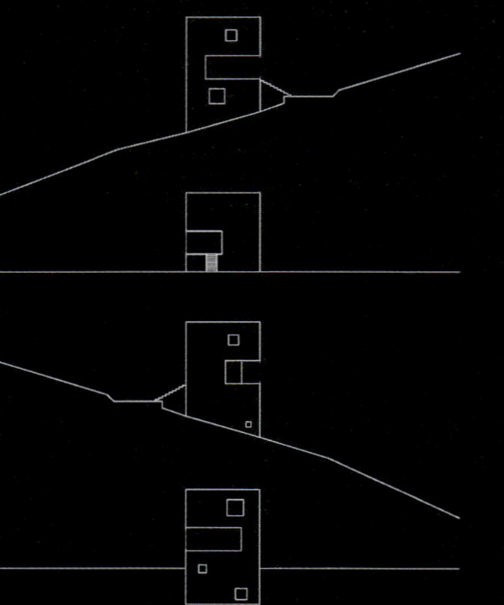

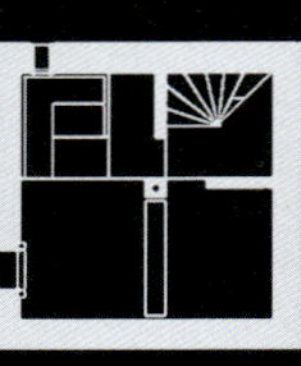

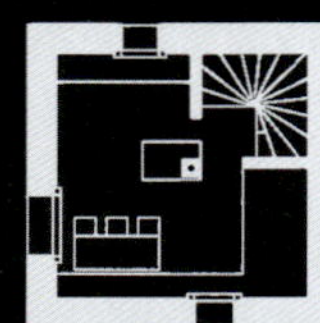

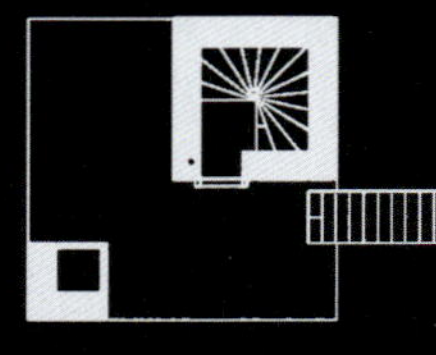

Concrete walls and wood finishing—including on the floors—give some warmth to the interiors that look out onto the natural spectacle of the mountains.

The architects insist on the fact that aside from an approach, the landscape of the 485-square-meter site for this cabin was not changed, likening it to traditional farm buildings in that respect. Approached via a stairway on the upper side, the tower-like building has a hollowed-out center where the front door is located. Built with rough concrete, heavy oak front doors, and anthracite-colored handrails, the cabin has square windows of different sizes with matte, solid-oak window frames. The tower-like structure has a 43-square-meter footprint. A spiral wood and steel staircase connects the living area on the upper level with two private spaces—bedrooms and relaxation areas. Inside, raw concrete surfaces, untreated oak floors, doors and fixtures, contrast with black metal surfaces in a "harmonious, austere combination of materials." Austerity is indeed the rule, both inside and out, and yet the interiors with their generous views of the mountain scenery create a kind of protected serenity—in the heart of what must be compared to a fortified building.

Simple furnishings and limited décor may bring to mind the aesthetic of some mountain huts, which are in a kind of symbiosis with the natural environment outside.

Die Architekten legen Wert darauf, dass die Landschaft des 485 m² großen Grundstücks bei der Konstruktion dieser Minilodge, abgesehen von der Zufahrt, nicht verändert wurde. Insofern folgte ihr Bauprinzip jenem der traditionellen Bauernhäuser. Der Zugang zur Turmstruktur erfolgt über eine Treppe, die zur Eingangstür im freiliegenden Mittelteil führt. Das aus rauem Beton errichtete und mit schweren Eichentüren und anthrazitfarbenen Handläufen ausgestattete Haus öffnet sich seiner Umgebung durch quadratische, unterschiedlich große Fenster mit matten Rahmen aus massiver Eiche. Das turmähnliche Gebäude hat eine Grundfläche von 43 m². Eine Wendeltreppe aus Holz und Stahl verbindet den Wohnbereich des Obergeschosses mit Schlafzimmern und Ruheräumen. Im Inneren herrscht ein „harmonischer, aber strenger Materialmix" aus rohen Betonoberflächen und unbehandelten Eichenböden, die mit Türen und Einbauten mit schwarzen Metalloberflächen kontrastieren. Strenge ist in der Tat die Regel, sowohl innen als auch außen, aber obgleich das Gebäude einer Festung nicht unähnlich ist, bilden die Innenräume dank der weiten Ausblicke auf die Berglandschaft eine Art geschützte Gelassenheit.

Les architectes insistent sur le fait que, sauf du côté de l'accès, le paysage du terrain de 485 m² où est construit le refuge n'a pas été modifié, ce qui le rapproche à cet égard des bâtiments de fermes traditionnels. Accessible par un escalier du côté le plus haut de la pente, la construction en forme de tour présente un centre évidé où se trouve la porte de devant. La petite maison en béton brut aux lourdes portes d'entrée en chêne et balustrades anthracite a des fenêtres carrées de différentes tailles aux encadrements en chêne massif mat. Son empreinte au sol est de 43 m². Un escalier en colimaçon en bois et acier relie l'espace séjour du niveau supérieur aux deux espaces privés – chambres et lieux de relaxation. À l'intérieur, les surfaces de béton brut et les planchers, les portes et le mobilier en chêne non traité contrastent avec les surfaces métalliques noires pour former une « association austère et harmonieuse de matériaux ». L'austérité est de rigueur, à l'intérieur comme à l'extérieur, ce qui n'empêche pas l'intérieur et ses larges vues sur les montagnes de créer comme une sérénité protectrice – au cœur de ce qu'il faut comparer à une construction fortifiée.

TAKAHIRO MORIYA

Setoyama
Shizuoka, Japan, 2020
Area: 101 m²

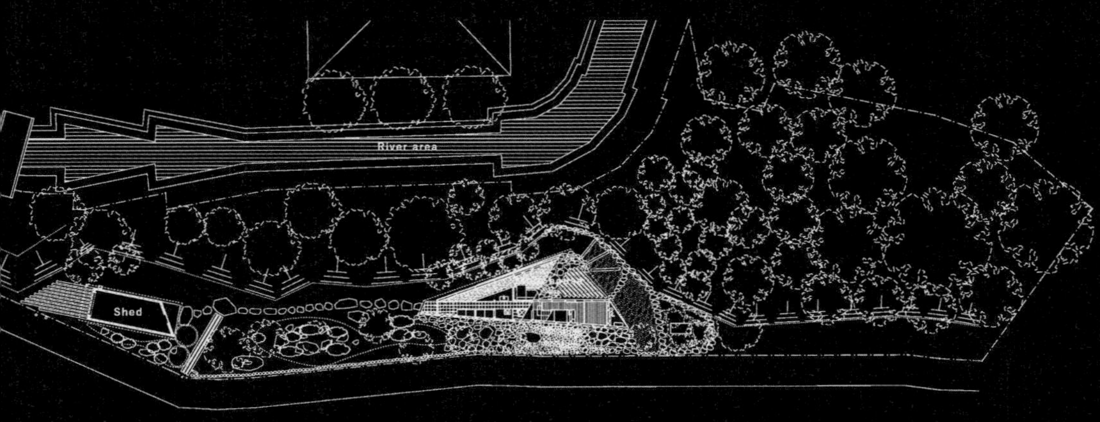

The house is perched on a cliff over a river. It is approached from above in its quite natural wooded setting.

Built on a 2061-square-meter site on a riverside cliff, Setoyama is a small villa with a 91-square-meter footprint. The site is an otherwise untouched plateau of layers of lava. The architect explains: "The client's request was for 'a view of the sea from the living room.' Therefore, in order to frame the seascape and groves seen through the trees, we planned to separate the main living room from the ground and project the upper structure to the cliffside. Since the foundation was on a steep slope, it was necessary to keep it away from the cliffs as much as possible." The reinforced-concrete base carries a locally sourced wood-frame structure in a triangular form that overhangs the slope. A living room and terrace face the slope, with the entrance, kitchen, and bathroom to the rear of the building. The bedroom is on the upper level. According to the architect: "We try to reduce the environmental impact of our buildings by not changing the shap of the land. We are committed to respecting and utilizing the natural environment and have made an important commitment to sustainability..."

Setoyama ist eine kleine Villa mit 91 m² Grundfläche, errichtet auf einem 2061 m² großen Grundstück an einer Flussuferklippe, einem ansonsten unberührten Plateau aus Lavaschichten. „Der Bauherr wünschte sich ein Wohnzimmer mit Blick aufs Meer", erzählt der Architekt. „Daher hoben wir den Hauptwohnraum vom Boden an und schufen so eine Klippenstruktur, deren Ausblick durch die Bäume hindurch auf das Meer und die Haine fällt. Da wir an einem steilen Hang bauten, mussten wir das Haus so weit wie möglich von den Klippen entfernt platzieren." Die dreieckige Rahmenkonstruktion auf dem Stahlbetonsockel ist aus lokal produziertem Holz und ragt über den

The wooden upper level extends in the direction of the slope. Below: *drawings with the first floor below the second-floor plan with its extended triangular living room.*

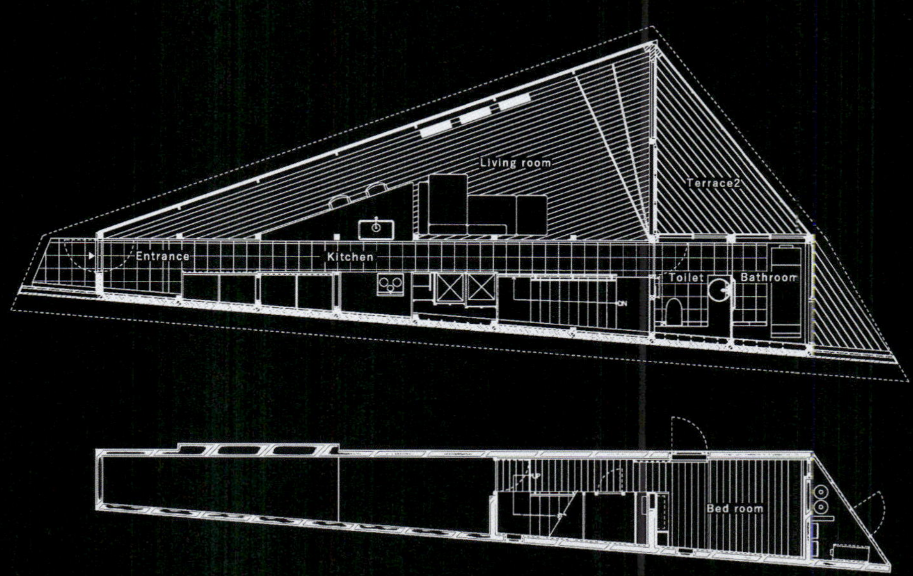

The sloping roof offers selected views of the landscape from the largely wooden-clad living and bathroom spaces seen on this double page.

Hang hinaus. Wohnzimmer und Terrasse sind dem Hang zugewandt, während sich Eingang, Küche und Bad auf der Rückseite des Gebäudes befinden. Das Schlafzimmer ist auf der oberen Ebene. „Wir reduzieren die Umweltauswirkungen unserer Gebäude, indem wir die Grundstücke unverändert lassen. Der Nachhaltigkeit verpflichtet sind wir stets bestrebt, äußerste Rücksicht auf die Natur zu nehmen und sie so wenig wie möglich für unsere Zwecke einzuspannen."

Construite sur un terrain de 2061 m² sur la berge à pic d'une rivière, Setoyama est une petite villa dont l'empreinte au sol est de 91 m². Le site est un plateau intact formé de couches de lave. L'architecte explique que « le client désirait "une vue sur la mer depuis le salon". Pour cela, afin de mieux encadrer le paysage marin et les bosquets qu'on voit à travers les arbres, nous avons imaginé de séparer le salon du sol et d'avancer la structure supérieure du côté de la falaise. Comme les fondations sont creusées dans une pente raide, il fallait les éloigner le plus possible de la falaise ». La base en béton armé porte une structure à charpente en bois d'origine locale dont la forme triangulaire surplombe la pente. Un salon et une terrasse lui font face, tandis que l'entrée, la cuisine et la salle de bains sont placées à l'arrière. La chambre est à l'étage. L'architecte précise encore que « nous essayons de réduire l'impact sur l'environnement de nos constructions, et pour cela, nous ne modifions pas la forme du terrain. Nous sommes tenus de respecter et d'utiliser la nature environnante et nous avons pris un engagement fort en faveur de la durabilité ».

NORGESHUS

The Bolder
Stavanger-Lysefjord, Norway, 2020
Area: 22 m²

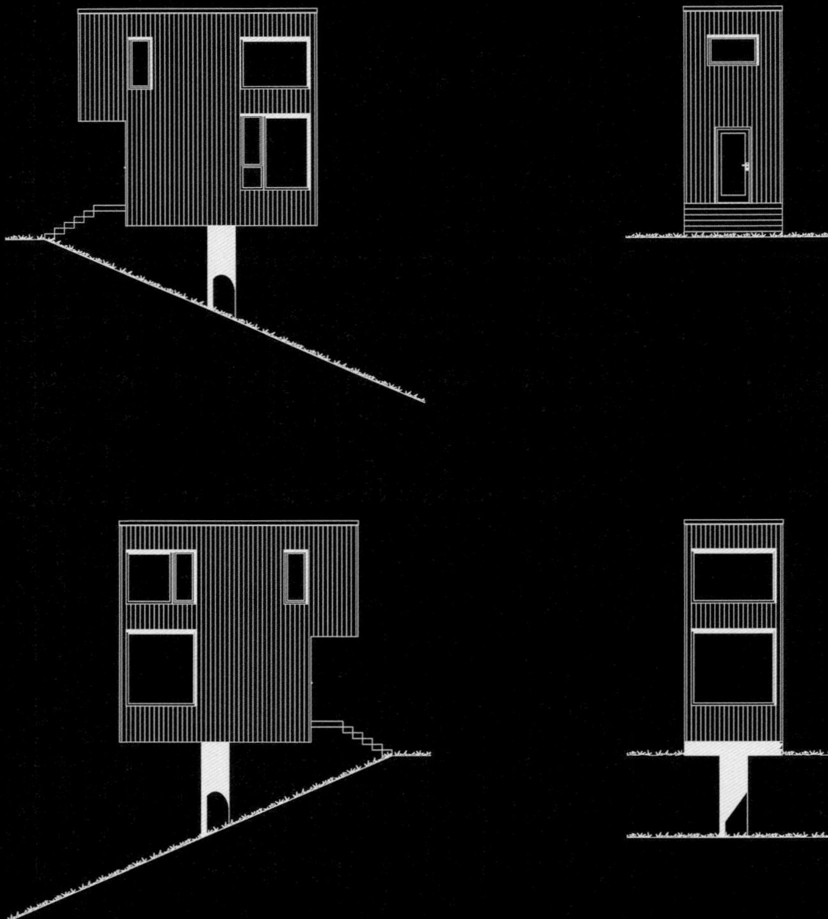

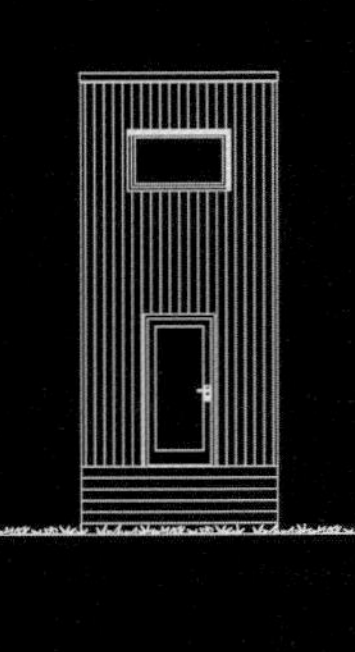

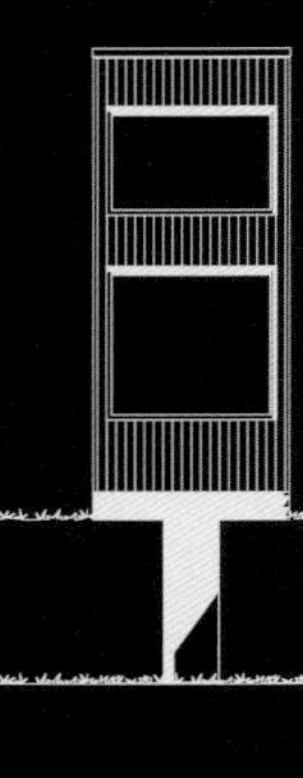

These cabins are built on an inspiring site overlooking the fjord—a steel pillar and lower structure carry the wooden volume above.

Lysefjord is a 42-kilometer-long fjord located in the Ryfylke area of southwestern Norway. The Bolder Sky Lodges are small rental cabins built on load-bearing steel pillars overlooking the fjord. The actual structure of the cabins is in prefabricated wood, mounted on a steel "undercarriage" calculated to resist the force of the wind. The interior design intentionally adapts to a minimal size, divided between two floors. The kitchen and living room are on the lower level (11 m²), with a bathroom and two bedrooms with double beds on the upper floor. Large, glazed surfaces are placed to best appreciate the views in the cabins, which have naturally gray wood exterior cladding.

Der Lysefjord ist ein 42 Kilometer langer Fjord in der Region Ryfylke im Südwesten Norwegens. Die Bolder Sky Lodges sind kleine zweistöckige Miethütten, die auf tragenden Stahlsäulen errichtet wurden. Ihre Grundstruktur aus vorgefertigtem Holz wurde auf ein „Untergestell" aus Stahl montiert, um den starken Winden standzuhalten. Außen mit natürlich grauem Holz verkleidet, sind sie auch innen bewusst minimalistisch gehalten. Küche und Wohnzimmer befinden sich auf der unteren Ebene (11 m²), ein Badezimmer und zwei Schlafzimmer mit Doppelbetten auf der oberen Etage. Durch die großzügigen Fenster öffnen sich den Bewohnern weite Ausblicke über den Fjord.

The kitchen and the living room are on the lower floor, while the bedrooms—one with a corner view and the other, with the bathroom in the foreground—are on the upper level. Plans show the straightforward design.

Le Lysefjord est un fjord de 42 km situé dans la région de Ryfylke, au sud-ouest de la Norvège. The Bolder Sky Lodges consiste en de toutes petites maisons de location portées par des piliers d'acier qui surplombent le fjord. Leur structure est en bois préfabriqué monté sur un « chariot » en acier calculé pour résister à la force du vent. L'intérieur est délibérément conçu pour s'adapter à une taille minimale, répartie en deux niveaux. La cuisine et le salon sont en bas (11 m²), tandis qu'une salle de bains et deux chambres avec des lits doubles occupent l'étage. De grandes surfaces vitrées permettent de profiter au mieux de la vue depuis les maisonnettes revêtues à l'extérieur de bois naturellement gris.

OJT

Starter Home No. 1, 3106 St. Thomas
New Orleans, Louisiana, USA, 2015
Area: 90 m²

Collaboration: Charles Rutledge
(Development Partner)

Echoing the corrugated metal façade of a neighboring warehouse, the house nonetheless offers a sophisticated, modern appearance and a real home to people with low budgets.

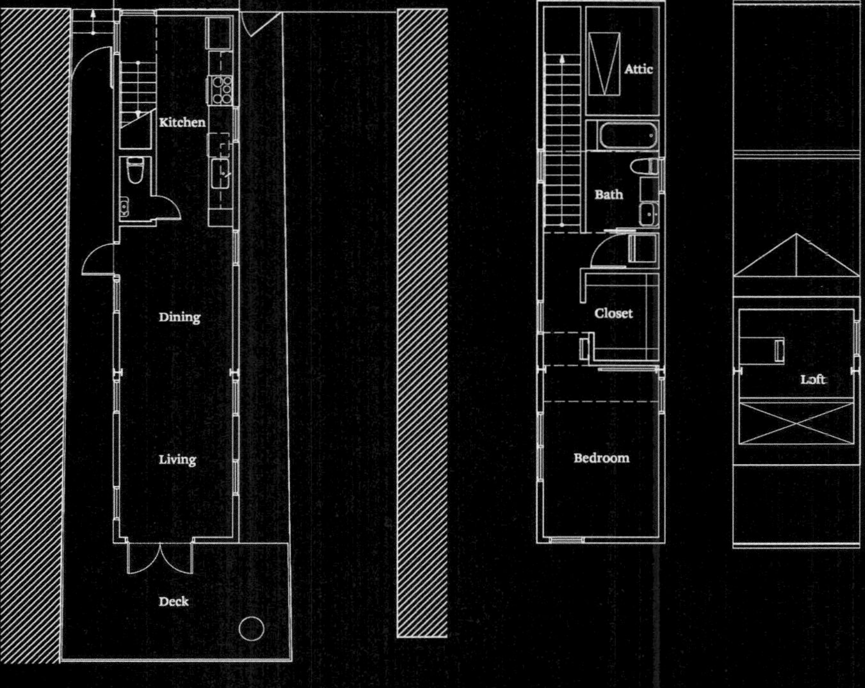

This single-family home was built for a budget of $200 000. It was classified as "infill housing for existing vacant parcel in historic neighborhood," which is to say the Irish Channel area of New Orleans near the Mississippi River. This is a "Starter Home," meaning that it is intended to increase opportunities for first-time homeowners, and in this instance seeks no government subsidies, instead relying on the architect and a local developer (Charles Rutledge). No zoning variances were requested, and the house is next to a warehouse and a two-family house and has a long narrow footprint but a more generous maximum height of 12 meters. This three-story wood-and-steel-frame house has one bedroom, one and a half bathrooms, and an office space. Its exterior walls are in corrugated metal, and the structure has a distinctive profile because of site constraints, meaning that its street elevation appears to be single story. OJT hopes to build other homes of this nature.

Dieses Einfamilienhaus wurde mit einem Budget von 200 000 US-Dollar gebaut. Eingestuft als „Bebauung einer bestehenden Baulücke in einem historischen Viertel" befindet es sich im Irish Channel von New Orleans nahe des Mississippi. Das sogenannte „Starter Home" richtet sich an jene, die erstmalig den Bau ihrer eigenen vier Wände planen. Das Projekt wurde gemeinsam vom Architekten und dem ansässigen Bauunternehmer Charles Rutledge finanziert und ohne staatliche Zuschüsse umgesetzt. Eine Änderung des Bebauungsplans war nicht notwendig, da das Häuschen zwischen einem Lagerhaus und einem Zweifamilienhaus eingefügt wurde. Sein Grundriss ist lang und schmal, die maximale Höhe beträgt beachtliche 12 m. Es wurde

The interior is bright, and its double-height area, generated by the raked form of the house, gives the impression that it is spacious. Wood cabinetry also gives a warm feeling in contrast to the white walls and ceilings.

in Holz- und Stahlrahmenbauweise konstruiert und mit einer Wellblechfassade versehen. Im Inneren finden ein Schlafzimmer, eineinhalb Badezimmer und ein Arbeitszimmer Platz. Aufgrund der besonderen Grundstücksform dreht das dreistöckige Gebäude der Straßenseite sein einstöckiges Profil zu und wirkt so nach außen noch kleiner als es ist. OJT hofft, mit den Starter Homes weitere Klein- und Zwischenflächen urbar zu machen.

Cette maison individuelle a été construite pour un budget de 200 000 dollars. Elle a été définie comme « un logement de remplissage d'une parcelle vacante dans un quartier historique », à savoir celui de l'Irish Channel à La Nouvelle-Orléans, près du Mississippi. Il s'agit d'un « Starter Home », destiné à donner des chances aux primo-accédants à la propriété sans chercher de subventions, mais en comptant sur l'architecte et un promoteur local (Charles Rutledge). Aucune dérogation au règlement de zonage n'a été exigée, la maison jouxte un entrepôt et une maison jumelée, son empreinte au sol est longue et étroite pour une hauteur maximale plus généreuse de 12 m. Elle a trois niveaux, une ossature de bois et d'acier, et possède une chambre, une salle de bains et demie et un coin bureau. Ses murs extérieurs sont en métal ondulé et les contraintes locales lui ont donné son profil spécifique qui ne laisse apparaître qu'un seul étage côté rue. OJT espère construire d'autres maisons de ce type.

OLSON KUNDIG

Gulf Islands Cabin
Gulf Islands, British Columbia, Canada, 2008
Area: 18 m²

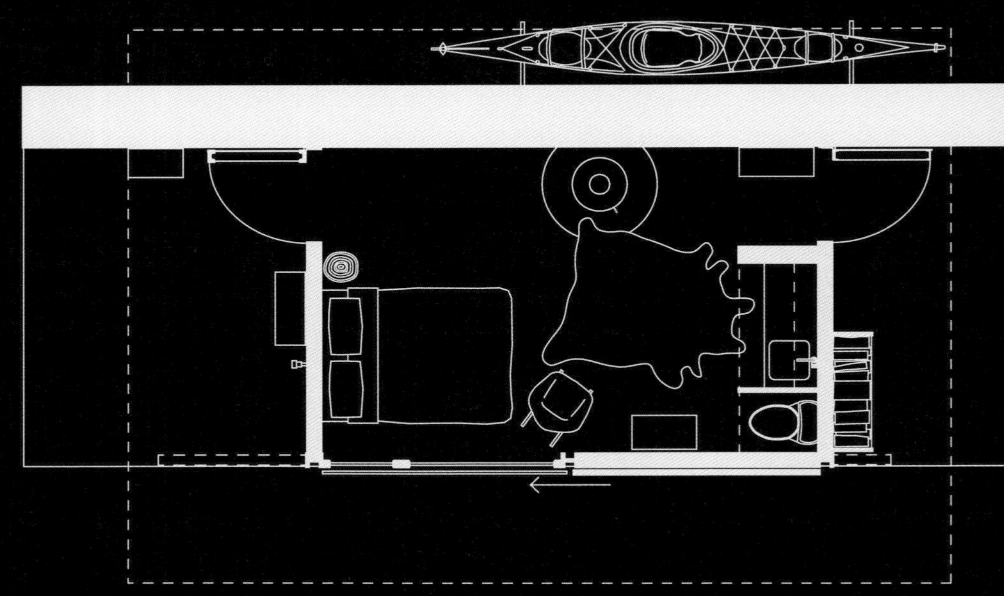

An outdoor shower and terrace are reached directly from the bedroom area seen within. A wood-burning stove provides the necessary heat.

Although this is the oldest project published in this book, it retains an originality and a solidity that is exemplary for a very small home. It was built on a previously occupied site using a rammed-earth retaining wall, mild steel cladding, and wood floors and ceilings, mostly cedar-milled from salvaged timber. It uses a high-efficiency RAIS wood-burning stove. The Gulf Islands are located between Vancouver Island and the mainland coast of Canada. The design is intended to require no maintenance, and a large, weathered steel panel can be slid in front of the glazed façade to protect the cabin when it is empty. The interior includes a kitchenette, toilet, and bed.

Trotz seines Alters – es ist das älteste der in diesem Buch vorgestellten Projekte – hat Gulf Islands Cabin bis heute nichts von seiner Originalität, Solidität und seinem Vorbildcharakter für kleine Häuser verloren. Die Stützmauer der auf dem Grundstück einer abgerissenen Hütte errichteten Minilodge ist aus Stampflehm, die Verkleidung aus Baustahl und die Holzböden und -decken wurden größtenteils aus wiedergewonnenem Zedernholz gefertigt. Für Wärme sorgt ein hocheffizienter RAIS-Holzofen. Die Gulf Islands liegen zwischen Vancouver Island und dem kanadischen Festland. Eine große verwitterte Stahlplatte, die sich vor die Glasfassade schieben lässt, bietet der wartungsfreien Konstruktion Schutz vor Wind, Wetter und Eindringlingen. Der Innenraum beherbergt eine Küchenzeile, eine Toilette und ein Bett.

The bedroom and outdoor shower are seen here again. Opposite: *the kitchen and toilet fit into closet-like spaces near the bed and the stove.*

Ce projet a beau être le plus ancien publié ici, il n'en conserve pas moins une originalité et un caractère exemplaires pour une toute petite maison. Elle a été construite sur un site déjà occupé et comprend un mur de soutènement en pisé, un revêtement en acier doux et des murs et plafonds en bois, surtout du cèdre scié dans du bois d'œuvre de récupération. Le chauffage est assuré par un poêle à bois RAIS haute efficacité. Les îles Gulf sont situées entre l'île de Vancouver et la côte du Canada. L'ensemble est conçu pour ne nécessiter aucune maintenance et un grand panneau d'acier patiné peut coulisser devant la façade vitrée pour protéger la maison lorsqu'elle est inoccupée. L'intérieur comporte une kitchenette, des toilettes et un lit.

ORTRAUM

Kynttilä
Savonlinna, Finland, 2020
Area: 16 m²

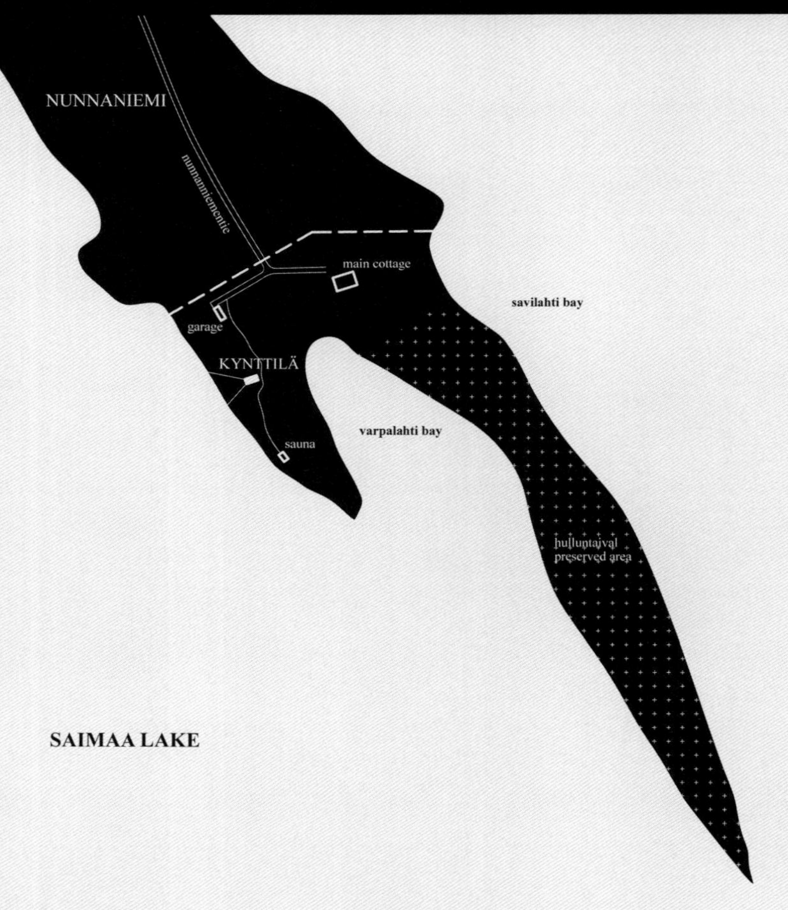

In a way the epitome of a small house for times of ecological troubles, this A-frame cabin has an entire wall made of glass to allow for generous views from the simple space.

This CLT structure with Siberian larch cladding was built on the Nunnanniemi peninsula in Lake Saimaa near Savonlinna in eastern Finland, close to the Russian border. On a property near a nature reserve, an existing summer cottage had additional building rights for just 15 square meters, and it was decided to create Kynttilä (Candle) as a guesthouse and meditation cottage. Construction was carefully planned in order not to disturb the forest setting. According to the architects: "The concept of Kynttilä is Zen, in the definition of 'nothing.' The space aims to provide focus, visually and spiritually, by stripping the content and design intention to a bare minimum. The dimensions of the five enveloping elements are identical, creating a calm space and framing the carefully chosen view toward the water with maximized simplicity." A large window allows for views of the surroundings. Cross-laminated timber (CLT) was used not only for the structure, but also for furnishings and the entrance door.

Diese Konstruktion aus Brettsperrholz mit einer Verkleidung aus sibirischer Lärche wurde auf der Halbinsel Nunnanniemi im ostfinnischen Saimaa errichtet, einem See bei Savonlinna, unweit der russischen Grenze. Auf dem Grundstück in der Nähe eines Naturschutzgebietes stand bereits ein nur 15 m² großes Sommerhaus, das sein Baurecht noch nicht ausgeschöpft hatte, und so wurde ihm Kynttilä (Kerze) als Gäste- und Meditationshaus zur Seite gestellt. Der Bau wurde sorgfältig geplant und umgesetzt, um die Waldumgebung nicht zu stören. „Kynttilä richtet sich ganz nach dem Zen, das ‚nichts' bietet und voraussetzt", erklären die Architekten. „Der Raum fördert den visuellen und spirituellen Fokus, da er seinen Inhalt und seine Gestaltungsabsicht auf ein

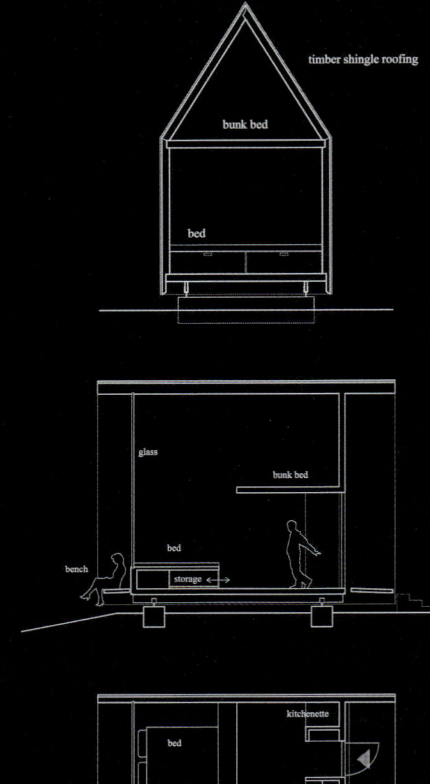

As the section drawing and plan indicate, the house is stripped down to the bare essentials, but, with 16 square meters of floor space, it offers a magnificent view of the forest.

absolutes Minimum reduziert. Die ihn umhüllenden fünf Elemente üben eine beständige Kraft auf ihn aus, füllen ihn mit Ruhe und öffnen leise und gezielt den Blick auf das Wasser." Ermöglicht wird diese Aussicht durch ein großes Fenster. Grundstruktur, Mobiliar und Eingangstür sind aus Brettsperrholz gefertigt.

Cette construction en bois lamellé-croisé (CLT) revêtue de mélèze de Sibérie a été bâtie sur la péninsule de Nunnanniemi qui s'avance dans le lac Saimaa, près de Savonlinna – dans l'est de la Finlande, à proximité de la frontière russe. La propriété est proche d'une réserve naturelle et une petite maison d'été déjà existante disposait d'un permis de construire pour encore 15 m². Les propriétaires ont donc décidé de créer Kynttilä (bougie) pour servir de maison d'hôtes et d'abri de méditation. La construction a été conçue avec soin pour ne pas nuire à la forêt tout autour. Les architectes expliquent que « le concept de Kynttilä est le zen dans sa définition qui signifie "rien". Le lieu est destiné à favoriser la concentration, visuellement et spirituellement, en dépouillant jusqu'au strict minimum le contenu et le design. Les dimensions des cinq éléments de l'enveloppe sont identiques afin de créer un espace de calme et un cadre pour la vue sur l'eau soigneusement choisie, avec une simplicité optimale ». Une vaste fenêtre donne sur la nature environnante. Le bois lamellé croisé a été utilisé pour la structure, mais aussi pour le mobilier et la porte d'entrée.

GUSTAVO PENNA

Sustainable House
Ouro Branco, Minas Gerais, Brazil, 2019
Area: 45 m^2

Collaboration: Norberto Bambozzi,
Laura Penna, Oded Stahl

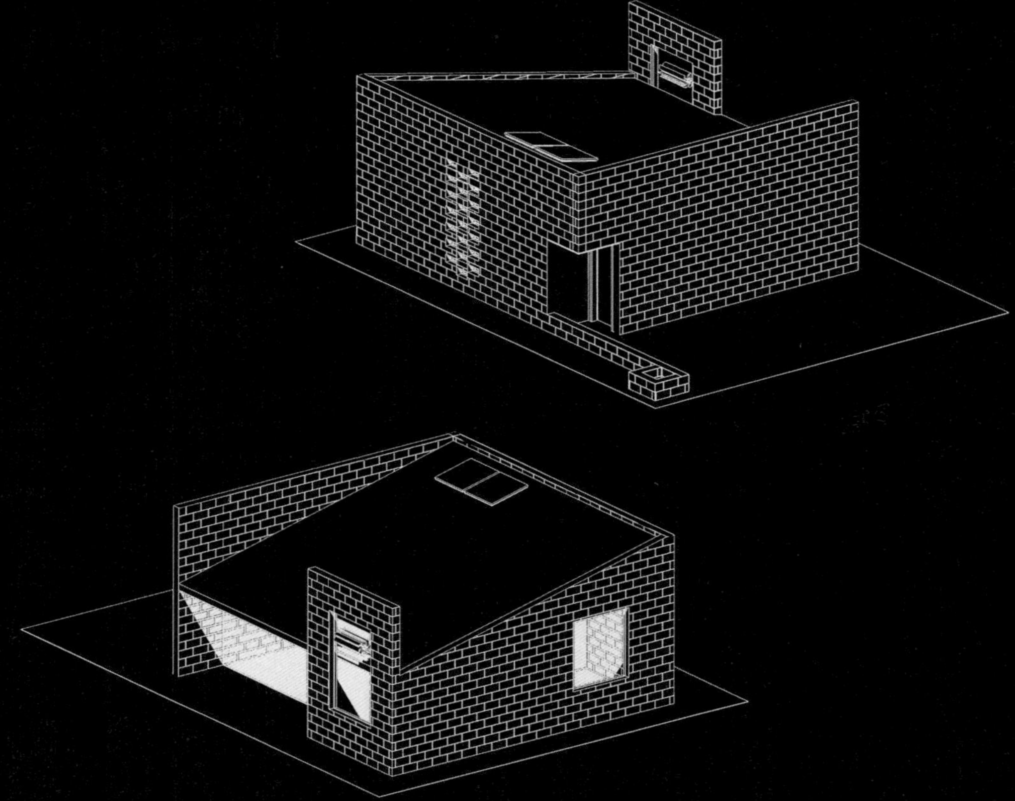

Making unexpected use of mining residue for the construction materials, this sustainable house adapts a low profile and simple design, taking full advantage of outdoor spaces.

Gustavo Penna Architect & Associates and Gerdau imagined the first house to be built from by-products of mining operations in Ouro Branco. Both sustainability in mining and the idea of a circular economy for housing are part of this concept. The Mining Engineering Department of the Federal University of Minas Gerais (UFMG) in partnership with Gerdau developed blocks, draining floors, and mortar made with iron ore tailings, elements intended to upgrade mining waste management in the future. The Sustainable House uses environmentally friendly systems that were readily accessible, such as solar heating, power generation, biodigesters, composting tanks, and rainwater collection. Researchers and students can visit the house at the Gerdau Germinar Biocenter. The space acts as an environmental education tool, and its main objective is to show the relevance of mining in the contemporary world and the technologies that can be adopted in our homes in order to make them more sustainable. Gerdau, which is headquartered in Porto Alegre, is a steelmaker whose core business is to transform steel scrap and iron ore into steel products. Ouro Branco, a city of about 40 000 people, has been an important point on the transportation route from mines in Minas Gerais to the coast.

Jsed in part as a teaching space, the house inte-
rates various types of ecologically oriented systems,
lthough this "green" aspect has been made to fully
lend into the architecture.

Mit diesem Gebäude entwarfen Gustavo Penna Architect & Associates gemeinsam mit dem brasilianischen Stahlkonzern Gerdau das erste Haus, das aus Nebenprodukten des Bergbaus von Ouro Branco erbaut wurde. Sein Konzept berücksichtigt sowohl die Nachhaltigkeit im Bergbau als auch die Idee einer Kreislaufwirtschaft im Wohnungsbau. Gerdau und die Abteilung für Bergbauingenieurwesen der Bundesuniversität von Minas Gerais entwickelten Blöcke, Drainageböden und Mörtel aus Eisenerzabfällen, das heißt aus Elementen, die künftig zu einer verbesserten Abfallwirtschaft im Bergbau beitragen sollen. Das nachhaltige Haus nutzt umweltfreundliche Systeme leicht zugänglicher Ressourcen, wie zum Beispiel Solarheizung, Stromerzeugung, Biogasanlagen, Kompost- und Regenwassertanks. Forscher und Studenten können das Haus im Biozentrum Gerdau Germinar besichtigen. Es dient der Umwelterziehung und soll vor allem die heutige Bedeutung des Bergbaus und jene Technologien aufzeigen, die unsere Wohnungen nachhaltiger machen können. Gerdau mit Hauptsitz in Porto Alegre ist ein Stahlhersteller, dessen Kernkompetenz in der Verarbeitung von Stahlschrott und Eisenerz zu Stahlprodukten besteht. Ouro Branco, eine Stadt mit etwa 40 000 Einwohnern, war früher ein wichtiger Punkt auf dem Transportweg von den Minas Gerais-Minen zur Küste.

The blocks made from iron ore tailings characterize both the interior and the exterior of the house. Furnishings and décor are minimal, in keeping with the strong, simple lines of the architecture.

Gustavo Penna Architect & Associates et Gerdau ont imaginé la première maison construite à partir de produits dérivés de l'exploitation minière à Ouro Branco. Le concept associe la durabilité de la mine et l'idée d'une économie circulaire pour le logement. Le département de génie minier de l'université fédérale de Minas Gerais (UFMG) a développé, en partenariat avec Gerdau, des blocs de construction, des planchers drainants et un mortier fait de résidu de minerai de fer, autant d'éléments destinés à valoriser à l'avenir la gestion des déchets de la mine. La Maison durable a recours à des systèmes respectueux de l'environnement facilement accessibles, notamment le chauffage solaire, la production d'électricité, des biodigesteurs, des composts et la récupération de l'eau de pluie. Elle est ouverte aux visites d'étudiants et de chercheurs au Biocenter Germinar de Gerdau. Elle tient lieu d'outil éducatif environnemental dont l'objectif principal est de monter la pertinence de l'exploitation minière dans le monde contemporain et les technologies auxquelles nous pouvons recourir chez nous pour les rendre plus durables. Gerdau, dont le siège se trouve à Porto Alegre, est un fabricant d'acier dont l'activité principale consiste à transformer les déchets d'acier et le minerai de fer en produits en acier. Ouro Branco, une ville d'environ 40 000 habitants, a été un passage important sur la route qui transportait les produits de la mine de Minas Gerais à la côte.

CHARLES PICTET

Atelier and Residence in a Garden Shed
Geneva, Switzerland, 2021
Area: 24 m^2 + 5 m^2 (chicken coop)

Despite its bucolic appearance, this small building is located very close to the center of Geneva in a wooded residential area. The former shed is just inside a stone wall that runs along the street.

This former shed is located close to the architect's house near central Geneva. He explains: "During 2020, experiencing confinement, I came to the idea of making it a place for myself to work from home and experiment with my ceramics. The project grew as it was under construction, without preconceived plans. Every morning discussing with the workers, I improvised with sketches on the back of the envelopes I had in hand from emptying my mailbox. In the process I added a tiny mezzanine to sleep above the shower and loo and the small kitchen, and from an atelier I managed to turn the tiny space into a complete living area. The furnishing enables the presence of a living room, dining room atelier, kitchen, bedroom, and bathroom in 20 square meters." Two large windows bring in southern light, while skylights add northern cool light from the roof. The architect adds: "At the other end, the space opens onto the ancient flower garden with a bench, an apple tree, and a beautiful magnolia."

„2020 war ein Jahr der Enge und Isolation, und ich wünschte mir einen Ort, an dem ich von zu Hause aus arbeiten und mit meiner Keramik experimentieren konnte", erzählt der Architekt über den ehemaligen Gartenschuppen seines Wohnhauses unweit des Genfer Stadtzentrums. „Es gab keine vorgefassten Pläne und das Projekt entwickelte sich während der Bauphase. Jeden Morgen diskutierte ich mit den Arbeitern und improvisierte mit Skizzen auf der Rückseite von Briefumschlägen, die ich nach dem Leeren meines Briefkastens noch in der Hand hielt. Auf diese Weise fügte ich ein winziges Zwischengeschoss als Schlafbereich ein, das über der Dusche, dem WC und der kleinen Küche

The long interior façade of the structure faces an internal courtyard, which is also next to the main house.

eingezogen wurde. So entstand aus einem Atelier ein vollausgestattetes Wohnhäuschen mit Wohn- und Essbereich, Atelier, Küche, Schlaf- und Badezimmer – auf nur 20 m².“ Durch zwei großzügige Fenster fällt Südlicht, während Oberlichter kühles Nordlicht ins Innere einladen. „Nach hinten hinaus öffnet sich der Raum zu einem alten Blumengarten mit einer Sitzbank, einem Apfelbaum und einer wunderschönen Magnolie.“

L'ancien abri est proche de la maison de l'architecte, non loin du centre de Genève. Il explique : « En 2020, pendant le confinement, j'ai eu l'idée d'en faire un endroit à moi pour travailler de la maison et faire des expériences avec mes céramiques. Le projet a grandi pendant sa construction, sans plan préconçu. Tous les matins, je discutais avec les ouvriers et j'improvisais en dessinant au dos des enveloppes que j'avais en main après avoir vidé ma boîte aux lettres. J'ai ainsi ajouté une minuscule mezzanine avec un lit au-dessus de la douche et des toilettes et la petite cuisine, et en partant d'un atelier, j'ai réussi à transformer ce minuscule espace en un lieu de vie complet. Le mobilier permet de faire entrer un salon, une salle à manger atelier, une cuisine, une chambre et une salle de bains dans 20 m². » Deux grandes fenêtres font entrer la lumière au sud, complétée par l'éclairage froid du Nord qui entre par les lucarnes dans le toit. L'architecte poursuit : « À l'autre extrémité, la maison ouvre sur l'ancien jardin fleuri avec un banc, un pommier et un superbe magnolia. »

The interior of the house includes a sitting and working area for the owner with a kitchenette and elevated bed at the far end. The plan shows the main space as well as a small residual area used for other purposes to the right.

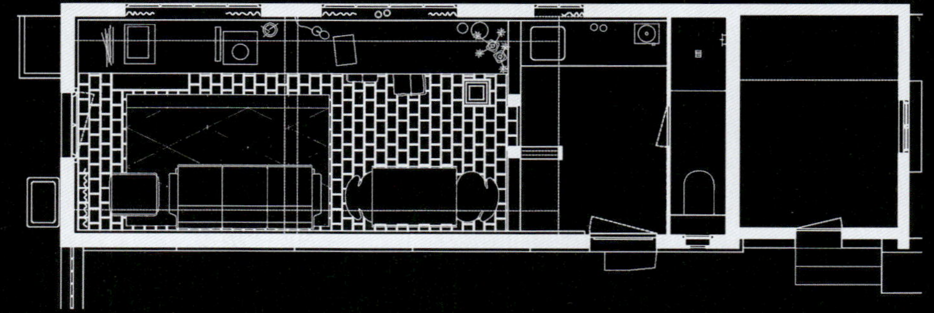

PRENTISS + BALANCE + WICKLINE

Boathouse
Orcas Island, Washington, USA, 2021
Area: 61 m²

Collaboration: Philip Burkhardt (Project Architect), Kelby Riegsecker (Architect)

Set up on very thin steel supports, the Boathouse has a light, metallic presence on the waters of the Salish Sea close to the Canadian maritime border in northwest Washington.

This boathouse replaced an existing "dilapidated, haphazardly constructed structure." The project involved the removal of 37 square meters of concrete and creosote-coated piles from the water. The new structure is supported by just 0.37 square meters of thin steel supports. Windows of the new building are placed to accentuate views of trees and moss-covered stones. Steel is used in the kitchen, fireplace, and shelves. The architects emphasize the material continuity between interior and exterior materials—"resilient materials able to weather the harsh environment." A steel structure and railings form the exterior, with Thermory (thermally modified) decking and screens, stained tight-knot cedar siding, and a metal roof. Interiors have ash ceilings and floors, cedar siding, steel cabinets and fireplace, and a Milestone-plaster bathroom. Orcas Island is the largest of the San Juan Islands, which are south of Vancouver.

Dieses Bootshaus ersetzte ein bestehendes „baufälliges, willkürlich konstruiertes Gebäude". Für seinen Bau wurden 37 m² Beton und mit Kreosot beschichtete Pfähle aus dem Wasser entfernt und durch 0,37 m² dünne Stahlstützen ersetzt, auf denen Boathouse heute ruht. Seine Fenster geben den Blick auf Bäume und moosbewachsene Steine frei. Küche, Kamin und Regale werden von Stahl dominiert. Die Architekten betonen die materielle Kontinuität der „widerstandsfähigen Materialien, die der rauen Umgebung standhalten". So wird der Außenraum von einer Stahlkonstruktion und Geländern geprägt sowie von thermisch behandelten Terrassendielen und Sichtblenden, gebeizten Zedernholzverkleidungen und einem Metalldach. Die Innenräume verfügen über Decken und Böden aus Eschenholz, Zedernholzverkleidungen, Stahlschränke, einen Kamin sowie ein Badezimmer aus Milestone-Fliesen. Orcas Island ist die größte der südlich von Vancouver liegenden San-Juan-Inseln.

Large, glazed openings and the external deck emphasize the idea that residents are floating above the water; furnishings are simple and sparse.

Le hangar à bateaux remplace une structure existante « construite au hasard et délabrée ». Le projet comprend le retrait de l'eau de 37 m² de piliers recouverts de béton et de créosote. La nouvelle construction est uniquement portée par 0,37 m² de fins poteaux en acier. Les fenêtres du nouveau bâtiment ont été placées pour mettre en valeur la vue des arbres et des pierres couvertes de mousse. L'acier est présent dans la cuisine, le foyer et les étagères. Les architectes insistent sur la continuité de matériaux entre l'intérieur et l'extérieur – « des matériaux résistants qui supportent des conditions difficiles ». Une structure et des balustrades en acier forment l'extérieur avec un ponton et des panneaux de Thermory (bois modifié thermiquement), un bardage de cèdre teinté à nœuds sains solides et une toiture métallique. Les plafonds et les sols de l'intérieur sont en frêne, le bardage en cèdre, les placards et la cheminée en acier et la salle de bains en Plaster Milestone. L'île Orcas est la plus grande des îles San Juan, au sud de Vancouver.

REIULF RAMSTAD

Breitenbach Landscape Hotel – 48° Nord
Breitenbach, France, 2020
Area: 20 to 41 m²

Collaboration: ASP Architecture

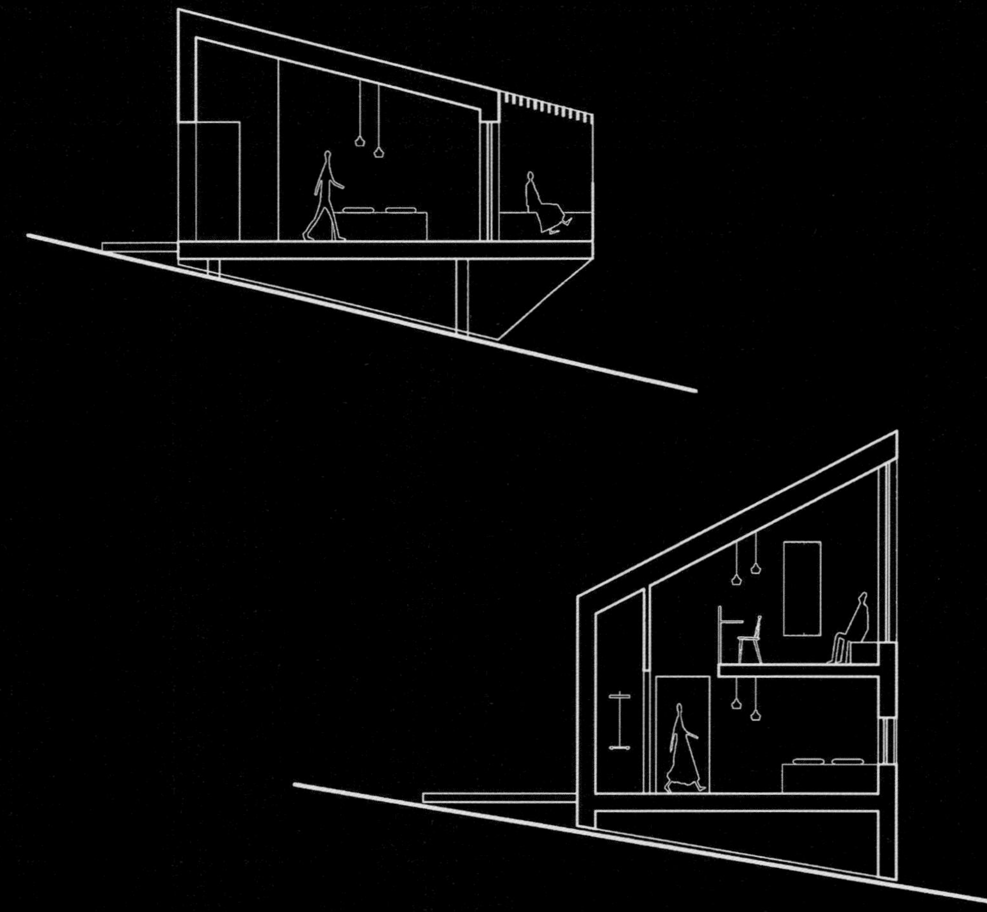

REIULF RAMSTAD

Breitenbach Landscape Hotel – 48° Nord
Breitenbach, France, 2020
Area: 20 to 41 m²

Collaboration: ASP Architecture

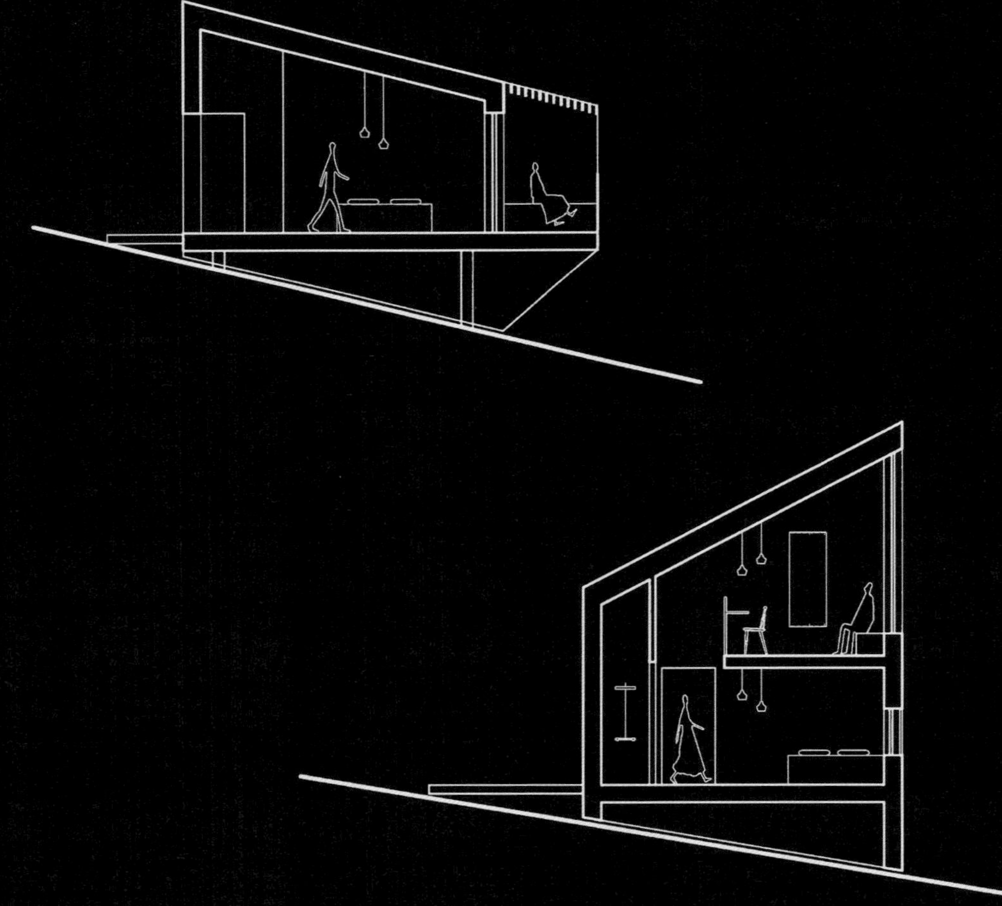

The 14 guest accommodations range in size from 14 to 20 square meters. They are clad in vertically laid strips of locally sourced chestnut wood.

The Breitenbach Landscape Hotel – 48° Nord seeks to propose a "true eco-tourism experience in Alsace, inspired by Scandinavian traditions." The project reinterprets the traditional Scandinavian *hytte*, a place of retreat and reconnection with nature. At the heart of a protected Natura 2000 site, the project was designed to fit into a preserved setting without disturbing it. The design includes a main building for the reception, restaurant, wellness, and director's housing, as well as 14 *hytte* for hotel guests. The total area of the project covers two hectares. Outdoor cladding of the structures is in sweet chestnut wood (*Castanea sativa*)—cut in the neighboring forest—while indoors, poplar (*Populus*) is used. Though not specifically individual houses, the *hytte* are inspired by residential holiday structures.

Das Breitenbach Landscape Hotel – 48° Nord stellt sich als „echtes Ökotourismuserlebnis im Elsass, inspiriert von skandinavischen Traditionen" vor. Es ist eine Neuinterpretation der traditionellen skandinavischen *hytte*, einem Ort des Rückzugs und der Rückverbindung mit der Natur. Gelegen inmitten eines Natura-2000-Schutzgebiets fügt sich die Anlage auf einer Gesamtfläche von zwei Hektar bewusst unaufdringlich in die geschützte Umgebung ein. Sie umfasst ein Hauptgebäude mit Rezeption, ein Restaurant, einen Wellnessbereich, die Direktionswohnung sowie 14 *hytte* für Gäste. Die Außenverkleidung besteht aus Kastanienholz (*Castanea sativa*) aus den umliegenden Wäldern, während für den Innenbereich Pappelholz (*Populus*) verwendet wurde. Auch wenn sie als Gruppe eine Einheit bilden, lassen die *hytte* erkennen, dass ihr Entwurf auf der Idee von Einzelferienhäusern beruht.

The structures vary in form as well as size, but all share openings to the natural setting that preserve the privacy of guests. Below: *Floor plans for one house on two levels* (above) *are juxtaposed with a plan for another of the houses.*

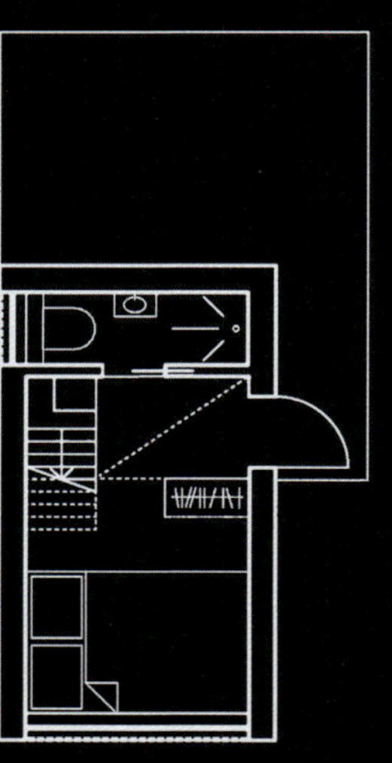

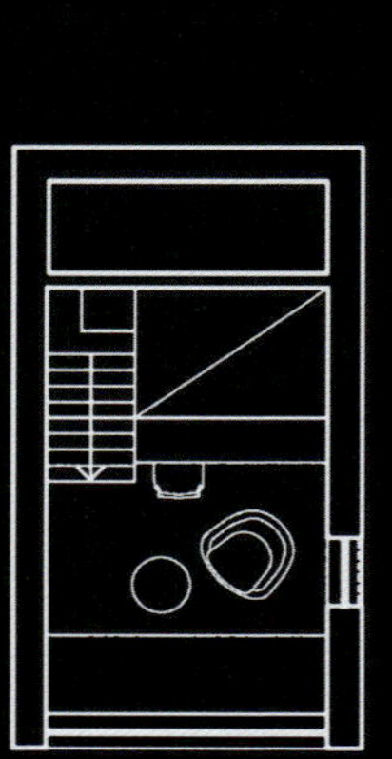

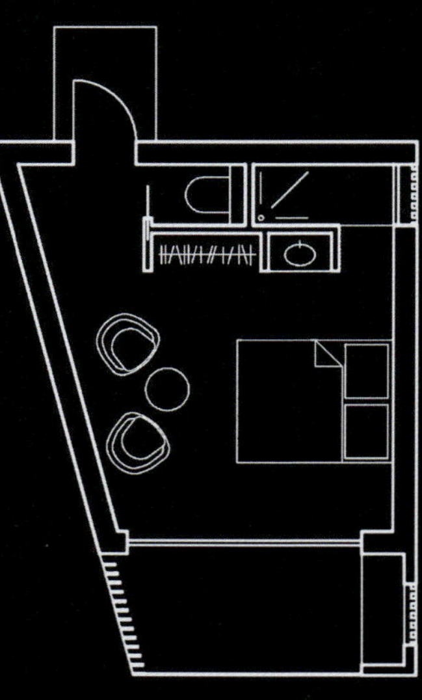

Wood and glass are the only materials used to generate this inspiring, sheltered view of the northeastern French landscape.

L'hôtel paysager de Breitenbach – 48° Nord propose une « véritable expérience d'éco-tourisme en Alsace, inspirée par les traditions scandinaves ». Le projet réinterprète la *hytte* traditionnelle scandinave, une retraite pour reprendre contact avec la nature. Au cœur d'un site protégé Natura 2000, il a été conçu pour s'intégrer à un cadre préservé sans lui nuire. L'ensemble comprend un bâtiment principal qui abrite la réception, un restaurant, l'espace bien-être et le logement du directeur, ainsi que 14 *hytte* destinés aux clients. La surface totale est de 2 ha. Les petites cabanes sont recouvertes à l'extérieur de bois tendre de châtaignier (*Castanea sativa*) coupé dans la forêt voisine, tandis que l'intérieur est en peuplier (*Populus*). Les *hytte* ne constituent pas spécifiquement des maisons individuelles, mais s'inspirent néanmoins des structures résidentielles de vacances.

JOÃO MENDES RIBEIRO

Chestnut House
Valeflor, Mêda, Portugal, 2020
Area: 25 m²

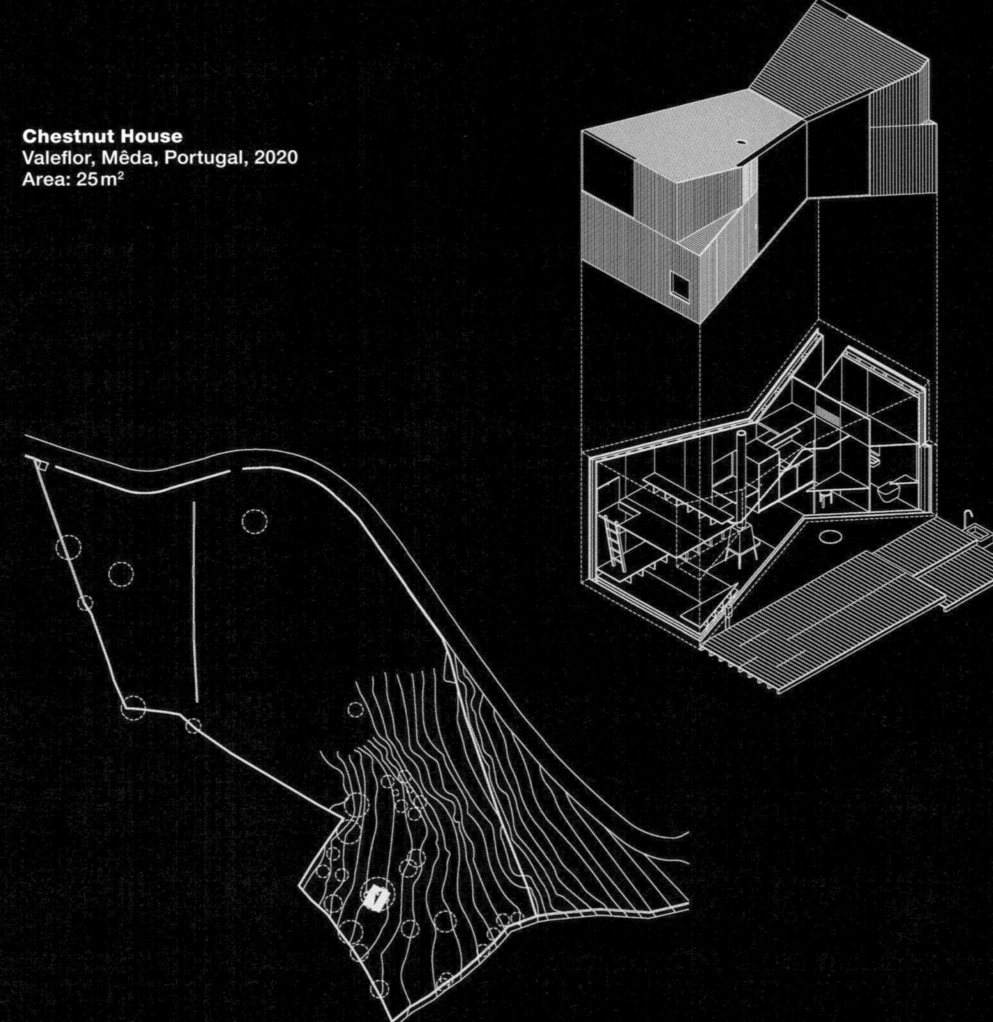

Large windows and an outdoor deck assure real contact with the forested setting.

The Chestnut House is in a rural area, near Valeflor, in the north of Portugal. The site, which has numerous chestnut and oak trees, is on an east-facing slope with a view of the Serra da Marofa ridge. The architect sought to intrude on the site as little as possible. "For this reason," he says, "the design considered the implantation of a light and over-elevated structure, whose morphology and materiality relate to the terrain in the most harmonious way possible." Sustainability and low carbon emissions were another goal. The certified wood structure is painted black on the exterior with birch plywood and cork inside. With its roof sloping inward, the house is formed from two "associated" 4.1-meter cubes. Part of the building is given over to a small kitchen, shower, and toilet, and, on the other hand, a living area with a bedroom. There is no living room per se, instead, a "meditation space" was created between the interior and the exterior. A large window in the living area assures a continual connection with the natural setting.

Chestnut House liegt in einer ländlichen Gegend nahe Valeflor im Norden Portugals auf einem Grundstück mit zahlreichen Kastanien- und Eichenbäumen. Von seiner nach Osten ausgerichteten Hanglage öffnet sich der Blick auf den Gebirgskamm der Serra da Marofa. Da dem Architekten sehr daran gelegen war, so wenig wie möglich in die Natur einzugreifen, „sah der Entwurf eine leichte und erhöhte Struktur vor, die sich in ihrer Morphologie und Materialität so harmonisch wie möglich in das Gelände einfügt". Als weitere Leitlinien dienten ihm Nachhaltigkeit und ein geringer Kohlenstoffausstoß. Die Grundstruktur aus zertifiziertem Holz ist außen schwarz gestrichen und innen mit Birkensperrholz und Kork

A drawing shows the importance given to a large existing tree, in the middle of the site.

Interiors are simple and bright, with plywood cladding. A wood-burning stove provides heat when it is required. Natural light fills the house during the day.

verkleidet. Mit seinem einwärts geneigten Dach ähnelt das Häuschen zwei miteinander verbundenen 4,1-Meter-Würfeln. Ein Teil beherbergt eine kleine Küche, eine Dusche und eine Toilette, im anderen Teil befinden sich ein Wohnbereich mit Schlafzimmer. Anstelle eines klassischen Wohnzimmers schuf der Architekt einen „Meditationsraum", der zwischen Innen und Außen vermittelt. Auch das große Fenster des Wohnbereichs hält die ständige Verbindung mit der Natur aufrecht.

La maison se trouve dans une zone rurale près de Valeflor, dans le nord du Portugal. Le site, planté de nombreux chênes et marronniers, est situé sur un versant qui fait face à l'est avec vue sur la crête de la Serra da Marofa. L'architecte a essayé d'être le moins intrusif possible. « Pour cela, explique-t-il, nous avons imaginé une structure et la matérialité dialoguent avec le terrain le plus harmonieusement possible. » La durabilité et les émissions de dioxyde de carbone réduites étaient un autre de ses objectifs. La construction en bois certifiée est peinte en noir à l'extérieur, tandis que l'intérieur est en contreplaqué de bouleau et en liège. La maison est constituée de deux cubes « associés » de 4,1 m avec la pente du toit vers l'intérieur. Une partie abrite une petite cuisine, une douche et des toilettes, l'autre côté comprend un espace avec une chambre. Il n'y a pas de salon à proprement parler, mais un « espace de méditation » a été créé entre l'intérieur et l'extérieur. Par ailleurs, une grande fenêtre du côté séjour forme une continuité avec le cadre naturel.

The roofs slope upwards from the center, providing extra ceiling height near the upper-level bedroom window seen here.

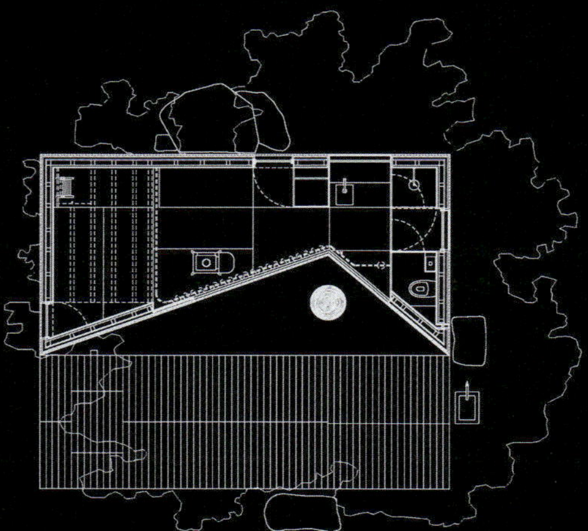

A wooden stepladder provides access to the upper-level bedroom, which occupies part of the area beneath the sloped roof on one side.

Drawings show the concept of the form of the house.

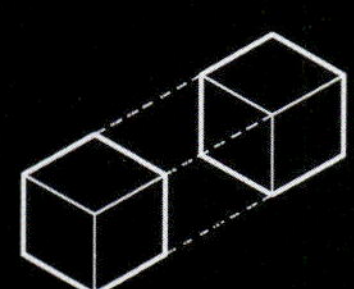
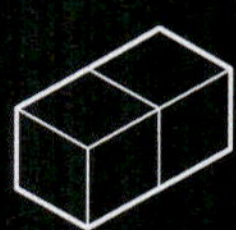
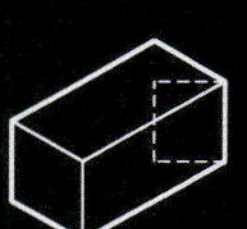
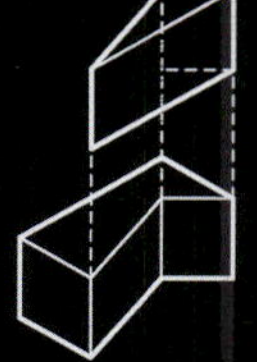
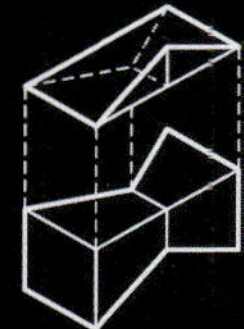
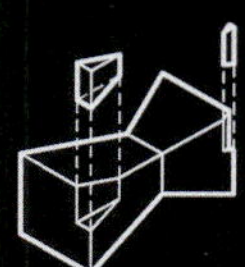

CLAUDIA RODRÍGUEZ & ROZANA MONTIEL

Cosmos Pavilions
Valle de Bravo, Mexico, 2019
Area: 65 m² (public pavilion),
70 m² (private pavilion)

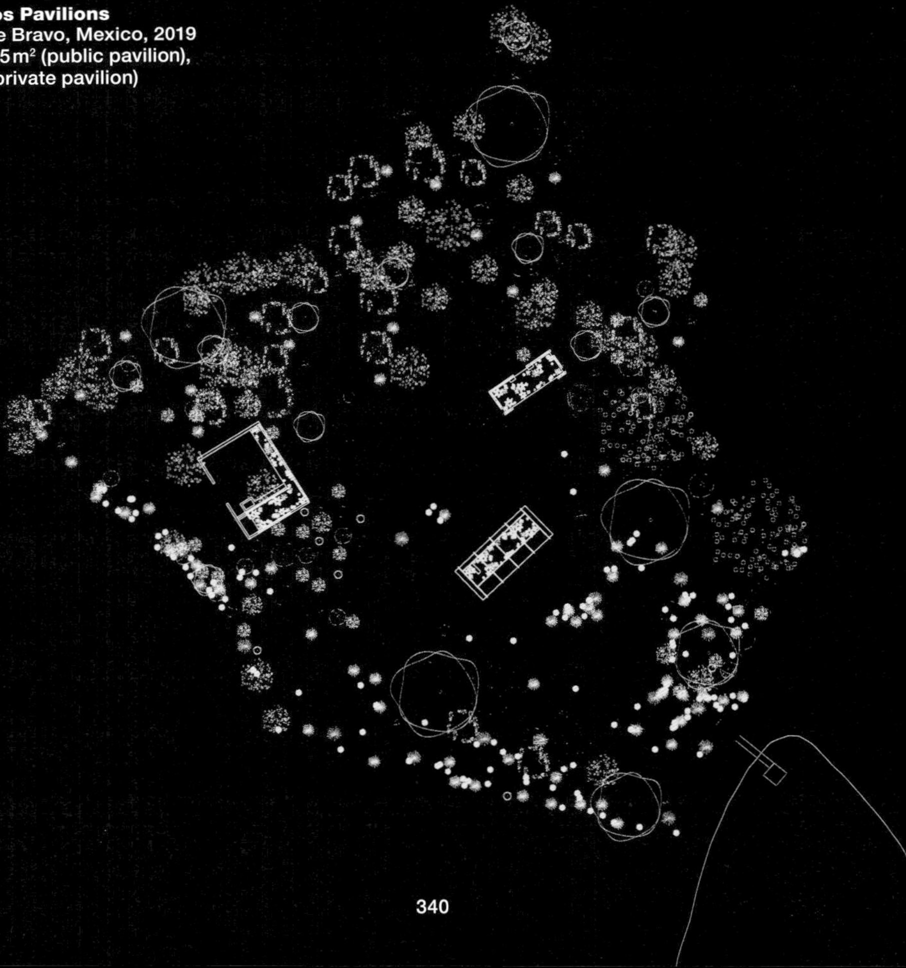

The public pavilion sits lightly on the ground and provides shelter under an extended roof. The outdoor terrace has a wood-burning stove for comfort in cool weather.

This project is in the forest of Valle de Bravo, a town on the shore of Lake Avándaro, about 155 kilometers southwest of Mexico City. Built on a one-hectare site, the two single-floor pavilions are located close to each other. The architects explain: "The public pavilion rises above the landscape and opens to a portico that connects to the exterior. The private one built in stone lies on the ground, where the bathroom becomes a special place that looks to the lake and to a private garden." The main materials used are stone, wood, and concrete. A close connection is established between the natural setting and the discrete architecture. According to the architects: "The client was an elderly woman who required these pavilions to have a simple program because she already has a house in the area. She asked to have private rooms spread around the property; the original project envisaged building more than just one private room, in fact we are building a new pavilion. She also wanted to have a separate public pavilion where all her guests could gather."

Die Cosmos Pavilions liegen im Wald von Valle de Bravo, einer Stadt am Ufer des Avándaro-Sees, etwa 155 Kilometer südwestlich von Mexiko-Stadt. Die beiden einstöckigen Strukturen aus den Hauptmaterialien Stein, Holz und Beton wurden unweit voneinander entfernt auf einem ein Hektar großen Grundstück errichtet. „Der öffentliche Pavillon erhebt sich über die Landschaft und hält dank seines Säulengangs eine enge Verbindung mit der Natur", schildern die Architektinnen. „Der private, aus Stein gebaute Pavillon ist ‚bodenständig'. Sein Badezimmer ist ein ganz spezieller Ort mit Blick auf den See und einen nicht öffentlichen Garten." Die Verbindung

Warm wood characterizes the kitchen space. The surrounding green environment is visible from all parts of the house.

zwischen der natürlichen Umgebung und der diskreten Architektur ist deutlich spürbar. „Die Bauherrin, eine ältere Dame, die bereits ein Haus in der Gegend besaß, wünschte sich für diese Pavillons ein schlichtes Profil", erzählen die Architektinnen. „Der ursprüngliche Entwurf sah mehr als nur einen privaten Raum vor und in der Tat bauen wir derzeit einen weiteren Pavillon. Der separate öffentliche Pavillon dient als Gästehaus."

Le projet est situé dans la forêt de Valle de Bravo, une ville au bord du lac Avándaro, à environ 155 km au sud-ouest de Mexico. Les deux pavillons à un étage ont été construits à côté l'un de l'autre sur un terrain d'un hectare. Les architectes expliquent que « le pavillon commun se dresse au-dessus du sol et ouvre sur un portique qui fait le lien avec l'extérieur. Le pavillon privé, en pierre, est au niveau du sol et la salle de bains prend un caractère très spécial avec vue sur le lac et sur un jardin privé ». Les principaux matériaux sont la pierre, le bois et le béton. L'architecture discrète est en lien étroit avec le décor naturel. Les architectes racontent encore que « la cliente est une dame âgée qui souhaitait des pavillons aménagés simplement, car elle possède déjà une maison dans la région. Elle nous a demandé de construire des espaces privés disséminés sur toute la propriété. Le projet d'origine prévoyait d'en réaliser plusieurs, nous sommes d'ailleurs en train d'en construire un autre. Elle voulait aussi un pavillon commun séparé où tous ses hôtes pourraient se retrouver ».

The bathroom space with a sliding glass opening. Below: a plan of the house in its forested setting.

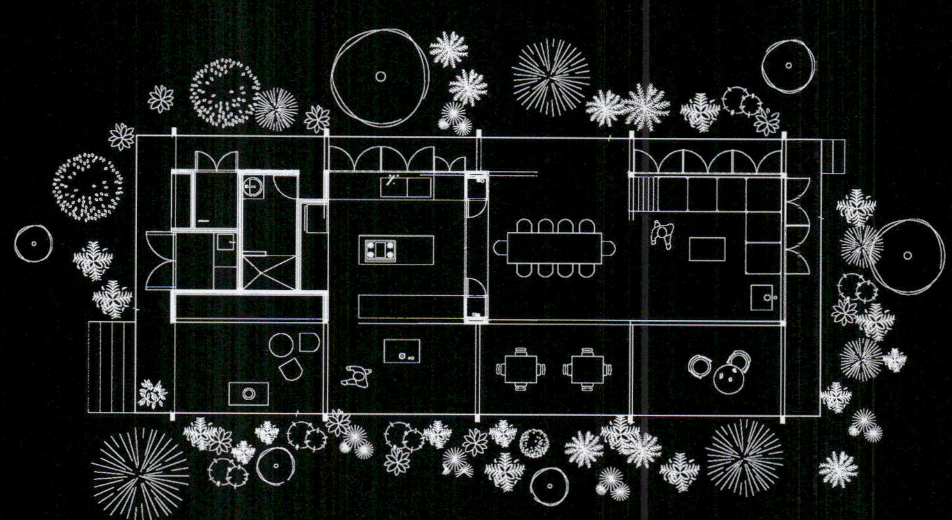

Cosmos House
Puerto Escondido, Oaxaca, Mexico, 2019
Area: 85 m²

Collaboration: Maria Sevilla,
Carlos Morales, Luis De la Garza

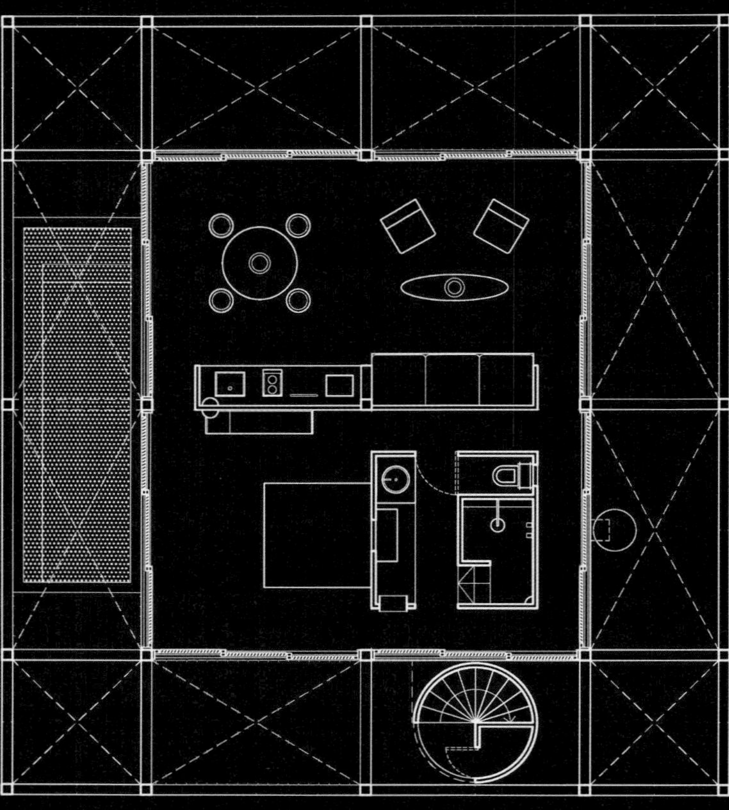

As the aerial view shows, the plan is based on a post-and-beam concrete grid, around a square central area. It is set in sandy brush near the Pacific.

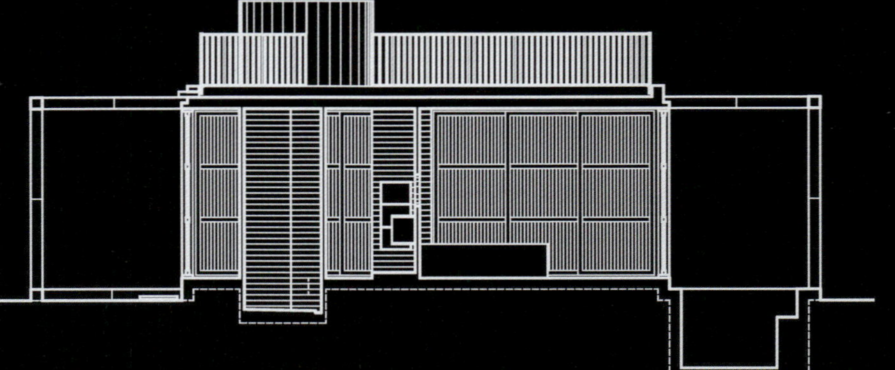

Sliding wooden doors open into the outdoor grid spaces that allow for gardens and pools to be integrated into the living area of the house.

Cosmos House is near the resort of Puerto Escondido on the Pacific Ocean. The house is composed of three main elements. The first of these is a "center or hard nucleus," built with concrete walls, slabs, and columns with a "brutal finish." It shelters the habitable space under the roof, which is to say a reduced program that includes a bedroom, kitchen-dining room, living area, and bathroom. Each of these occupies a quadrant of the almost perfectly square floor plan. The second element is an external grid made of concrete beams and columns with a smooth finish. This is connected to the central nucleus, which allows the extension of activities of the house to the exterior terraces and a pond. The final part of the scheme is the roof, which functions as a "lookout toward the landscape."It houses a water mirror for "reading the stars, constellations and the cosmos that surround us at night." The house was built with concrete and locally harvested macuil (*Tababuia chrysantha*) wood.

Cosmos House liegt nahe des Ferienortes Puerto Escondido am Pazifischen Ozean und besteht aus drei Hauptelementen. Das erste ist das „Zentrum beziehungsweise der harte Kern“ aus Betonwänden, -platten und -säulen mit „brutalem Finish“. Er birgt den überdachten Wohnraum, der auf Schlafzimmer, Essküche, Wohnbereich und Badezimmer reduziert ist. Jede dieser Zonen nimmt einen Quadranten des fast perfekt quadratischen Grundrisses ein. Das zweite Element ist ein Außenraster aus Betonbalken und -stützen mit glatter Oberfläche. Es ist mit dem zentralen Kern verbunden und ermöglicht so die Ausweitung der Innenzonen auf die Terrassen und einen Teich. Das finale Element ist das Dach, die „Aussichtswarte“, auf dem ein Wasserspiegel zum

The kitchen, with its wooden furnishings, is entirely open to the exterior with the sliding wooden walls pushed aside. Following spread: *a bedroom can be equally open.*

„Lesen der Sterne, der Sternbilder und des nächtlichen, sich über uns wölbenden Kosmos“ einlädt. Für die Konstruktion wurden hauptsächlich Beton und lokal geschlagenes Macuil-Holz (*Tabebuia chrysantha*) verwendet.

La maison est proche du complexe de Puerto Escondido, au bord de l'océan Pacifique. Elle se compose de trois éléments principaux. Le premier est le « centre ou noyau dur » fait de murs en béton, dalles et colonnes aux « finitions brutes », il abrite l'espace d'habitation sous le toit, réduit à une chambre, une cuisine-salle à manger, un espace de vie et une salle de bains, chacun occupant un quart du plan presque parfaitement carré. Le second élément est un quadrillage extérieur de poutres et colonnes en béton au fini lisse, relié au noyau central et qui permet d'étendre les activités domestiques aux terrasses et à l'étang. Enfin, la dernière partie de l'ensemble est le toit qui tient lieu de « poste d'observation du paysage » et comprend un miroir d'eau pour « lire les étoiles, les constellations et l'univers qui nous entoure la nuit ». La maison est en béton et bois d'araguaney (*Tababuia chrysantha*) local.

SAVIOZ FABRIZZI

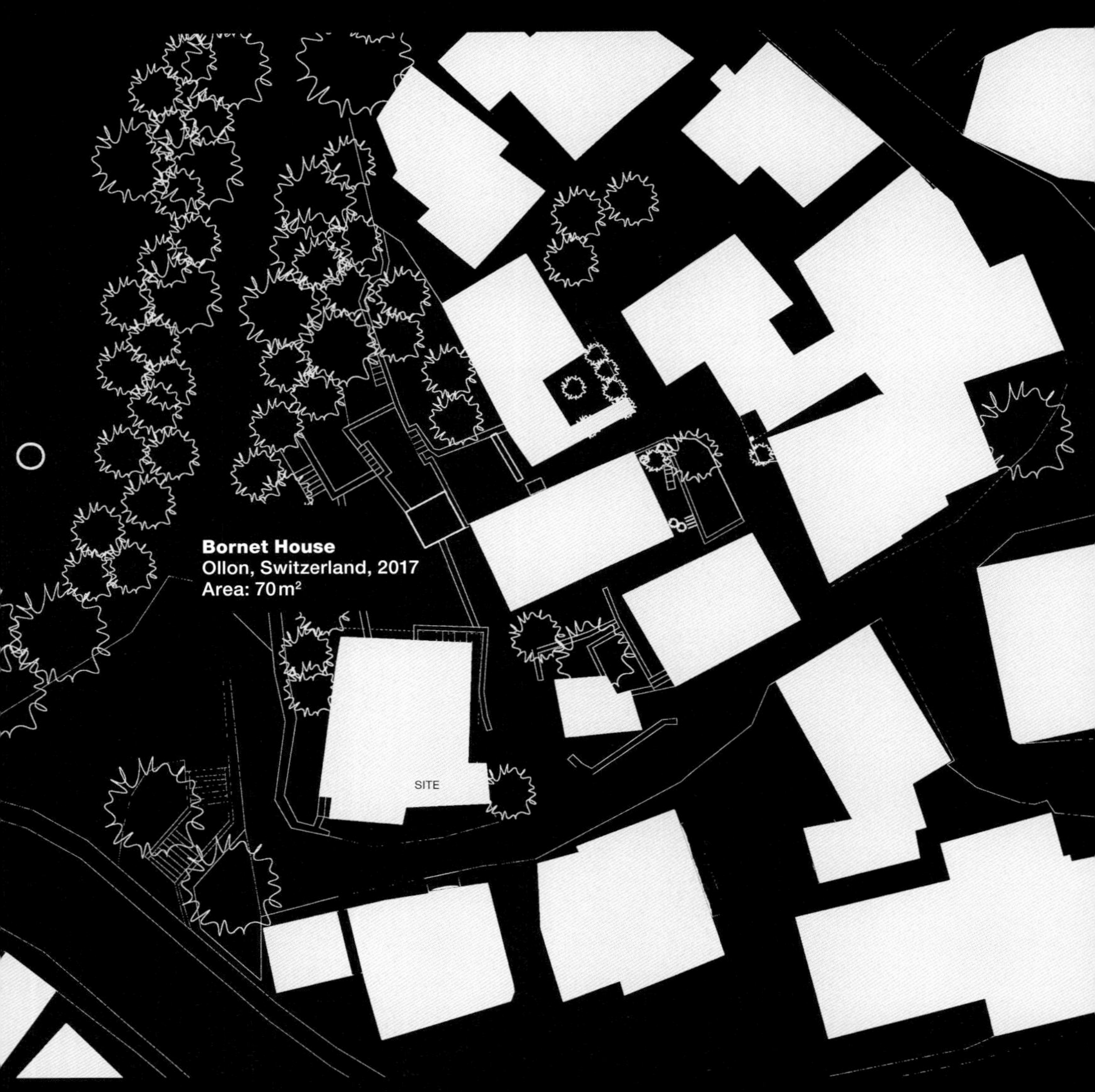

Bornet House
Ollon, Switzerland, 2017
Area: 70 m²

As they have in villages in the neighboring Canton of Valais, the architects successfully converted an existing stone farm structure into a small modern house. The unobtrusive renovation fits into the town with no contradictions.

This transformation of an existing stone barn contains a living area, kitchen, two bedrooms, two bathrooms, and a basement. It is in the center of Ollon, a small village in the Canton of Valais. The ground floor is a single space with the day side on the western side and an elevated bed area opposite. The bed area has direct access to a small outdoor terrace. The structure of the existing building was maintained except on the west, where a new wall had to be built and a large window was added. The house was built with black concrete, three-ply fir plywood cladding indoors with a dark stain, unglazed ceramic tiles, and larch outside. The lateral openings were part of the original structure, and the vertical wood bars used evoke the language of agricultural architecture in the area, where these openings provided ventilation. A small office and bathroom, together with technical equipment, occupy the basement.

Dieser Umbau einer Steinscheune umfasst einen Wohnbereich, eine Küche, zwei Schlafzimmer, zwei Bäder und einen Keller. Er liegt im Zentrum von Ollon, einer Kleinstadt im Kanton Wallis. Das Erdgeschoss ist ein einziger Raum mit einer Tagseite nach Westen und einem erhöhten Schlafbereich gen Osten, der sich zu einer kleinen Terrasse öffnet. Mit Ausnahme der Westseite, wo eine neue Wand errichtet und ein großes Fenster hinzugefügt wurde, blieb die Struktur der einstigen Scheune unverändert. Das Haus wurde mit schwarzem Beton gebaut, mit einer Innenverkleidung aus dreilagigem dunkelgebeizten Tannensperrholz, und unglasierten Keramikfliesen sowie einer Außenverkleidung aus Lärche. Die Öffnungen mit vertikalen Holzbalken an den Seitenwänden sorgten einst für die Belüftung der Steinscheune. Sie stellen ein für die Region typisches landwirtschaftliches Architekturelement dar. Das Untergeschoss beherbergt ein kleines Büro, ein Bad sowie die technischen Anlagen.

Une grange en pierre a ici été transformée pour accueillir un espace séjour, une cuisine, deux chambres, deux salles de bains et un sous-sol. Elle est située au centre d'Ollon, un petit village dans le canton de Valais. Le rez-de-chaussée est composé d'un espace unique, ouvert au jour du côté ouest avec un lit en hauteur de l'autre côté, qui bénéficie d'un accès direct à une petite terrasse. La structure du bâtiment existant a été conservée, sauf à l'ouest où un nouveau mur a dû être construit et une grande fenêtre a été ajoutée. La maison a été construite en béton noir, contre-plaqué de sapin trois couches pour le revêtement intérieur à la teinte sombre, carreaux céramique non vitrifiés et mélèze à l'extérieur. Les ouvertures latérales étaient présentes dans la structure d'origine tandis que les barres de bois verticales évoquent l'architecture agricole de la région où les ouvertures assurent la ventilation. Un petit bureau et une salle de bains occupent le sous-sol avec les équipements techniques.

Fir plywood cladding and concrete floors inside give this house a solid and warm interior. Natural light is brought in through windows, but also wooden slats and the array of pentagonal openings seen here.

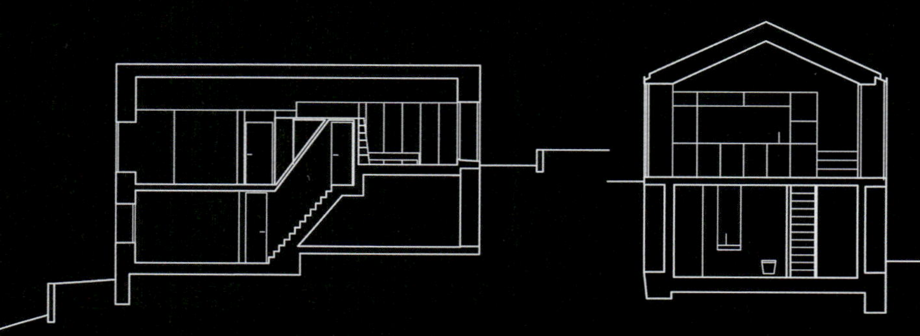

SELGASCANO

House in Los Rincones (The Nooks)
La Vera, Spain, 2021
Area: 85 m²

Collaboration: Luismi Quintana,
Ruben Criba

In this unexpected setting, the architects, known for their bright colors and innovative designs, have repurposed a group of rural buildings.

This house is located in the La Vera region of Extremadura, Spain. The project consists of preserving and reusing each of the existing spaces on the property—the 21-square-meter main house in stone with a tile roof, and a fig drying room on the upper floor, to which a kitchen was added. Other existing structures, such as chicken coops, stables, and toolsheds, were converted to more modern uses. The house was entirely off-grid, with no running water, drains, electricity, or heating. The former fig drying room saw its collapsing roof raised by 80 centimeters to become a living area. The lower part of the house was used for a bedroom, bathrooms, and a pantry. A cooking island was placed in the old kitchen. By lowering the floor and raising the roof, the part above the kitchen could be used as a dining room, connected with the living room in the same space. A 12-square-meter bedroom was created in the former chicken coop. New openings were created by removing stones from the existing walls, while the wood and tiles found on site were used to rebuild the roof. A nearby spring brings water into the house and also fills a pond that can be used for bathing in summer.

Combining existing spaces with added elements, he architects took a heterogenous approach o surfaces and materials, blending old stone vith modern windows and stairs such as those seen here.

Space was made for the upper-level kitchen by raising the existing roof by 80 centimeters. The rough appearance of some elements is more of a reminiscence of the past than it is the real nature of this new design.

Dieses Haus befindet sich in der Region La Vera in der spanischen Extremadura. Sein Konzept umfasste die Erhaltung und Wiederverwendung der auf dem Grundstück bereits vorhandenen Strukturen, darunter das 21 m² große Haupthaus aus Stein mit Ziegeldach samt Trocknungsraum für Feigen, angebauter Küche, Hühnerverschlag, Ställe und Geräteschuppen. Das Steinhaus glich einer abgeschotteten Insel: ohne fließendes Wasser, Abflüsse, Strom oder Heizung. Um Wohnraum zu schaffen, wurde das eingestürzte Dach des ehemaligen Trocknungsraums um 80 Zentimeter angehoben. Im Untergeschoss befinden sich nun Schlafzimmer, Badezimmer und Speisekammer. Die alte Küche erhielt eine Kochinsel und durch Absenken des Bodens und Anheben des Daches konnte der Teil über der Küche als offener Essbereich eingerichtet werden, der ins Wohnzimmer übergeht. Geschlafen wird auf 15 m² im ehemaligen Hühnerstall. Unregelmäßige Fenster entstanden durch die Entfernung von Steinen aus den Wänden, während Holz und Ziegel, die auf dem Grundstück gefunden wurden, für den Wiederaufbau des Daches verwendet wurden. Eine nahe gelegene Quelle versorgt das Haus mit Wasser und füllt einen Teich, der im Sommer zum Baden einlädt.

La maison est située dans la région de La Vera, en Estrémadure (Espagne). Le projet consiste à préserver et réutiliser tous les espaces existants sur la propriété – l'habitation principale en pierre de 21 m² au toit de tuiles et son séchoir à figues à l'étage, à laquelle une cuisine a été ajoutée – tandis que d'autres structures comme le poulailler, l'étable et les cabanes à outils ont été reconverties pour des usages plus modernes. La maison était entièrement hors réseau sans eau courante ni la moindre canalisation, électricité ou chauffage. Le toit de l'ancien séchoir à figues qui s'effondrait a été surélevé de 80 cm pour en faire un lieu de vie. La partie basse de la maison sert désormais de chambre, salle de bains et garde-manger. Un îlot de cuisson a été placé dans l'ancienne cuisine. Le sol a été abaissé et le toit surélevé pour transformer l'espace au-dessus de la cuisine en salle à manger, reliée au salon qui se trouve au même niveau. Une chambre de 12 m² a été aménagée dans l'ancien poulailler. De nouvelles ouvertures ont été obtenues en retirant des pierres des murs, tandis que le bois et les tuiles trouvés sur place ont servi à refaire le toit. Une source voisine fournit l'eau et remplit un bassin où il est possible de se baigner en été.

Rocks on the site, like the old stone walls, were maintained in position, and ideas such as a plank roof were used to create a new and unexpected seating area.

FRAN SILVESTRE

NIU N70
Valencia, Spain, 2021
Area: 70 m²

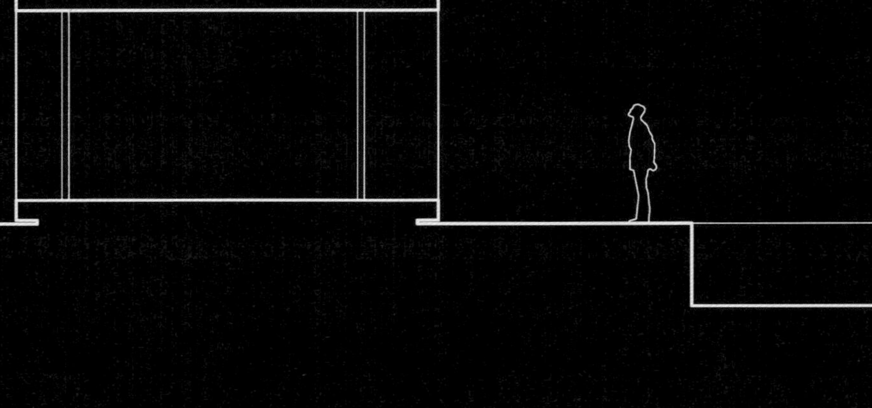

Fran Silvestre has made rigorously geometric white forms his signature, and this 70-square-meter house is no exception. It is largely transparent with opacity introduced only in the lateral walls and more private areas.

The NIU houses designed by Fran Silvestre are intended to provide "a comprehensive response to architectural and construction processes," centered on a "system to build houses in the most efficient and effective way." These are essentially prefabricated homes that retain the design quality of more elaborate and original houses designed by Fran Silvestre. The range of very contemporary, largely automated houses runs from N70 (published here), which has one room and a bathroom for 151 200 euros, to N150, a more substantial 157-square-meter home with three rooms and two baths that sells for 313 600 euros, and finally to N160 at just five square meters less than N150 which is priced at 301 000 euros. The architect explains that "the N70 is the smallest model of the NIU project. The wet areas in which all the facilities are located divides the day zone from the night zone." "It is," he says, "a new version of a known typology that continues to fascinate us."

Eine „umsichtige Reaktion auf architektonische und bautechnische Prozesse“ nennt der Architekt seine NIU-Entwürfe. Diese Prozesse laufen sämtlich unter der Prämisse: „Häuser so effizient und effektiv wie möglich zu bauen“. Auch wenn die NIU-Häuser im Wesentlichen Fertigkonstruktionen sind, stehen sie in Sachen Designqualität den von Fran Silvestre entworfenen aufwendigeren und individuelleren Gebäuden in nichts nach. Dem interessierten Kunden steht eine breite Auswahl an modernsten, weitgehend automatisierten Häusern zur Verfügung: von N70 (hier vorgestellt) als Einraumentwurf mit Bad für 151 200 Euro über das größere N150 mit 157 m², drei Zimmern und zwei Bädern für 313 600 Euro bis hin zum 152 m² messenden N160 zum Preis von 301 000 Euro.

„Das N70 ist das kleinste NIU-Modell. Das Badezimmer, in dem alle Einrichtungen vorhanden sind, trennt den Tag- vom Nachtbereich“, erklärt der Architekt. Die NIUs sind, wie er sagt, „eine neue Version einer bekannten Typologie, die uns weiterhin fasziniert“.

Les maisons NIU conçues par Fran Silvestre ont pour but de fournir « une réponse globale aux processus architecturaux et de construction » centrée sur un « système destiné à construire des maisons de la manière la plus efficace ». Il s'agit pour l'essentiel de maisons préfabriquées, avec cependant un design de qualité tel qu'on le trouve dans les maisons plus complexes et originales de Fran Silvestre. La gamme de maisons très contemporaines et très automatisées va de N70 (publiée ici) composée d'une pièce unique et d'une salle de bains, pour 151 200 euros, à N150 et ses 157 m², trois pièces et deux salles de bains, vendue pour 313 600 euros, et N160 qui compte seulement 5 m² de moins que N150, dont le prix est fixé à 301 000 euros. L'architecte explique que « le modèle N70 est le plus petit du projet NIU. Les zones humides où se trouvent tous les équipements séparent l'espace jour de l'espace nuit. C'est une nouvelle version d'une typologie bien connue qui continue de nous fasciner ».

White blocks inside the house create space for a small kitchen and the bathroom. Spare whiteness is also the rule inside and out.

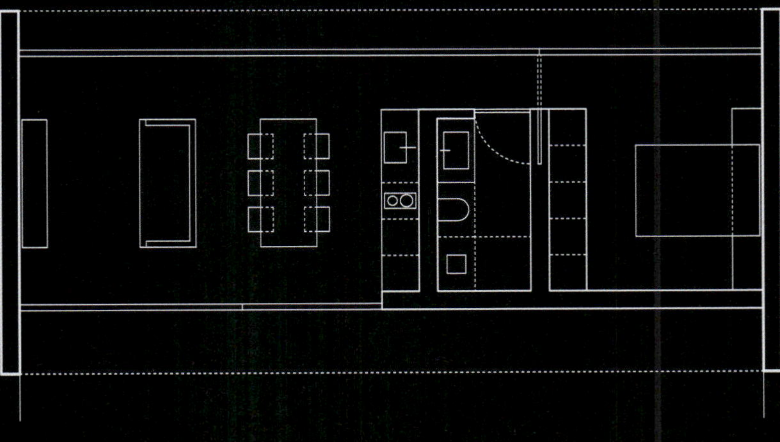

SMALLER ARCHITECTS

Seroro
Seoul, South Korea, 2020
Area: 66 m^2

Collaboration: Ahyoung Jeong

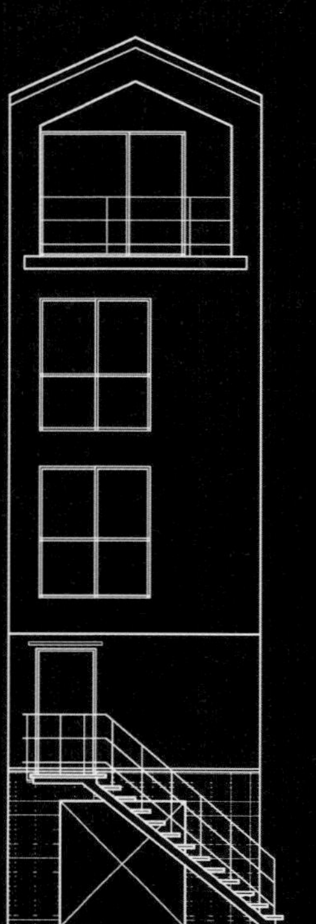

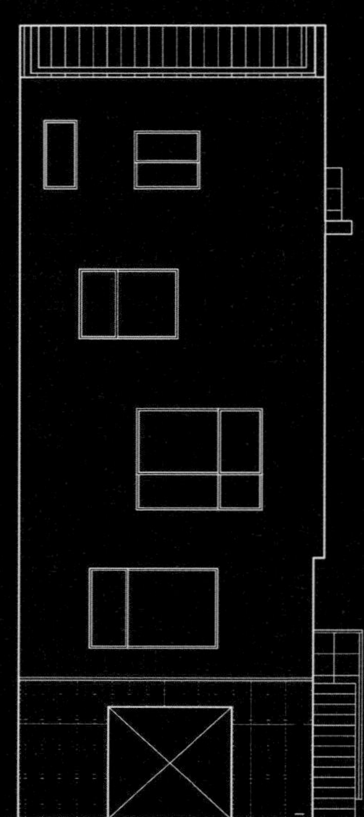

Although the image here gives an impression that the house is in a wooded area, it is in fact near the center of Seoul, where land values imposed the high structure with a small footprint.

Seroro means "vertically" and this structure is a stacked building located in the center of Seoul. As is the case in Tokyo, for example, land prices in Seoul are extremely high—nonetheless this site was considered too small to build on, so it was left unbuilt. It is located near several public transportation lines and is near the Fortress Wall of the old city. A parking space is located at ground level, and above it there is a living space and bathroom. The second floor houses a kitchen and dining space, while a bedroom and another bathroom are on the third level. A dressing room and bathtub occupies the fourth 16-square-meter floor. Windows face mostly to the south and west to admit natural light and views of a park. The curvature of the building is related to the form of the site.

Seroro bedeutet „vertikal", und in der Tat wurden für dieses Gebäude im Herzen Seouls die Räume aufeinanderstapelt. Wie beispielsweise auch in Tokio sind die Grundstückspreise in Seoul extrem hoch. Da jedoch dieses Grundstück in sehr gut erschlossener Lage nahe der alten Stadtmauer als zu klein für eine Bebauung bewertet wurde, blieb es zunächst unbebaut. Auf Straßenebene wurde Raum für einen Parkplatz gelassen, im ersten Stock befinden sich der Wohnbereich und ein Bad. Darüber liegen Küche und Esszimmer, während die dritte Etage ein Schlafzimmer und ein weiteres Badezimmer beherbergt. Das Ankleidezimmer und eine Badewanne sind im vierten, 16 m² großen Stockwerk untergebracht. Die meisten Fenster mit Aussicht auf einen Park blicken nach Süden und Westen und lassen natürliches Licht herein. Die Form des Hauses folgt in seiner Krümmung jener des Grundstücks.

The house is curved and quite closed on its street-side façade and quite open on the opposite side, allowing in natural light, as seen in these images and the floor plans.

Seroro signifie « verticalement » et on a ici un immeuble à empilement, situé dans le centre de Séoul. Le prix du terrain est extrêmement élevé à Séoul, comme c'est aussi le cas à Tokyo, par exemple, mais la parcelle avait malgré tout été considérée comme trop petite pour être construite et était vacante. Elle est proche de plusieurs lignes de transports publics et des remparts de la vieille ville. Une place de stationnement a été aménagée au rez-de-chaussée, surmonté d'un

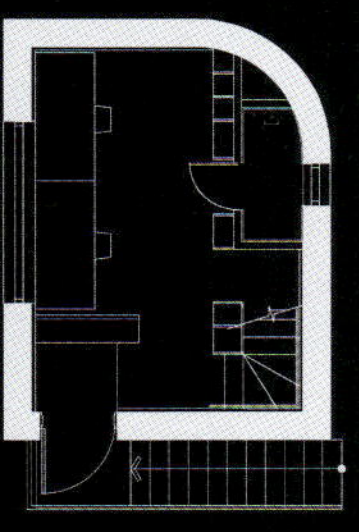

First floor

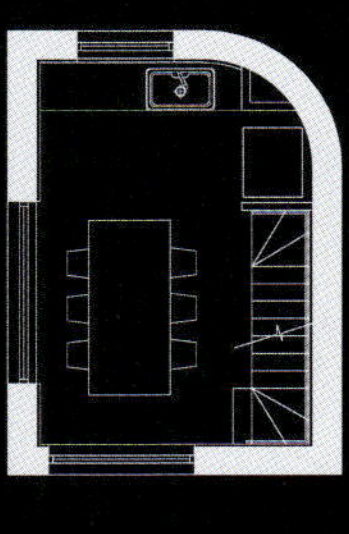

Second floor

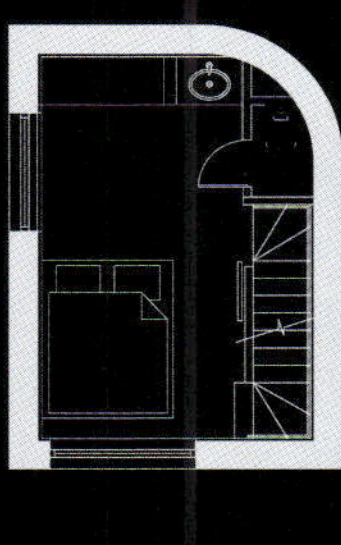

Third floor

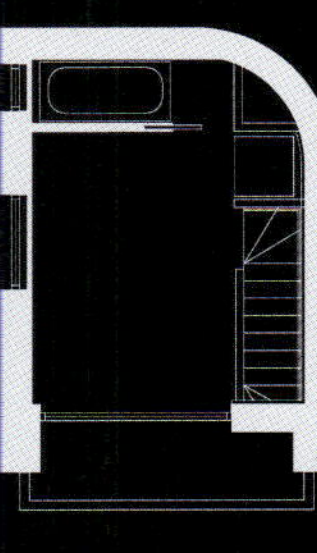

Fourth floor

LINE SOLGAARD

Weekend House
Fredrikstad, Norway, 2020
Area: 90 m²

The interiors are wrapped in wood cladding, a choice of materials that also applies to the furnishings in most cases.

This cabin is located about 200 meters from the sea, near large rocks, and has a view of the water to the southwest. Fredrikstad is near the Glomma river and the Skagerrak strait, about 20 kilometers from the border with Sweden. Most of the trees on the site were preserved during construction. The structure was built on an *in-situ* concrete base, which keeps the interior cool even at the height of summer because of its thermal mass. A glass sunroof can be used to provide natural ventilation. The ceiling is finished in oak paneling and the entire interior is in wood. Blown spruce chip fiber was used for insulation of the home. Cladding is largely in burnt cedar with a metal roof. The plan of the house is a square.

Diese Minilodge wurde etwa 200 m vom Meer entfernt errichtet, unweit großer Felsen. Von hier blickt im Südwesten aufs Wasser hinaus. Fredrikstad liegt nahe des Flusses Glomma und der Skagerrak Meerenge, etwa 20 Kilometer vor der schwedischen Grenze entfernt. Beim Bau blieben die meisten Bäume auf dem Gelände erhalten. Das quadratische Haus ruht auf einem Ortbetonsockel, der aufgrund seiner thermischen Masse das Innere auch im Hochsommer kühl hält. Ein gläsernes Sonnendach ermöglicht bei Bedarf auch natürliche Belüftung. Die Decke ist mit Eichenholz vertäfelt und der gesamte Innenraum in Holz ausgeführt. Für die Dämmung wurde geblasene Fichtenspanfaser verwendet. Die Verkleidung besteht vorwiegend aus gebranntem Zedernholz und einem Metalldach.

The relatively simple volume of the house is lifted off the sloped site, making for minimal impact on the environment.

Vood is employed on nearly every available urface, laid vertically on the walls. Below: *the plan of the house is a notched square.*

La petite maison est située à environ 200 m de la ner, à côté de grands rochers, et a vue sur l'eau u sud-ouest. Fredrikstad est proche du fleuve Glomma et du détroit du Skagerrak, à une 20 km e la frontière suédoise. La construction a veillé conserver la plupart des arbres sur le site. Le bâtiment a été placé sur un socle de béton coulé ur place qui garde l'intérieur frais jusqu'au plus ort de l'été grâce à sa masse thermique. Un toit uvrant en verre peut apporter une ventilation aturelle. Les finitions du plafond sont en panneaux de chêne et l'intérieur est entièrement en bois. De la fibre de copeaux d'épicéa soufflée servi à l'isolation. La maison est revêtue pour essentiel de cèdre brûlé et le toit est en métal. Son plan est carré

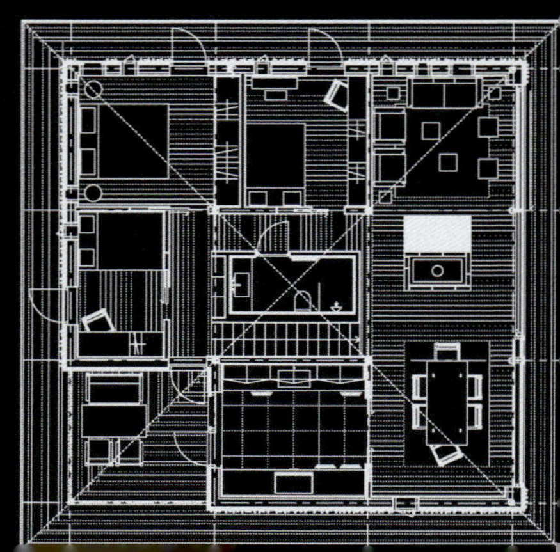

SOTAMAA

Meteorite
Kontiolahti, Finland, 2020
Area: 65 m²

Collaboration: Filippo Fabi

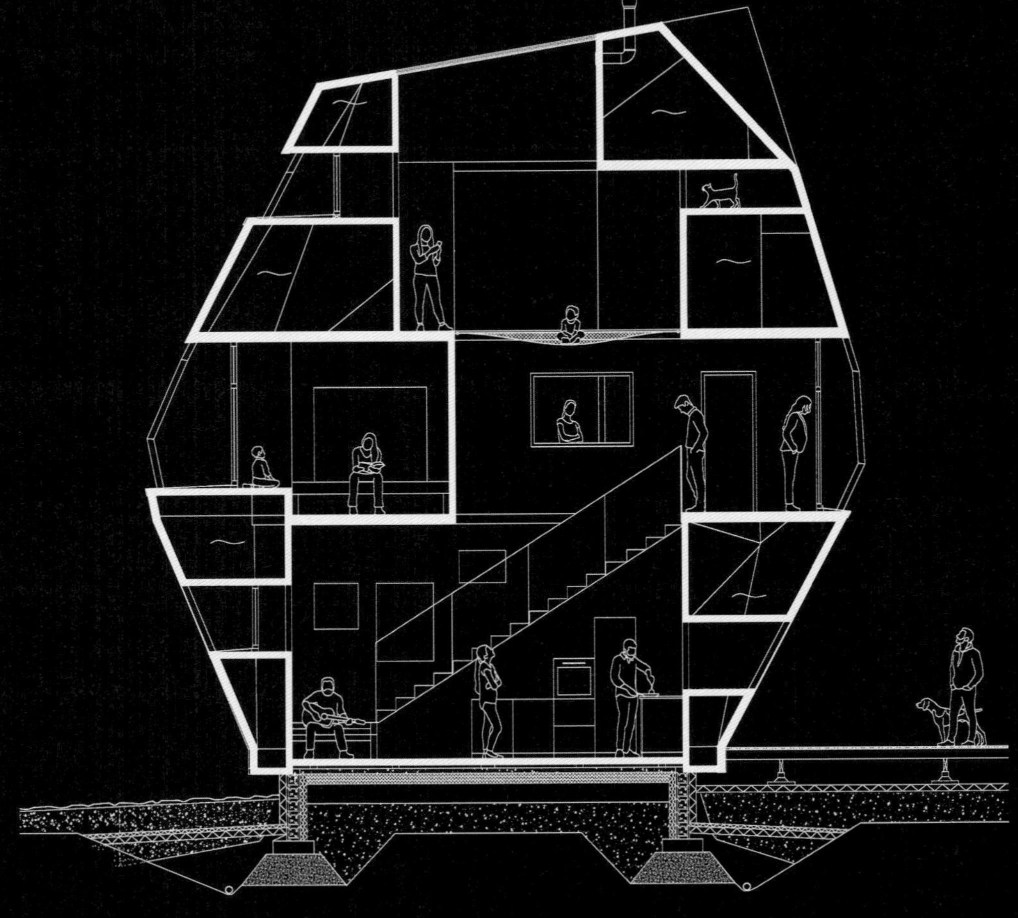

Despite the unusual exterior form of the house, interiors are agreeable and light filled, reaching up with the stairway seen here to offer double height and more.

This small and very unusual three-story house was built in eastern Finland on a forest site that is approached on foot. An atrium in the middle of the structure has a large, electrically heated (10 m^2) skylight providing "an unobstructed view of the stars," even in winter. A catamaran net strung at a height of seven meters allows the residence to "float" in the space. Meteorite was made with prefabricated cross-laminated timber (CLT) panels. According to the architects, it is insulated by air and uses natural ventilation. Building services and technology are hidden in the massive wood walls of the building. The roof of the house is also in solid, oiled wood. Kivi Sotamaa states: "Unlike traditional houses where each room has a specific predetermined purpose, Meteorite's architecture supports the more dynamic relationships of its residents and a variety of life situations. Digital design and new prefabrication and construction technologies enable the creation of unique, aesthetically high-quality ecological wood buildings that add experiential value to their locations."

Interiors are largely covered in wood and include a good deal of built-in furniture. Natural light is admitted from windows that are frequently placed in the higher part of the volumes.

Die ungewöhnliche Form dieses dreistöckigen Häuschens macht seinem Namen alle Ehre. Meteorite wurde in Ostfinnland auf einem nur zu Fuß erreichbaren Waldgrundstück errichtet. Die Decke des zentralen Atriums bildet ein 10 m² großes, elektrisch beheiztes Oberlicht, das selbst im Winter „freien Blick in den Sternenhimmel“ bietet. Ein in 7 m Höhe gespanntes Katamaran-Netz lädt die Bewohner ein, im Raum zu „schweben“. Nach Angaben der Architekten ist Meteorite, das aus vorgefertigten Brettsperrholztafeln gebaut wurde, luftgedämmt und profitiert von natürlicher Belüftung. Die technische Gebäudeausrüstung liegt in den massiven Holzwänden verborgen. Auch das Hausdach besteht aus massivem, geöltem Holz. „Anders als bei traditionellen Häusern, in denen jeder Raum einem vorher festgelegten Zweck dient, fördert Meteorites Architektur eine dynamischere Nutzung und kann auf vielfältigste Lebenssituationen eingehen“, so Kivi Sotamaa. „Digitales Design und neue Vorfertigungs- und Bautechnologien ermöglichen einzigartige, ästhetisch hochwertige ökologische Holzhäuser, die ihre Standorte durch einen besonderen Erlebniswert veredeln.“

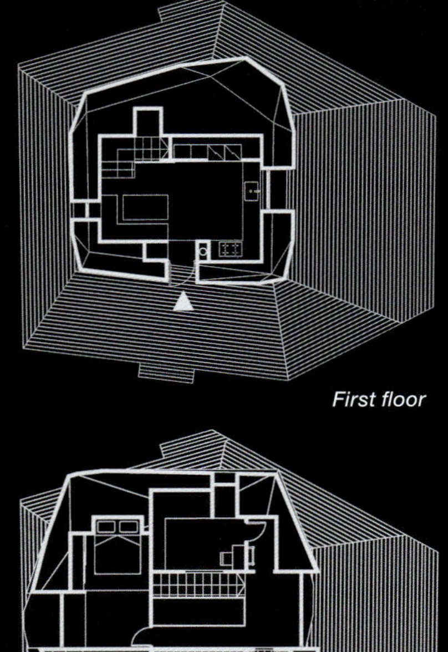

Plans show how more strictly geometric rectangles are inserted into the irregular exterior periphery of the house. Opposite: *a net allows residents to relax as they hang above the high interior volume.*

Cette petite maison très originale à trois niveaux a été construite dans l'est de la Finlande sur un site forestier accessible à pied. Au centre de la structure, un atrium dispose d'une grande lucarne à chauffage électrique (10 m²) qui offre « une vue parfaitement dégagée sur les étoiles », même en hiver. Un filet de catamaran suspendu à une hauteur de 7 m fait « flotter » l'habitation dans l'espace. Meteorite est faite de panneaux préfabriqués en bois lamellé croisé (CLT). Les architectes expliquent qu'elle est isolée par l'air et utilise la ventilation naturelle. Les équipements et éléments techniques sont dissimulés dans les épais murs de bois. Le toit est également en bois massif huilé. Kivi Sotamaa présente le projet en ces termes : « À la différence des maisons traditionnelles où chaque pièce a une fonction spécifique prédéterminée, l'architecture de Meteorite favorise des rapports plus dynamiques entre ses occupants et un grand nombre de situations. La conception numérique et les nouvelles technologies de préfabrication et de construction permettent de créer des bâtiments en bois uniques, écologiques et d'une grande qualité esthétique qui offrent une expérience des sites qu'elles occupent. »

STUDIO DIAA

Portage Bay Float Home
Seattle, Washington, USA, 2020
Area: 60 m²

Collaboration: Dovetail GC (General Contractor), Forrest Taylor and Geoff Gamsby (Interior and Exterior Finishes Build), BUILT Engineering (Structural Engineer)

Set on the water, the house has nearly as much outdoor deck area as it does interior space. The floor plan of the residence is square.

This home, intended for a family of three, is situated at the north end of Seattle's Lake Union. It continues the city's long tradition of floating homes and houseboats. The structure includes two compact bedrooms, with an emphasis on common areas that remain connected to the exterior through floor-to-ceiling window doors and a motorized skylight system. The interior area is augmented by a further 56 square meters of cedar deck. The building is covered by an open rainscreen with blackened-stained cedar siding. The architect states: "The design captures the poetic quality of light reflecting off the surrounding water, an aspect heightened by overhead aluminum-lined sky vessels that softly reflect the colors of the changing sky. Amplifying contrasts between the home's dark cedar and Richlite exterior and the soft, light interior of pine and oak means the home embodies a feeling of lightness—a sensibility perfectly suited for a floating home."

Dieses Haus für eine dreiköpfige Familie liegt am nördlichen Ende des Lake Union in Seattle und setzt die lange Tradition schwimmender Häuser und Hausboote in dieser Stadt fort. Es beherbergt zwei Schlafzimmer und einen besonders sorgfältig geplanten Gemeinschaftsbereich, der durch raumhohe Fenstertüren sowie ein motorisiertes Oberlichtsystem in ständiger Verbindung mit der Außenwelt ist. Die Innenfläche verlängert sich ins Freie durch ein 56 m² großes Zedernholzdeck. Das Gebäude umgibt eine vorgehängte Fassade mit geschwärzter Zedernverkleidung. „Sein Design fängt die poetische Qualität des vom Wasser widergespiegelten Lichts ein", so die Architekten, „ein Effekt, der durch die Oberlichter verstärkt wird, deren

JAMES TURRELL
EARTH
La Collezione Panza
structures
Mechanical and Electrical Manual
SEAMANSHIP
The VISUAL HANDBOOK of BUILDING and REMODELING

Bright and light thanks to the color of the wood cladding and numerous windows (including some set in the roof), the interior also benefits from the higher sloped areas beneath the ceiling.

Aluminiumverkleidung die Farben des sich verändernden Himmels weich reflektiert. Die deutlichen Kontraste zwischen dem dunklen Äußeren aus Zedernholz und Richlite und dem sanften, hellen Inneren aus Kiefer und Eiche verleihen dem Haus eine Leichtigkeit, eine Sensibilität, wie sie einem schwimmenden Haus gebührt."

La maison destinée à une famille de trois personnes est située à l'extrémité nord du lac Union de Seattle. Elle s'inscrit dans une longue tradition de maisons flottantes et house-boats dans la ville. L'ensemble comprend deux chambres compactes et met l'accent sur les parties communes qui restent en lien avec l'extérieur grâce à des portes-fenêtres sur toute la hauteur de la pièce et un système de lucarne électrique. L'intérieur est prolongé par un ponton en cèdre de 56 m². Le bâtiment est couvert d'un écran pare-pluie ouvert et bardé de cèdre teinté noirci. L'architecte explique que « le concept capture la qualité poétique de la lumière qui se reflète sur l'eau tout autour, mis en valeur par les lucarnes à cadre en aluminium qui font écho en douceur aux couleurs changeantes du ciel. Les contrastes amplifiés entre le cèdre sombre de la maison, l'extérieur en Richlite et l'intérieur doux et clair de pin et chêne se traduisent par un sentiment de légèreté incarné par la maison – une sensibilité qui convient parfaitement à une maison sur l'eau ».

STUDIO PUISTO

Kivijärvi Resort/Niliaitta Prototype
Kivijärvi, Finland, 2020
Area: 30 m²

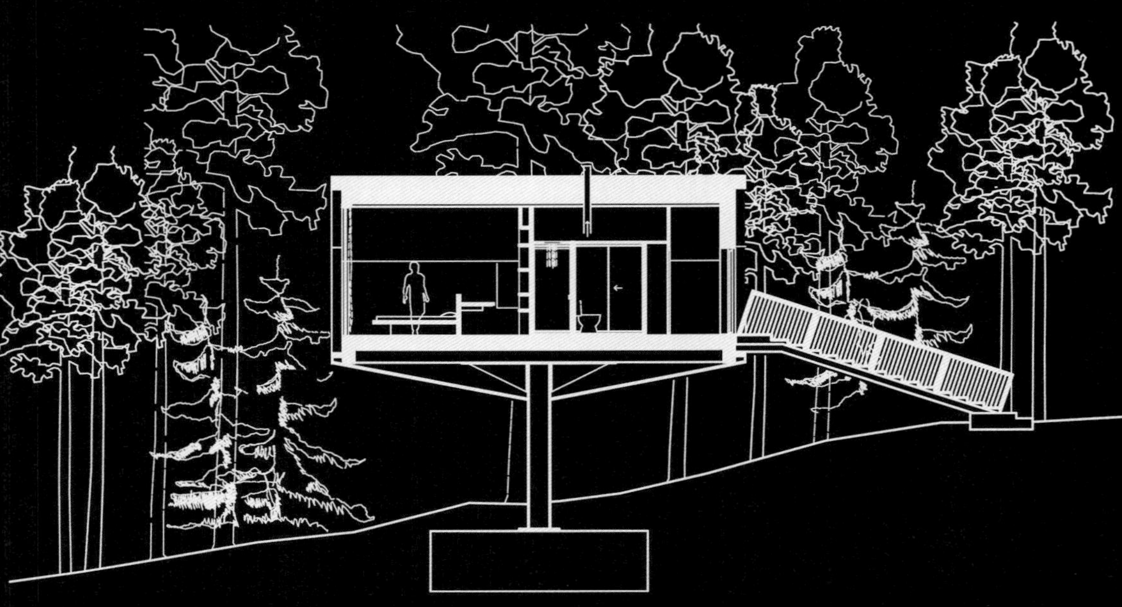

The site of the Kivijärvi Resort is near Salamajärvi National Park, which required careful attention in order not to disturb the natural environment. Given the varied habitats and landscapes of the site, the architects proposed three types of accommodation for the resort. The Niliaitta prototype (seen here), is lifted off the ground to "provide a more secluded perspective through which to connect with nature." A full-height window offers immediate views of the landscape. The structure is raised on a single pillar to disturb the site as little as possible. Its coloring and exterior materials were also chosen for this reason. Eco-wool was used for insulation, and there is no plastic in the design. A bathroom, shower, and kitchenette are located in a rotating core in the middle of the cabin. In the future it is planned to build about 50 accommodation units as well as a sauna and conference center on the site.

Die Nähe des Salamajärvi-Nationalparks forderte für die Planung des Kivijärvi-Resorts besondere Sorgfalt. Um die Natur zu schonen und angesichts der diversen Lebensräume und Landschaftsarten auf dem Baugelände, entschieden sich die Architekten für drei Unterkunftsvarianten, darunter der Prototyp Niliaitta (hier gezeigt). Indem sie vom Boden angehoben wird, bietet diese Struktur ihren Bewohnern eine „distanziertere Perspektive auf die Natur, um sich dieser auf ganz eigene Art zu nähern". Durch das raumhohe Fenster lässt sich die Landschaft ungehindert überblicken. Das Bauwerk balanciert auf einem einzigen Pfeiler, um seinen Standort so wenig wie möglich zu belasten. Ebenso unaufdringlich sind seine Farbgebung und Außenmaterialien. Als Dämmung dient Ökowolle, auf Kunststoff wurde bei der Konstruktion komplett verzichtet. Badezimmer, Dusche sowie Kochnische befinden sich in einem

The structure was inspired by a traditional Lapland building type called the niliaitta, which was designed "as a safe place to store food outdoors in habitats with bears and other wild animals."

rotierenden Kern in der Mitte der kleinen Hütte. Pläne sehen vor, dem Gelände etwa 50 Wohneinheiten sowie eine Sauna und ein Konferenzzentrum hinzuzufügen.

Le site qu'occupe le complexe de Kivijärvi est proche du parc national de Salamajärvi qui a imposé une grande vigilance pour ne pas troubler l'environnement naturel. Compte tenu des habitats et paysages très divers dans la zone, les architectes ont proposé trois types de logement. Le prototype Niliaitta (vu ici) est surélevé pour « une perspective plus retirée qui permet le contact avec la nature ». Une fenêtre pleine hauteur offre une vue directe sur le paysage. La construction repose sur un pilier unique afin de porter le moins possible atteinte au site. C'est aussi dans cette perspective que la couleur et les matériaux extérieurs ont été choisis. De la laine Eco-wool assure l'isolation et l'ensemble ne comprend aucun plastique. La salle de bain la douche et une kitchenette occupent un noya rotatif au centre de la maison. Une cinquantain d'unités doivent être construites sur le même si ainsi qu'un sauna et une salle de conférences.

The interiors are clad in light-colored wood and have generous glazed openings with views of the forest, as seen on the previous spread and the opposite page. Below: *a floor plan.*

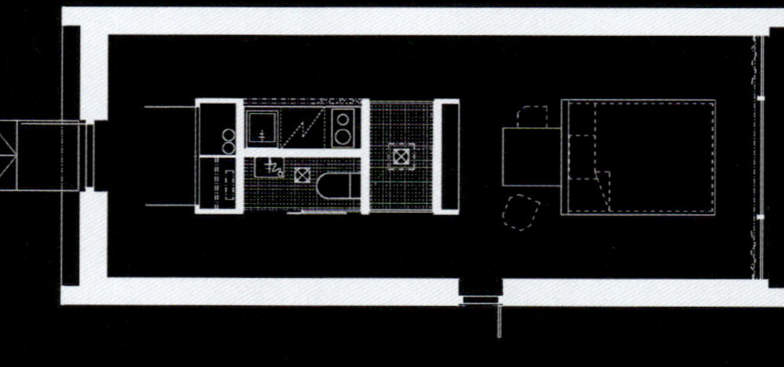

SUMMARY

Paradinha
Alvarenga, Portugal, 2021
Area: 28 to 58 m²

Collaboration: João Meira, Inês Rodrígues

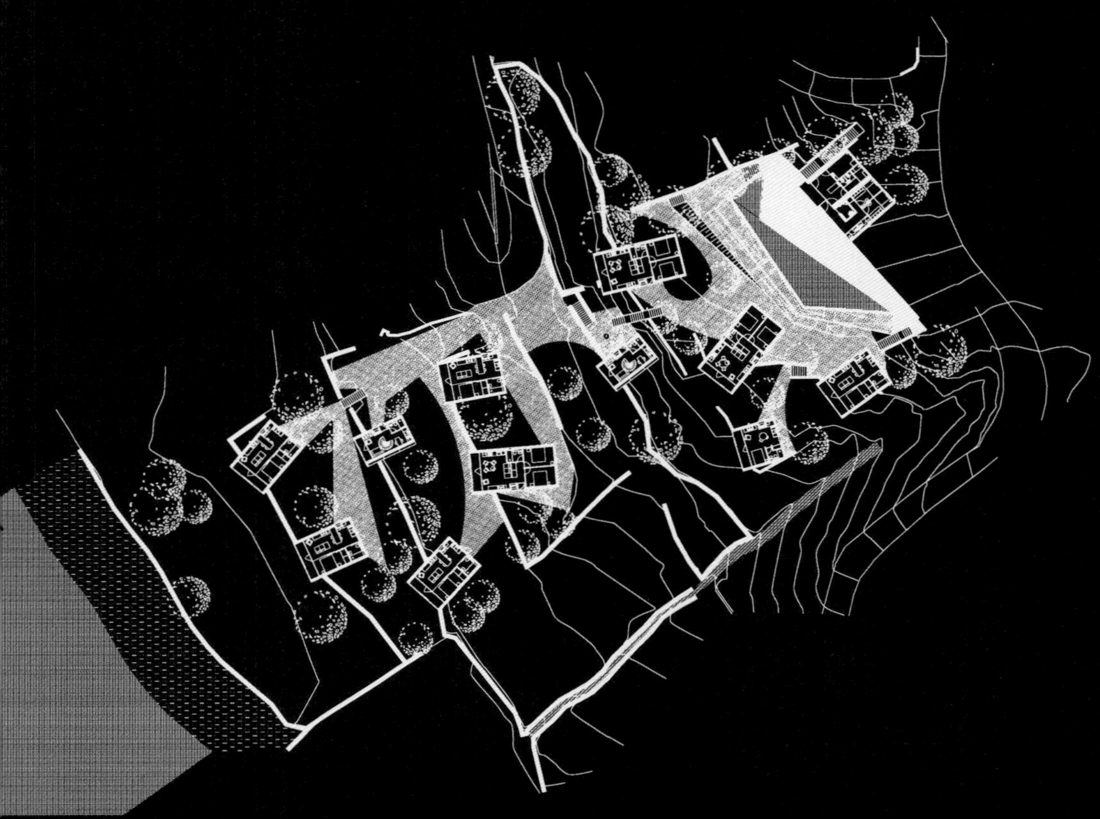

Previous spread: *in their verdant hillside setting, these cabins do not appear to be the result of a prefabrication system, and yet they are—different but provided with the same core elements.*

Wood and stone but also shaded terraces and a peaceful atmosphere characterize the project, which is inserted into sloping terrain.

Alvarenga is in north-central Portugal, 72 kilometers southeast of Porto. This project involves a total of 11 prefabricated retreat cabins in the woods. Some of the structures are to be inhabited during the whole year and others only in vacation periods. The Gomos building system, created by SUMMARY, was used to assure that services (water, electricity, climate control) were concentrated in a single module, accelerating the production and assembly process. Four cabin types in reinforced concrete and wood were distributed on the site "according to the natural configuration of the terrain, altering it as little as possible." Existing stone walls and trees were preserved.

Dieses Projekt in den Wäldern des nordportugiesischen Alvarenga, 72 Kilometer südöstlich von Porto, umfasst insgesamt elf vorgefertigte Minilodges. Einige dieser Rückzugsorte sind ganzjährig, andere nur in den Ferienzeiten bewohnbar. Das SUMMARY Gomos-Gebäudesystem sieht vor, zwecks Beschleunigung des Produktions- und Montageprozesses alle Dienstleistungsanlagen (Wasser, Strom, Klimatisierung) in einem einzigen Modul unterzubringen. Die Standorte der vier Hüttentypen aus Stahlbeton und Holz sind über das Grundstück verteilt, um „den natürlichen Begebenheiten des Geländes zu folgen und es so wenig wie möglich zu beeinträchtigen". In der Tat wurde beim Bau weder in den Baumbestand noch in vorhandene Mauerstrukturen eingegriffen.

Despite being quite small (28 to 58 m²), the structures are comfortable and modern, with natural light. Opposite: a sloping roof offers generous ceiling height, as well as a broad view into neighboring greenery.

SZCZ
JAKUB SZCZĘSNY

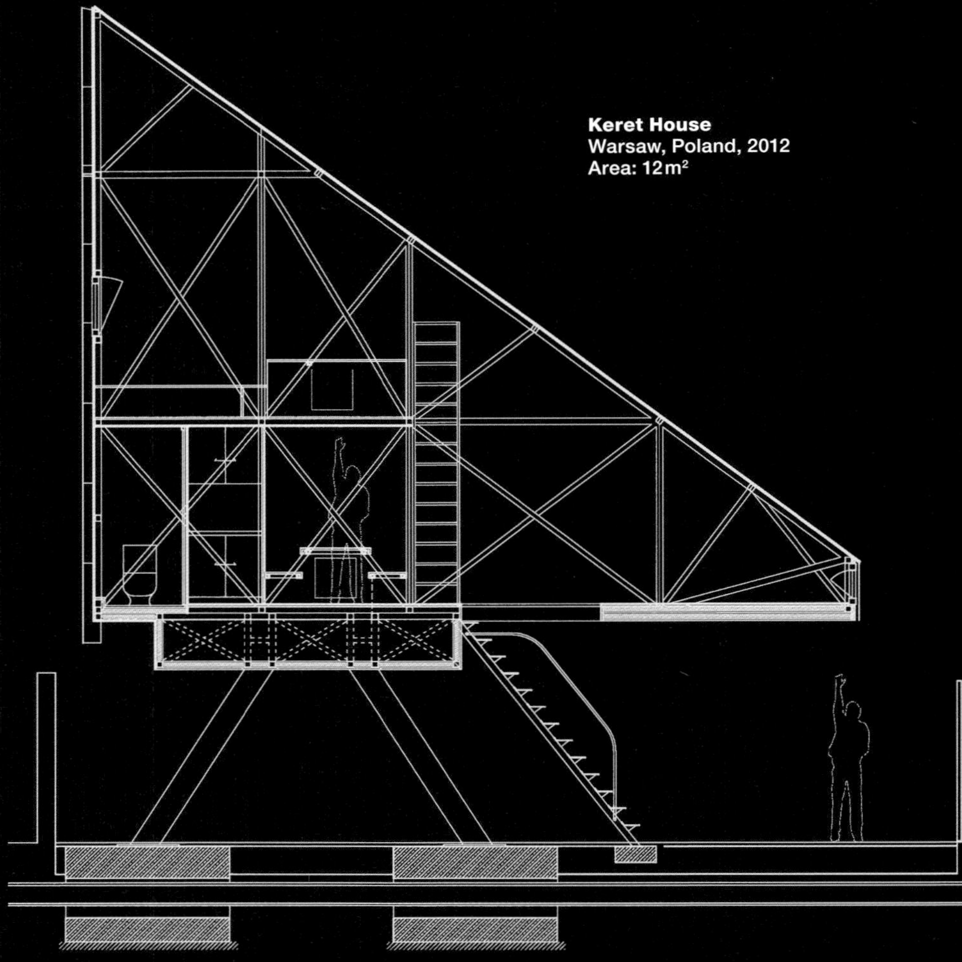

Keret House
Warsaw, Poland, 2012
Area: 12 m²

and®
AMA
TEJ ZIEMI!
CZYNNE
Pon. - Piąt.
14.00 - 17.00
18265

The extreme narrowness of the house is emphasized in the computer-generated image above and in the two photos of the stairway, which occupies almost the entire width of the structure.

This project was presented as an artistic concept by Jakub Szczęsny at the Wola Art Festival in Warsaw in 2009. With the assistance of the Foundation of Polish Modern Art, the tiny house was built "in a crack between buildings at 22 Chłodna Street and 74 Żelazna Street in Warsaw" in 2012. The house is 133 centimeters wide at its largest point. The designer named it after the Israeli-Polish writer Etgar Keret, and stated that the structure would "fulfill a function of a studio for invited guests—young creators and intellectuals from all over the world. The residential program, conducted in the heart of Wola, is supposed to produce creative work conditions and become a significant platform for world intellectual exchange." The prefabricated steel structure has a polycarbonate roof and external wall, two PVC windows, perforated stainless-steel skin, concrete footing, and MDF interior walls.

Though imagined as an ephemeral structure, the Keret House still exists. A model of the Keret House was the first Polish architectural design to be included in the permanent collection of the Museum of Modern Art (MoMA, New York, 2013).

Dieses Projekt wurde 2009 als künstlerisches Konzept von Jakub Szczęsny auf dem Wola Art Festival in Warschau präsentiert. Mit Unterstützung der Stiftung für Moderne Polnische Kunst wurde das Häuschen 2012 „in eine Ritze zwischen den Gebäuden Chłodna-Straße 22 und Żelazna-Straße 74 in Warschau" eingefügt. An seiner breitesten Stelle misst das Gebäude 133 Zentimeter. Benannt nach dem israelisch-polnischen Schriftsteller Etgar Keret „dient es ausgewählten jungen Kreativen und Intellektuellen aus aller Welt als Atelier", so der Architekt. „Die Wohnbauinitiative für Wolas Zentrum soll kreative

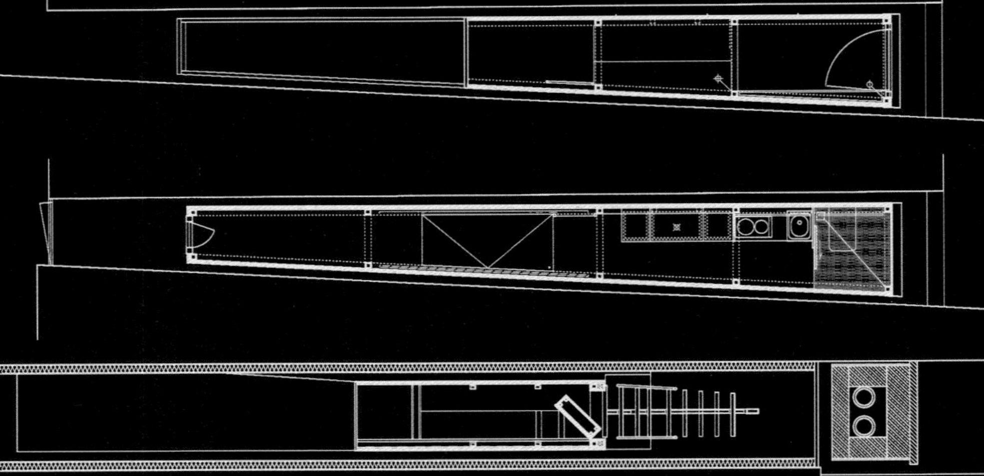

A cross section and the ground- and upper-floor plans of the structure. The interior views show the carefully thought-out structure and use of space.

Arbeitsbedingungen schaffen und eine wichtige Plattform für den weltweiten intellektuellen Austausch werden.“ Die vorgefertigte Stahlkonstruktion verfügt über ein Dach und eine Außenwand aus Polycarbonat, zwei PVC-Fenster, eine perforierte Edelstahlhaut, ein Betonfundament und Innenwände aus MDF. Obwohl nur als temporäre Struktur geplant, steht das Häuschen noch immer. Ein Modell von Keret House befindet sich als erster polnischer Architekturentwurf in der ständigen Sammlung des Museum of Modern Art (MoMA, New York, 2013).

Jakub Szczęsny a présenté ce projet comme un concept artistique au festival d'art Wola de Varsovie en 2009. La minuscule maison a été construite avec l'aide de la Fondation pour l'art moderne polonais « dans une fente entre deux immeubles au 22 rue Chłodna et 74 rue Żelazna à Varsovie » en 2012. Sa largeur maximale atteint 133 cm. Le designer lui a donné le nom de l'écrivain israélo-polonais Etgar Keret et explique qu'elle peut « servir de studio pour les invités – jeunes créateurs et intellectuels du monde entier. Le programme de résidence au cœur de l'action de Wola doit en effet fournir des conditions de travail propices à la créativité et devenir une importante plate-forme d'échanges pour les intellectuels du monde entier ». La structure en acier préfabriqué possède un toit et un mur extérieur en polycarbonate, deux fenêtres en PVC, une enveloppe perforée en acier inoxydable, une semelle de fondations en béton et des murs intérieurs en panneaux MDF. Bien qu'elle ait été conçue pour être temporaire, elle existe encore. Le modèle réduit de la maison Keret a été le premier concept architectural polonais à entrer dans la collection permanente du Museum of Modern Art (MoMA, New York, 2013).

HIROYUKI UNEMORI

House Tokyo
Tokyo, Japan, 2019
Area: 51 m²

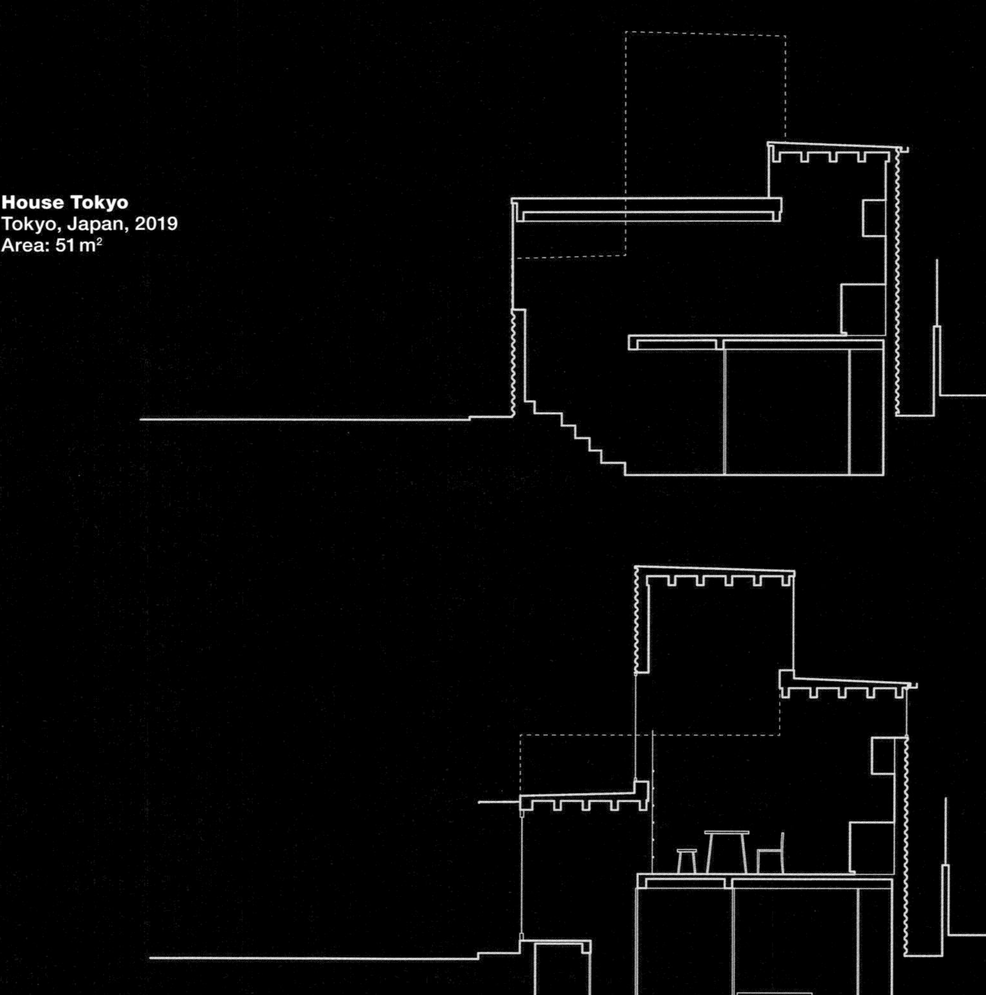

From the exterior, the house appears to be essentially made of metal, but its frame is in wood. External cladding is in corrugated, galvanized steel plate, and its interiors also give a rather industrial feeling.

Below: the first-floor plan shows the entrance to the house on the left.

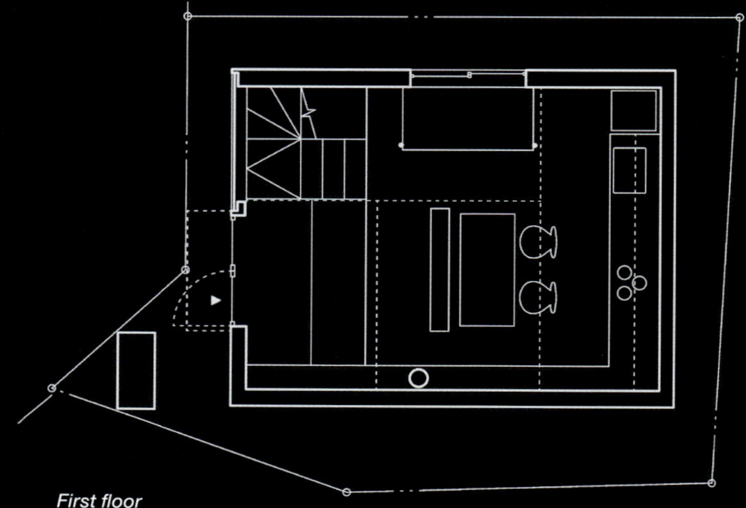

First floor

The unusual articulation of the volumes of the house makes for unexpected interiors with light coming from different angles, combined with views through the spaces as seen in the image above.

This wooden house was built on a 52-square-meter site in Tokyo. It has a footprint of just 27 square meters and includes a basement and one upper story. The basement set at just one meter below grade includes a storage space, a shower and toilet, and the bedroom. The entrance is through the upper level, which also has a dining area. The architect explains: "By setting back the outer walls even more than the regulations required, we created various heights with ceilings that range from about 1.9 meters to 4.7 meters and opened many large windows on the increased surface of the outer walls." The house is in a narrow alley and has "four roofs aimed to create a space that feels like a small crevice between buildings by suspending one part of the structure and balancing it evenly throughout, while applying different types of finishes on the inner walls." The somewhat indeterminate nature of the space corresponds to what the architect calls the "fluid lifestyle and freedom of the client." Corrugated galvanized-steel plate is used for the exterior walls while interior walls are in calcium silicate board and water-resistant plasterboard.

Dieses Holzhaus wurde auf einem 52 m^2 großen Grundstück in Tokio errichtet. Mit einer Grundfläche von nur 27 m^2 umfasst es ein Unter- sowie ein Obergeschoss. Die untere Ebene liegt einen Meter unter dem Erdboden und bietet Platz für eine Abstellkammer, eine Dusche mit WC und das Schlafzimmer. Der Eingang sowie ein Essbereich befinden sich im oberen Stockwerk. „Indem wir die Außenwände noch weiter zurücksetzten als vorgeschrieben, schufen wir verschiedene Deckenhöhen von etwa 1,9 m bis 4,7 m", erklärt der Architekt. „So konnten wir zahlreiche große Fenster in die vergrößerte Außenfläche einfügen." Das Haus in einer engen Gasse verfügt

The same space as the one on the left page seen from a different angle.

über „vier Dächer und einen teilweise abgehängten Boden, um einen Raum zu schaffen, der wie ein schmaler Spalt zwischen den Gebäuden wirkt. Unterstützt wird dieser Eindruck durch die unterschiedlichen Oberflächen der Innenwände". Die etwas unbestimmte Natur des Raums entspricht dem – so der Architekt – „fließenden Lebensstil und Freiheitsgefühl des Bauherrn". Die Fassade ist aus verzinktem Stahlblech, die Innenwände sind aus Kalziumsilikatplatten und wasserfesten Gipsplatten gefertigt.

La maison en bois a été construite sur une parcelle de 52 m² à Tokyo. Son empreinte au sol est de seulement 27 m², elle comprend un sous-sol et un étage. Le sous-sol, un mètre seulement sous le niveau du sol, comporte un espace de rangement, une douche, des toilettes et une chambre. L'entrée est située au niveau supérieur où se trouve aussi un coin repas. L'architecte explique qu'« en reculant les murs extérieurs plus encore que ne l'exigent les règles de construction, nous avons pu créer différentes hauteurs sous plafonds de 1,9 m à 4,7 m et ouvrir de nombreuses grandes fenêtres dans la surface agrandie des murs extérieurs ». La maison est située dans une allée étroite et ses « quatre toits forment un espace qui donne l'impression d'une petite fissure entre d'autres constructions, du fait de la structure, en partie suspendue et parfaitement équilibrée, et des finitions différentes des murs intérieurs ». La nature quelque peu indéterminée de l'espace correspond à ce que l'architecte désigne comme le « style de vie fluide et la liberté du client ». Les murs extérieurs sont en plaques d'acier galvanisé ondulé et les murs intérieurs en panneaux de silicate de calcium et placoplâtre résistant à l'eau.

WONDER

Intertwine House
Yanqing, Beijing, China, 2019
Area: 100 m²

Collaboration: Xuemei Gao, Tailin Jin

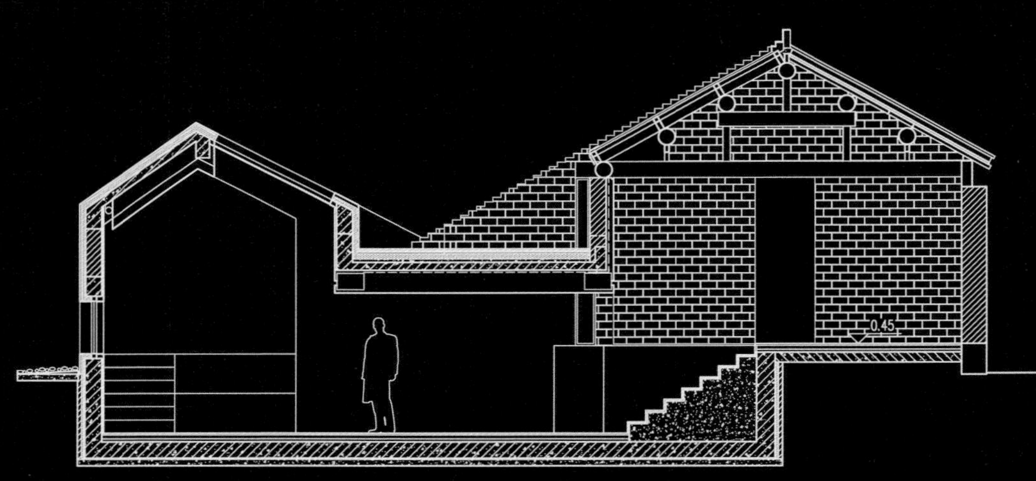

The green ceramic covering added by the architects to an existing brick house gives it an entirely renewed external appearance in an otherwise red-gray urban environment.

This project is located in the rural area of Houheilongmiao Village in Yanqing, Beijing. It is based on a single-story, three-room brick house of the 1980s, which was originally used as a wedding room. A new section with a gabled roof was added on the south side of the structure and covered in green ceramic tiles in contrast to the original red brick. The ground floor of the new area contains two bedrooms, a living area, a dining room, and a kitchen. The architects say: "Tear down and rebuild? Or worship history and keep it as it was? We feel that the dual relationship between the old and the new should be merged into a 'communisme formel'—giving a new meaning to an object that's already produced."

Dieses Projekt befindet sich in der ländlichen Umgebung des Dorfes Houheilongmiao in Yanqing, Peking. Es basiert auf einem einstöckigen Dreizimmerhaus aus Backstein aus den 1980er Jahren,das ursprünglich als Hochzeitssaal diente. An seine Südseite wurde ein neuer Gebäudeteil mit Satteldach angefügt, gedeckt mit grünen Keramikfliesen, die mit dem ursprünglichen roten Backstein kontrastieren. Im Erdgeschoss dieses neuen Bereichs befinden sich zwei Schlafzimmer, ein Wohnbereich, ein Esszimmer und eine Küche. „Abreißen und neu bauen? Oder die Geschichte verehren und alles belassen, wie es war?", fragten sich die Architekten. „Unserer Ansicht nach sollte die gegenseitige Beziehung zwischen Alt und Neu zu einem ‚formalen Kommunismus' verschmelzen und auf diese Weise einem existierenden Objekt eine neue Bedeutung verleihen."

The origin of the building is felt through exposed brick surfaces seen in the neighboring row house, or on the roof terraces (following spread). Below: the ground-floor plan.

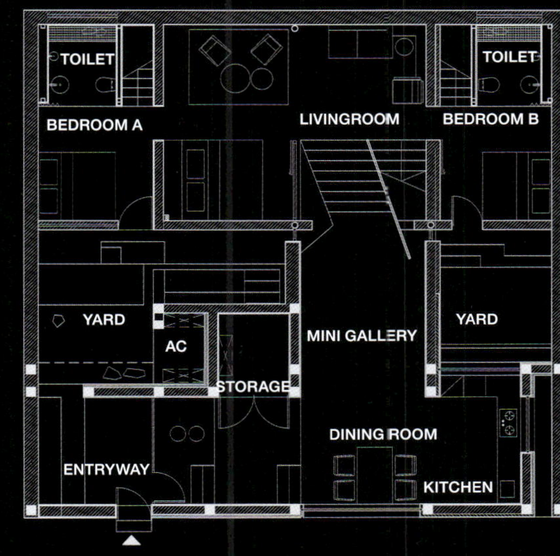

'he internal spaces flow into each other and through he different levels—dining table, bedroom, and roof errace.

.e projet se trouve dans la zone rurale du village le Houheilongmiao à Yanqing (Pékin). La base en ;st une maison de à un étage des années 1980 jui servait à l'origine de salle de mariages. Une ouvelle partie avec un toit à pignon a été ajoutée ιu sud et revêtue de carreaux céramiques verts jui contrastent avec la brique rouge d'origine. Le ez-de-chaussée de cette partie accueille deux :hambres, un salon, une salle à manger et une :uisine. Les architectes se sont demandé : « Tout lémolir et reconstruire ? Ou vénérer l'histoire et out laisser tel quel ? Nous avons senti qu'il fallait usionner en un "communisme formel" le rapport jual entre l'ancien et le neuf – et donner ainsi un ens nouveau à un objet déjà construit. »

YOSHIHIRO YAMAMOTO

Toolbox House
Miyakojima-ku, Osaka, Japan, 2021
Area: 90 m²

Collaboration: Kaori Mihashi

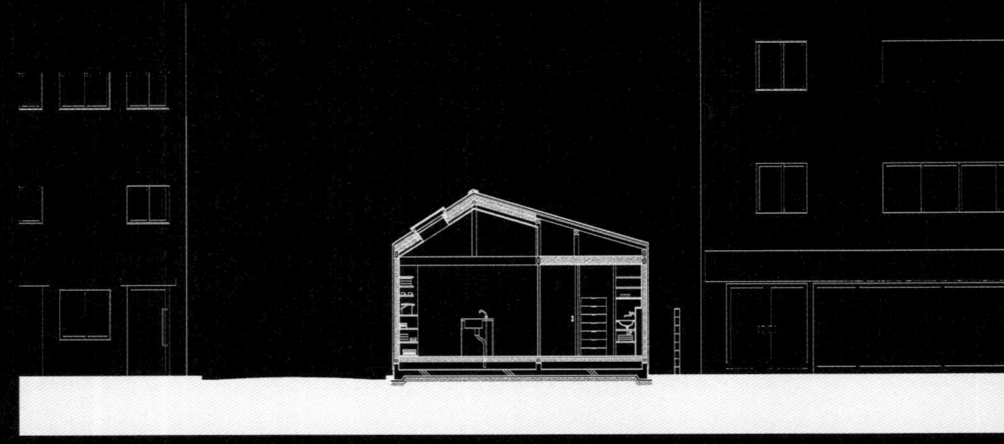

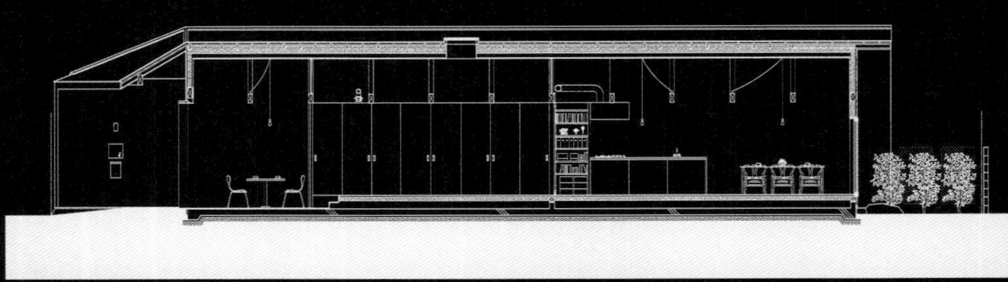

とおやま
Pet

This one-story house is described by the architects as “compact and easy to use like a toolbox.” An elongated floor plan was chosen to fit the site, and the building was covered with a simple triangular steel roof and several skylights to allow light to enter between neighboring buildings. The design includes an office on the west side. The entrance was conceived as a semi-outdoor multipurpose space for unloading, meetings, and machine maintenance. Public space inside is on the east side and is connected, like the office space, to the dining area and kitchen. The kitchen is made of plywood, and is large enough to allow work with family and friends, while the dining area faces a small garden on the north side. A room for the mother is located close to the bathroom so that she can live at a little distance from the couple who owns the house. The materials used are galvanized-steel sheet, plywood, tile, oak and Japanese cedar flooring, mortar, tatami mats, and cork.

„So kompakt und simpel zu benutzen wie ein Werkzeugkasten“ sei das einstöckige Toolbox House (toolbox = Werkzeugkasten) laut Aussage der Architekten. Als Hauptmaterialien wurden verzinkte Stahlbleche, Sperrholz, Fliesen, Eichen- und japanische Zedernholzböden, Mörtel, Tatami-Matten und Kork verwendet. Um das Häuschen an seinen Standort zwischen hohen, lichtraubenden Nachbargebäuden anzupassen, wählten die Architekten einen lang gestreckten Grundriss und fügten dem dreieckigen Stahldach mehrere Oberlichter hinzu, die für helle Innenräume sorgen. Auf der Westseite liegt ein Büro, dessen Eingang als halb offener Mehrzweckraum für das Entladen, Besprechungen und die Maschinenwartung dient. Der Gemeinschaftsbereich

A floorplan of the house shows the elongated form also seen in the images, as well as in the working area with the motorcycle (following page).

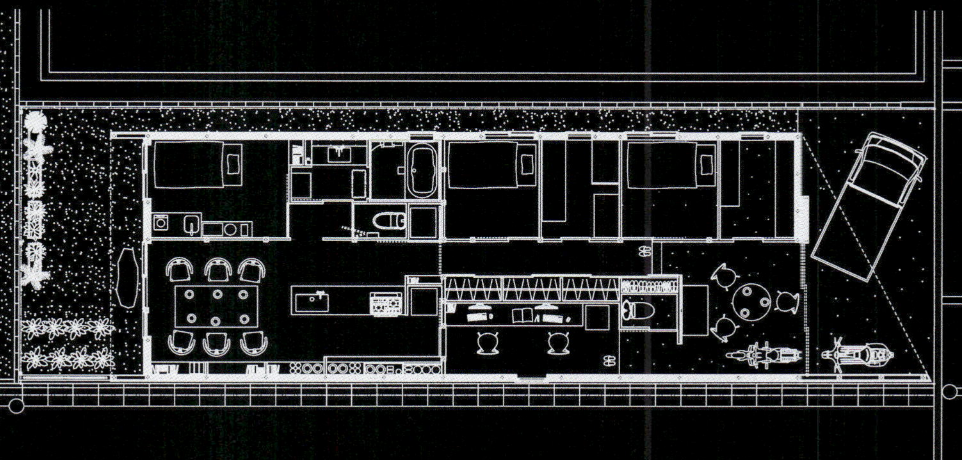

Despite its narrowness, the interior benefits from the extra height afforded by a sloped roof. Skylights also brighten the inside spaces.

auf der Ostseite ist, wie das Büro, mit Essbereich und Küche verbunden. Letztere ist aus Sperrholz gefertigt und bietet genügend Platz für Familie und Freunde. Der Essbereich auf der Nordseite blickt auf einen kleinen Garten hinaus. Ein Zimmer für die Mutter der Eigentümer ist unweit des Badezimmers eingerichtet, sodass sie für sich bleiben kann und doch ihre Familie unter demselben Dach um sich weiß.

Cette maison de plain-pied est présentée par les architectes comme « compacte et aussi facile à utiliser qu'une boîte à outils ». Le plan au sol en longueur est adapté au terrain et le bâtiment est couvert d'un simple toit triangulaire en acier avec plusieurs lucarnes pour laisser passer la lumière entre les immeubles voisins. Le concept comprend aussi un bureau du côté ouest. L'entrée forme un espace polyvalent semi-extérieur pour décharger, se réunir et effectuer des réparations. À l'intérieur, la partie commune est placée à l'est et reliée, comme le bureau, à la salle à manger-cuisine. La cuisine est en contreplaqué et suffisamment grande pour y travailler en famille ou entre amis, tandis que le coin repas donne sur un petit jardin au nord. Une pièce est réservée à la grand-mère à côté de la salle de bains pour lui permettre de vivre à quelque distance du couple de propriétaires. Les matériaux utilisés sont la feuille d'acier galvanisé, le contreplaqué, les carrelages, le chêne et le cèdre du Japon pour le sol, le mortier, les tatamis et le liège.

S 24 Oct

BIOGRAPHIES

ALPHAVILLE
KENTARO TAKEGUCHI graduated in 1994 from the School of Architecture, Faculty of Engineering at Kyoto University. He studied at the AA in London (1995–96) and worked with Foreign Office Architects. He received his M.Arch in 1998 (Kyoto University) and founded Alphaville Architects with Asako Yamamoto the same year. ASAKO YAMAMOTO also graduated from the School of Architecture, Faculty of Engineering (Kyoto University, 1994), before studying at ENSA-Paris La Villette (France, 1995–96). She obtained her Master's (Kyoto University, 1997) and worked the same year for the office of Riken Yamamoto & Field Shop. Their work includes the Suzuka Catholic Church (Suzuka, 2015); Studio Apartments (Hikone, 2015); Garden Alley House (Kyoto, 2017); the Kizunaya Building (Kyoto, 2017); and the House of 24mm Plywood (Kyoto, 2020, published here), all in Japan.

CAMERON ANDERSON ARCHITECTS
Born in 1981, CAMERON ANDERSON has been the director of Cameron Anderson Architects in Mudgee since 2011. He earned his Bachelor of Environmental Design from the University of Tasmania (2000–02) and a B.Arch from the same institution (2004–05). He worked at Hayball Architects in Melbourne (2006–10) before founding his own firm. His recent work includes the Glen Willow Junior League Clubhouse (Mudgee, 2019); Yeates Wine Cellar Door and Farmstay (Mudgee, 2020); Gawthorne's Hut (Mudgee, 2020, published here); Glen Willow Rugby Union Clubhouse (Mudgee, 2021); and the Griffith Community Center (Griffith, 2021), all in New South Wales, Australia.

ANDERSON ARCHITECTURE
SIMON ANDERSON graduated from the University of Technology Sydney UTS in 1996. His part-time degree program allowed him to work for a Sri Lankan architect, Pri De Fonseka, during his studies. He also travelled to Mexico to learn about the work of Luis Barragán. After his studies he worked for several Sydney firms, including Daryl Jackson Robin Dyke, Tony Caro Architecture, and Kennedy Associates Architects (KAA). He created Anderson Architecture in 2002. His recent projects include the Ferry Road House (Glebe, Sydney, 2018); Imprint House (Alexandria, Sydney, 2018); The Shed Studio (Naremburn, Sydney, 2018); the Sol House, a renovation of a California bungalow (Russel Lea, Sydney, 2019); the Off-Grid FZ House (Blue Mountains, Sydney, 2020, published here); and a new bushfire resilient home in the Blue Mountains (2020), all in Australia.

ARBOL
Arbol Design was founded by YOUSAKU TSUTSUMI in Osaka in 2009. Born in Tokyo in 1979, he grew up in Tokushima Prefecture and graduated from both the Anan National College of Technology (Anan, Tokushima) and Kobe Art College. He worked in the office of Kenji Tagashira (Osaka) before creating his own firm. Aside from the House in Akashi (Hyoto, 2018) published here, recent work includes House in Kawachinagano (Osaka, 2019); House in Ohasu (Osaka, 2019); an apartment building (Osaka, 2020); and Hareruya Café & Beer restaurants (Hyogo, 2021), all in Japan.

ARANZA DE ARIÑO
was born in Mexico City in 1989. She has been an independent architect since 2014, after receiving her B.Arch from the Universidad Iberoamericana (Mexico City, 2009–13). She worked as a researcher in the office of AMO at OMA (Rotterdam, 2017) during her studies for a Master's in Urban Design (Harvard GSD, Cambridge, MA, 2019). She followed up at the same university with another Master's in Design Studies (2019). Aside from her Casa Tiny (San Pedro Tututepec, 2016, published here), she has worked on the Cobarde Bar (Puerto Escondido), (San Pedro Tututepec, 2019); and the Restaurante Punta Pájaros (San Pedro Tututepec, 2020). Current work includes Casa LR (San Pedro Tututepec); and the Residencias CDP (Sisal, Yucatán, ongoing), a master plan and landscape project for a residential development of 14 hectares. Aranza de Ariño is based in Mexico City.

ARTE-1
KAZUYUKI YAMADA was born in 1947 in Tokyo. He graduated from Nihon University in 1970 and established Arte-1 in 1980 in Tokyo. A younger generation has since come to the fore in the firm. YUGO YAMADA, who was involved with the 6 Tsubo House (Shibuya, Tokyo, 2020, published here), was born in Tokyo in 1979. He received his Master's degree from Tokyo Denki University in 2007. He worked after that date with Toyo Ito, in particular on the Taichung Metropolitan Opera House (Taipei, 2016), and joined Arte-1 in 2017. Other recent work of the office includes the House with a Rocky Surface (Tokyo, 2018); and the Shinko Building (Tokyo, renovation, 2020), both in Japan.

BAUMRAUM
ANDREAS WENNING was born in 1965. He studied as a cabinetmaker in Weinheim, Germany (1982–85), and as an architect at the Technical University of Bremen, where he obtained his degree in 1995. He worked in various German architecture studios, and the office of José Garcia Negrette in Sydney, Australia, before creating his own office, baumraum, in Bremen in 2003. In 2008, Wenning exhibited during the architectural symposium ARTINDEX in St. Petersburg, Russia; and at La Triennale in Milan, Italy, with a spatial installation. He has completed tree houses and other landscape buildings in many European countries, North and South America, Russia, and China, including Casa Giraffa (Curitiba, Brazil, 2006); the Green Dwelling (near Hannover, Germany, 2019, which received the 2021 HÄUSER-Award); the Dark Room (Ruinen, the Netherlands, 2020, published here); and Black Crystal (Catskill Mountains, New York, USA, 2020).

ATTILA BÉRES
is the founder and owner of Béres Architects. He was born in 1982 in Zalaegerszeg, Hungary. He received his diploma from BME (Budapest University of Technology) in 2007. JUSZTINA BALÁZS, who worked on Cabin Moss (Kőszeg, 2021, published here), was born in 1983 in Budapest. She also received her degree from BME in 2008. Their work includes the Hideg House in Kőszeg (2013); Summer Cabin V2 (Tihany, 2016); the Niczky Apartment (Kőszeg, 2016); and Cabin Balaton (Vonyarcvashegy, 2020), all in Hungary.

BIANCHI-FUCILE
LEANDRO FUCILE is a founding partner of the Bianchi-Fucile studio. He graduated in 2010 from the Faculty of Architecture and Urbanism, Universidad Nacional de La Plata (FAU-UNLP), Argentina. The other founding partner of the firm is SANTIAGO NICOLAS BIANCHI, who graduated from the same institution, also in 2010. Aside from the House in Los Hornos (La Plata, 2018, published here), and the BA House (Brandsen, 2020), they have worked on designs for the government-funded Procrear housing scheme (Cordoba, 2019, and La Plata, 2021). Other work includes Casa BK2 (Chascomus, 2020), all in Argentina.

BIG
BJARKE INGELS was born in 1974 in Copenhagen, Denmark. He graduated from the Royal Academy of Arts School of Architecture (Copenhagen, 1999) and attended the ETSAB School of Architecture (Barcelona). He created his own office in 2005 under the name Bjarke Ingels Group (BIG), after having cofounded PLOT Architects in 2001 and collaborated with Rem Koolhaas at OMA (Rotterdam). Today, BIG is based in New York and Copenhagen and has 24 partners and 53 associates, with an international team of over 500 people. The Mountain (Copenhagen, Denmark, 2008), designed by BIG in collaboration with JDS Architects, received numerous awards. The firm has also designed the Danish Expo Pavilion (Shanghai, China, 2010); Superkilen Master Plan (Copenhagen, Denmark, 2011); and the Maritime Museum of Denmark (Elsinore, Denmark, 2013). Recent work includes W57 NY (New York, New York, USA, 2016); Shenzhen International Energy Mansion (Shenzhen, China, 2017); the Amager Bakke Resource Center (Copenhagen, Denmark, 2018); Klein A45 (Upstate New York, 2018, published here); The Spiral (Hudson Yards, New York, under construction); and a redevelopment of 120 Fleet Street (London, 2021–). BIG is co-designing the largest neighborhood in the world of 3D-printed homes with ICON and Lennar in Austin, Texas (2021–).

B.L.U.E.
SHUHEI AOYAMA is the founding partner and principal of B.L.U.E. Architecture Studio. He was born in Hiroshima in 1980, then graduated from Osaka University in 2003 and received his Master's from Tokyo University in 2005. He worked with SAKO Architects in Beijing from 2005 to 2012 before founding B.L.U.E. in 2014 in Beijing. Aside from Hutong 02 (Beijing, 2015, published here), his work includes the Dengshikou Hutong Residence (Dongcheng, Beijing, 2016); the renovation of a historic house (Suzhou, 2017); M WOODS Museum (Beijing, 2019); & Arabica Coffee (Shanghai, 2019); Forest Valley Hot Spring Center (Chengde, 2019); 1402 Coffee Shop in Aranya (Qinhuangda, 2021); and BAN Villa (Suzhou, 2021), all located in China.

BUREAU LADA
LADA HRŠAK is a Croatian-Dutch architect, researcher, educator, and founder of the cross-disciplinary studio Bureau LADA (Landscape, Architecture, Design, Action) created in 2010. Following her training at the Faculty of Architecture at the University of Zagreb, Hršak completed the postgraduate program at the Berlage Institute in Amsterdam in 1997. Her work includes the mirrored Archive Pavilion (Amsterdam, 2009); Pendopo House (Jogjakarta, Indonesia, 2015); "*Structuralism*," an exhibition held at the Nieuwe Instituut (formerly the Nai, Rotterdam, 2015); Zandpier, a landscape intervention (Amsterdam, 2017); Stargazing Platform (Marrakech, Morocco, 2018); the Towerhouse (Amsterdam, 2020, published here); and the Bustan Garden (Cairo, Egypt, 2021), all in the Netherlands unless otherwise indicated. She also created *Shallow Waters* magazine at the Venice Architecture Biennale (2021).

CASEY BROWN
ROBERT BROWN received his degrees in Architecture from the University of New South Wales (1976 and 1979) and from Columbia University Graduate School of Architecture in New York (1992–93). He worked with Fisher Lucas Architects in Sydney (1976), Julian Harap Architects in London (1983), and with the Heritage Council NSW (1984–86) before creating Dawson Brown Partnership (1986–89), Dawson Brown + Ackert Architecture (1989–92), and Dawson Brown Architecture (1993–2004). In 2004, he created the firm Casey Brown with partner CAROLINE CASEY. The James-Robertson House (Great Mackeral Beach, Sydney, 2001–03) won a 2004 Residential Architecture Award from the Royal Australian Institute of Architects (NSW Chapter). More recent work includes the Permanent Camping House (Mudgee, 2007); the Stanwell Park House (Stanwell Park Beach, Sydney, 2007); Eagles Rest Winery (Hunter Valley 2010); Jodie's House (Clifton Gardens, 2014); the Palm House (Sydney, 2016); Crackenback Stables (Crackenback, 2016); and Permanent Camping Two (Berry, 2020, published here), all in New South Wales, Australia.

JAIME CHIOCO
was born in Stanton, Virginia in 1972. He graduated from the University of Oklahoma School of Architecture in 1995 and worked with Dick Clark Architecture (Austin, 1997–2005), before creating his own firm in 2005. As well as Tiny Victories 2.0 (2019, published here), his built work includes Resignation Media Offices (2015); Torchy's South

Congress (2016); Uship Headquarters (2018); Better Half Coffee and Cocktails (2018); Hemlock House (2019); Paperboy Restaurant (2020); and 979 Springdale (2020), all in Austin, Texas.

BARRY CONNOR
Born in 1975 in Billinge, Widnes, UK, BARRY CONNOR received a B.A. in Architecture from Kingston University (London, 1993–96) and did further studies in Archicad at Christscurch Polytechnic University of Technology (New Zealand, 2006). He worked at 3-Architecture (Christchurch, 2006–08) and at Ray Hawthorne Design (Christchurch 2008–13) while founding his own firm in Christchurch in 2010. Connor gives a single name to his houses, which include Simpson (Merivale, Christchurch, 2018); Tinning (Twizel, Mackenzie, 2018); Patterson (Hawarden, Hurunui, 2020); the Skylark Cabin (Twizel, Mackenzie, 2020, published here); and Lear, which was still in the concept phase as this book went to press (Banks Peninsula, Canterbury, 2021–), all in New Zealand.

CROXATTO & OPAZO
FELIPE CROXATTO was born in Chile in 1979 and received his degree in Architecture from the Mayor University (Providencia, 2005), and a Master's from the University of Pamplona (Spain, 2006–08). NICOLAS OPAZO, born in Chile in 1981, also graduated from the Mayor University in 2005 and has a degree in Design from the Catholic University of Chile (PUC, 2018) as well. They created their present office in 2010. Their work includes the Alhué Nursing Home (Villa Alhué, Melipilla, 2010); Foneron House (Valdivia, Región de Los Ríos, 2015); Machagua House (Cachagua, Zapallar, 2016); Parrón House (Colina, Santiago, 2017); the Matzanas Cabins (Matzanas, 2018, published here); and the TS Marbella House (Marbella, Valparaíso, 2022), all in Chile.

EL SINDICATO
El Sindicato Arquitectura was founded by MARIA REINOSO, XAVIER DUQUE, and NICOLÁS VITERI in 2014. All three studied at the Architecture Faculty of the Catholic University of Ecuador in Quito, earning their degrees between 2014 and 2016. Their completed works include the Cacao Interpretation Center (Kichwa de Santa Rita, Archidona, 2014); Post-Earthquake Prototype (Los Horconcitos, Manabí, 2017); House in the Trees (Barrio Collas Cumbayá, Quito, 2019); Parasitic House (Quito, 2019, published here); and Mountain House (San Juan, Cumbayá, 2020), all in Ecuador.

TAKAAKI FUJI + YUKO FUJI
TAKAAKI FUJI was born in Hyogo Prefecture in 1982. He received his M.Arch from Waseda University (Tokyo, 2007) and worked starting that year with the architectural design, engineering, and consulting company Mitsubishi Jisho Design, cofounding his own firm in 2019 as well. YUKO FUJI was born in 1982 in Osaka. She received her M.Arch from the Graduate School of Waseda University (Tokyo, 2007) and worked as an architect with the general contractor Tasei Corporation from 2007, also cofounding Takaaki Fuji + Yuko Fuji Architecture in 2019 as well. As their firm was recently created, their first completed work is the Bay Window Tower House (Tokyo, 2020, published here).

SEAN GODSELL
was born in Melbourne, Australia, in 1960. He graduated from the University of Melbourne in 1984 and worked from 1986 to 1988 in London with Sir Denys Lasdun. He created Godsell Associates Pty Ltd. Architects in 1994. After receiving an M.Arch from RMIT University (Melbourne, 1999), he was a finalist in the Seppelt Contemporary Art Awards held by the Museum of Contemporary Art in Sydney for his work "*Future Shack*." He won the RAIA Award of Merit for new residential work for the Carter/Tucker House in 2000 (Breamlea, Victoria, 2000). His work also includes Peninsula House (Victoria, 2002); Lewis House (Dunkeld, Victoria, 2003); and he ACN Headquarters (Victoria, 2003). More recent work includes Tanderra House (Victoria, 2012); the RMIT Design Hub (Melbourne, 2012); House on the Coast (Mornington Peninsula, Victoria, 2017); a chapel for the Vatican (Venice Architecture Biennale, Italy, 2018); House in the Hills (rural Victoria, 2018); and Shack in the Rocks (Victoria, 2021, published here), all in Australia unless stated otherwise.

H&P
DOAN THANH HA was born in 1980 in Bac Ninh, Vietnam. He earned a B.Arch degree (1997–2002) and a Master's (2004–07), both from Hanoi Architectural University. Aside from AgriNesture (Quang Ninh, 2018, published here), his work includes S Space (Ha Nam, 2018); Tropical Cave (Bac Ninh, 2019); Human's Optional USE House

(Hai Duong, 2019); revitalization of the Mao Khe Mining Park (Quang Ninh, 2019); and Ngói Space (Hanoi, 2020), all in Vietnam.

TAKESHI HOSAKA
was born in Yamanashi in 1975. He graduated in Architecture from Yokohama National University and obtained his Master's degree in 2001. While studying, he created the Speed Studio architecture design office. He created his current firm in 2004. He is a professor at Waseda University, Art and Architecture School. The CEO and cofounder of his office is Megumi Hosaka. His work includes the original Love House (Yokohama, 2005); Hoto Fudo Restaurant (Minamitsuru, Yamanashi, 2009); Shonan Christ Church (Fujisawa, Kanagawa, 2014); Balcony House (Tokyo, 2016); the Love2 House (Tokyo, 2019, published here); Seesaw Coffee Shanghai (China, 2019); and the Cemetery of the Kamakura Yukinoshita Church (Kanagawa, 2020), all in Japan unless indicated otherwise.

I29
i29 architects was created by JASPAR JANSEN, who was born in 1972 in Amsterdam and studied at the Rietveld Academy (Amsterdam); JEROEN DELLENSON, also born in 1972 in Amsterdam, studied at the Utrecht School of Arts and Architecture; and CHRIS COLLARIS, born in 1981 in Heerlen and who graduated from the Technical University of Eindhoven. Aside from the Tiny Holiday Home (Vinkeveen, 2019, published here), their work includes De Bijenkorf Menswear Department Store (Amsterdam, 2019); Felix Meritis Cultural Venue (Amsterdam, 2020); a floating home (Amsterdam, 2021); the Booking.com Headquarters (Amsterdam, 2022); and RED7 Residential development (with MVRDV, Moscow, Russia, 2022), all in the Netherlands unless indicated otherwise.

PAULO AND BERNARDO JACOBSEN
PAULO JACOBSEN was born in 1954 in Rio de Janeiro and studied photography in London before graduating from the Bennett Methodist Institute in 1979 and then cofounding the office of Bernardes + Jacobsen in 1980. BERNARDO JACOBSEN was born in 1980 and joined his father's company in 2007 after graduating from the Federal University of Rio de Janeiro and working in the offices of Christian de Portzamparc and Shigeru Ban. Jacobsen Arquitetura was created in 2011 by Bernardo and Paolo Jacobsen and has since completed MAR—Art Museum of Rio (with Bernardes Arquitetura, Rio de Janeiro, 2013); the SW House (Porto Feliz, São Paulo, 2013); Kalabo Business Center (Fiji, 2015); OS House (São Paulo, 2016); RMA House (Portugal, 2016); AB House (Rio de Janeiro, 2016); GAF House (São Paulo, 2016); luxury resorts in the Caribbean (2016), and Indonesia (2017); the Marine Museum (Rio de Janeiro, 2017); ANM House (Melbourne, Australia, 2018); MPJ Cabin (Rio de Janeiro, 2020, published here); and the RDJ House (Porto Feliz, São Paulo, 2023), all in Brazil unless otherwise indicated.

MACKAY-LYONS SWEETAPPLE
BRIAN MACKAY-LYONS was born in Arcadia, Nova Scotia. He received his B.Arch from the Technical University of Nova Scotia in 1978, and his Master of Architecture and Urban Design at U.C.L.A. After studying in China, Japan, California, and Italy, working with Charles Moore, Barton Myers and Giancarlo De Carlo, Brian returned to Nova Scotia in 1983. In 1985 he founded the firm Brian MacKay-Lyons Architecture Urban Design in Halifax. Twenty years later, he created a partnership with Talbot Sweetapple under the name MacKay-Lyons Sweetapple Architects Ltd. TALBOT SWEETAPPLE was born in St. John's, Newfoundland. He graduated with an M.Arch from Dalhousie University. He worked with Shin Takamatsu in Berlin and with KPMB in Toronto prior to the creation of MacKay-Lyons Sweetapple. Their work includes the Canadian Chancery and Official Residence (with RDHA, Dhaka, Bangladesh, 2005); the Shobac Campus and Ghost Architectural Laboratory (Upper Kingsburg, Nova Scotia, 2019); Horizon, Summit Powder Mountain (Eden, Utah, USA, 2019); as well as numerous smaller structures and houses such as the Enough House (Upper Kingsburg, Nova Scotia, 2015, published here); Bigwin Island Cabins (Bigwin Island, Ontario, 2018); and the Smith Residence (Upper Kingsburg, Nova Scotia, 2019), all in Canada unless otherwise indicated.

MAGUIRE + DEVINE
HUGH MAGUIRE was born in Tasmania and studied at the University of Tasmania in Launceston (with an exchange year at the Robert Gordon University in Aberdeen, Scotland) and graduated with a B.Arch in 2003. Before establishing Maguire Architects in 2012, he worked with RMJM in Edinburgh as well as Jaws Architects and Morrison & Breytenbach Architects in Tasmania.

DAN DEVINE graduated from the University of Tasmania in Architecture (B.Arch, 2003). After working for seven years in London as an associate at Studio 54, he joined Maguire Architects (2013–15), which became Maguire + Devine in 2015, and he is now co-Director of the firm. Their recent work includes another very small residence, the Bruny Island Hideaway (Bruny Island, 2017); Sherwood Hill House (Pelverata, 2017); Periscope House (West Hobart, 2018); Di and Bernie's Place (Lindisfarne, 2019); Soho Small House (South Hobart, 2020); and the Boathouse (Hobart, 2021, published here), all in Tasmania, Australia.

MAKERS OF ARCHITECTURE
BETH CAMERON is a Director and cofounder of Makers of Architecture, as is JAE WARRANDER. Other cofounders are BEN SUTHERLAND and GRANT DOUGLAS. Their work has been concentrated on numerous small houses designed and built with cutting-edge computer-driven technology and includes the Warrander Studio (Governors Bay, 2014); Pearce Place (South Island, 2015); the Lynds Residence (Queenstown, 2016); the Akaroa Bach (Akaroa, Banks Peninsula, 2018, published here); Sonnhalde (Geraldine, 2019); and On Giants' Shoulders tasting room (Martinborough, 2019), all in New Zealand.

MAPA
MAPA Architects is a bi-national collective that works in Brazil and Uruguay. LUCIANO ANDRADES was born in Porto Alegre in 1972 and graduated from ULBRA (São José, Canoas, RS, 2002). MATÍAS CARBALLAL was born in Montevideo in 1979 and graduated from the Universidad de la República Uruguay in 2009. ROCHELLE CASTRO was born in Porto Alegre in 1978 and graduated from ULBRA in 2002. ANDRÉS GOBBA was born in Montevideo in 1978 and established the office MAAM in Montevideo in 2002. MAURICIO LÓPEZ was also born in Montevideo in 1978, graduating from the Universidad de la República in 2009. SILVIO MACHADO was born in Porto Alegre in 1977 and graduated from UniRitter (Porto Alegre) in 2004. They collectively established MAPA in 2013. Their work includes the Retreat in Finca Aguy (Pueblo Edén, Maldonado, Uruguay, 2015); Minimod Catuçaba (Fazenda Catuçaba, São Paulo, Brazil, 2015); a retreat in José Ignacio (José Ignacio, Maldonado, Uruguay, 2015); the Sacromonte Landscape Hotel (Maldonado, Uruguay, 2016–); Minimod Curucaca (Santa Catarina, Brazil, 2017, published here); and Smokewood Garzón (Rocha, Uruguay, 2020).

MAR PLUS ASK
was established in 2015 by the architects MAR VICENS FUSTER from Spain and ASK ANKER AISTRUP (Denmark). Born in 1985, Vicens received her M.Arch from the Polytechnic University of Valencia (UPV) and also studied at the Facultade de Arquitetura e Urbanismo in São Paulo (FAU). Born in 1980, Ask Anker Aistrup received his Master's from the Royal Danish Academy of Fine Arts School of Architecture (KADK). Prior to 2015, Ask worked for David Adjaye Architects (London), Praksis Arkitekter (Svendborg, Denmark), and Jean-François Bodin (Paris). Since 2022 he has been the sole owner of the firm. Their work includes the refurbishment of Casa Puerto Sóller (Mallorca, 2017); an apartment renovation on Glogauer Strasse (Berlin, Germany, 2017); the Olive Houses (Mallorca, 2019, published here); and Casa Sóller (Mallorca, 2021), all in Spain, unless indicated otherwise.

MARTE.MARTE
BERNHARD MARTE was born in 1966 in Dornbirn, Vorarlberg, Austria, and his brother, STEFAN MARTE, was born in the same locality in 1967. They obtained their M.Arch degrees from the Technical University of Innsbruck. Stefan Marte worked in the office of Gohm + Hiessberger in Feldkirch until Marte.Marte was created in Weiler in 1993. Their work includes the Schanerloch Bridge (Dornbirn, 2006); State Pathology Hospital (Feldkirch, 2008); Alfenz Bridge (Lorüns, 2010); Special Pedagogical Center (Dornbirn, 2011); Kärnten Diocesan Museum (Fresach, 2011); Mountain Cabin (Laterns, 2011, published here); Maiden Tower (Dafins, 2012); a tourism school (Villach, 2013); Schloss Hofen Seminar Hotel (Vorarlberg, 2016); the Landesgalerie Niederösterreich (Krems-Stein, 2019); and the refurbishment of their own Tschitscher Schlössle (Feldkirch, 2023), all in Austria.

TAKAHIRO MORIYA
was born in Kanagawa in 1983 and graduated from Tokai University with an M.Arch in 2011. He founded Moriya and Partners in 2011. He has been an adjunct Professor at Tokai University since 2014. His works include the Sannomiya

House (Kanagawa, 2014); Iriya House (Kanagawa, 2014); Office for Startups by Mistletoe Japan, Inc. (Tokyo, 2016); Setoyama (Shizuoka, 2020, published here); Dried Seafood Shop Yamayasu (Kanagawa, 2021); Nikaido House (Kanagawa, 2021); and Soutousan House (Shizuoka, 2021), all in Japan.

NORGESHUS
is a fairly large Norwegian engineering and architectural office. Created 30 years ago, the firm has built more than 18 500 homes on the basis of catalog designs. They have also designed and built commercial and public buildings and done rehabilitation, extension, and renovation work. Included in their kit-type houses are various small cabins and vacation homes. They have also designed such buildings as the recent Bruhagen Kindergarden on Averøy. The principal involved in The Bolder (Stavanger-Lysefjord, Norway, 2020, published here) was JOHN BIRGER GRYTDAL. Grytdal received his M.Arch from NTNU (Trondheim, 1999–2004). He worked in the office of Per Knudsen in Trondheim (2004–10) before joining Norgeshus, where he has been since 2010. His work includes Five Villas (Sveberg, 2015); Moment–Villa at Halhjem (2016); Villa Gundersen (Tjøme, 2016); and the Lillerønning Snekkerfabrikk (Kotsøy, 2016), all in Norway.

OJT
JONATHAN TATE was born in 1974 in Alabama. He earned his B.Sc. in Architecture from Auburn University (1997) and went on to receive a Master in Design Studies from the Harvard GSD (Cambridge, MA, 2008). He created his architectural practice, Office of Jonathan Tate, in 2011 in New Orleans. His work includes Starter Home No. 1, 3106 St. Thomas (New Orleans, Louisiana, 2015, published here); the Bastion (New Orleans, Louisiana, 2018); 3609-13 S. Saratoga (New Orleans, Louisiana, 2019); 1476 Magazine Street (New Orleans, Louisiana, 2021); and the Clarksdale Collegiate Public Charter School (Clarksdale, Mississippi, 2021), all in the USA.

OLSON KUNDIG
TOM KUNDIG received his B.A. in Environmental Design (1977) and his M.Arch (1981) degrees from the University of Washington. He was a principal of Jochman/Kundig (1983–84), before becoming a principal of Olson Kundig Architects, a firm founded by Jim Olson, in 1986. As Olson Sundberg Kundig Allen Architects, the firm received the 2009 National AIA Architecture Firm Award. Tom Kundig's design work includes the Gulf Islands Cabin (Gulf Islands, British Columbia, Canada, 2008, published here); The Pierre (San Juan Islands, Washington, 2010); Art Stable (Seattle, Washington, 2010); Sol Duc Cabin (Olympic Peninsula, Washington, 2011); the Berkshire Residence (New Marlborough, Massachusetts, 2014), Tillamook Creamery (Tillamook, Oregon, 2018); and the Burke Museum (Seattle, Washington, 2019), all in the USA unless stated otherwise. Internationally, the firm has designed the Shinsegae International Headquarters (Seoul, South Korea, 2015); and the JW Marriott Puerto Los Cabos Beach Resort and Spa (San José del Cabo, Mexico, 2016). Martin's Lane Winery (Kelowna, British Columbia, Canada), designed by Tom Kundig, received a 2021 American Institute of Architects (AIA) National Architecture Honor Award.

ORTRAUM
MARTIN LUKASCZYK was born in Gifhorn, Germany, in 1977. He received his Diploma in Architecture from the Technical University of Braunschweig in 2004. He spent an exchange year during that time in London at the University of East London (2002–03). He created ORTRAUM in Helsinki in 2012 and is currently the director of design at the firm. Recent work of the firm includes House MK5 (Helsinki, 2017); House 12 (Helsinki, 2019); House TAO (Helsinki, 2020); Kynttilä (Savonlinna, 2020, published here); House UP (Helsinki, 2021); and House T (Helsinki, 2021), all in Finland.

GUSTAVO PENNA
is an architect and urban planner born in 1950 in Belo Horizonte. He graduated from the EA-UFMG School of Architecture (Belo Horizonte, Minas Gerais, 1973). He has been the Director of Gustavo Penna Arquiteto & Associados since 1973, and is a member of the Board of Trustees of the Oscar Niemeyer Foundation. His work includes the Revitalization of the City Center of Araxá (Araxá, Minas Gerais, 2010); the All Saints Chapel (Martinho Campos, Minas Gerais, 2011); Sete Lagoas High School – Fundação Zerrenner (Sete Lagoas, Minas Gerais, 2012) and UNIFEI –Campus for the Federal University of Itajubá (Itajubá, Minas Gerais, 2011). More recent work includes the Casa Roca (Belo Horizonte, Minas

Gerais, 2016); the Sustainable House (Ouro Branco, Minas Gerais, 2019, published here); the Memorial Brumadinho (Brumadinho, Minas Gerais, 2020); and Edificio Prisma (Nova Lima, Minas Gerais, 2023), all in Brazil.

CHARLES PICTET

was born in 1963. He received his degree in Architecture from the École d'Architecture de Genève in 1996. He worked as an intern (1992–93) and as a project architect in the office of Klaus Theo Brenner (Berlin, 1996–97). He completed several projects in collaboration with François Frey between 1998 and 2001 and then created his own office in Geneva in 2002. He has taught at the EPFL (Lausanne, 2010, 2011–12). He has completed an atelier in an agricultural building (Landecy, Geneva, 2010); a building for Student Housing (Geneva, 2011); and a house in Anières (2011), all in Switzerland. Since January 2021 he has worked in partnership with Baptiste Broillet. As well as the project published here—Atelier and Residence in a Garden Shed (Geneva, 2021)—the main ongoing projects of the office are a new visitor center of the United Nations Headquarters in Geneva; a museum for a private collector in Jussy; a winery in Chateauneuf-du-Pape (France); apartment buildings in Zurich; and several private houses and buildings in Geneva.

PRENTISS + BALANCE + WICKLINE

DANIEL ALAN WICKLINE was born in Seattle, Washington, in 1974. He graduated with a B.A. in Architecture from the University of Washington (1996). After working for Carlson Architects in Seattle, he continued his studies, graduating from the University of California Los Angeles with an M.Arch (UCLA, 2003). Returning to Seattle, he began working with Prentiss Architects, becoming a partner at Prentiss Wickline Architects in 2014 and forming Prentiss + Balance + Wickline in 2016. His work includes Ballard Cut (Seattle, Washington, 2010); Houseboat J in Portage Bay (Washington, 2017); Tongass Ledge (Ketchikan, Alaska, 2019); Big Fir Vineyard (Dundee, Oregon, 2020); Wawona (Yosemite, California, 2021); Bramblewood (San Juan Island, 2021); Wallowa (Joseph Oregon, 2021); Lost River Meadow (Mazama, Washington, 2021); Boathouse (Orcas Island, Washington, 2021, published here); and Wallingford (Seattle, Washington, 2022). All houses are located in the USA.

REIULF RAMSTAD

REIULF DANIEL RAMSTAD was born in 1962 in Oslo. He graduated from the IUAV University in Venice (Italy, 1985–91) and created his own firm in 1995. KRISTIN STOKKE RAMSTAD graduated from the Norwegian NTNU and UiO in 1997, and then got a Master's from the Department of Public and International Law in 2004. ANJA HOLE STRANDSKOGEN was born in Oslo in 1972. She received an M.Arch from AHO (1993–2000) and joined the firm in 2000. CHRISTIAN SKRAM FUGLSET was born in 1976 in Molde, received his Master's from AHO in 2005, and has worked with Reiulf Ramstad since 2006. Their work includes the Troll Wall Visitor Center (Trollveggen, Møre og Romsdal, 2011); Holmenkollen Metro Station (Holmenkollen, Oslo, 2011); Selvika National Tourist Route (Havøysund, Finnmark, 2012); Recycling Plant (Isi, Akershus, 2012); the Trollstigen National Tourist Route (Rauma, Møre og Romsdal, 2012); the Stjørdal Cultural Center (Stjørdal, Nord-Trøndelag, 2014); and the ISI Romsdal Folk Museum (Molde, Møre og Romsdal, 2015), all in Norway. More recently, they created the Chemin des Carrières (Rosheim, France, 2019); the House of Grain (Hjørring, Denmark, 2020); and the Breitenbach Landscape Hotel—48° Nord (Breitenbach, France, 2020, published here).

JOÃO MENDES RIBEIRO

was born in Coimbra in 1960. He graduated from the Faculty of Architecture at the University of Porto in 1986. He received a Ph.D. in Architecture from the University of Coimbra in 2009. In 1990 he set up his own practice in Coimbra. His recent work includes Arquipélago–Contemporary Art Center (Ribeira Grande, Azores, 2014); Botanical Garden Tropical Greenhouses (Coimbra, 2016); Casa São Roque–Art Center (Porto, 2019); São Pedro do Sul Roman Baths (São Pedro do Sul, 2019); Arruda dos Vinhos House (Arruda dos Vinhos, 2020); Areeiro House (Coimbra, 2020); the Chestnut House (Valeflor, Mêda, 2020, published here); and Ourém Castle (Ourém, 2021), all in Portugal.

CLAUDIA RODRÍGUEZ AND ROZANA MONTIEL

CLAUDIA RODRÍGUEZ was born in Mexico City in 1972. She graduated in Architecture and Urbanism from the Universidad Ibero-americana in Mexico City in 1996. She studied for an M.A. Architectural Theory and Criticism at the

Polytechnic University of Cataluña UPC (Spain, 1999). Her built work includes Casa Bruma (with Fernanda Canales, Valle de Bravo, 2018); Cosmos Pavilions (with Rozana Montiel, Valle de Bravo, 2019, published here); Reserva el Peñón, a master plan and landscape project for 200 hectares in Valle de Bravo (with Daniel Jaramillo TNT, 2021); Casa K in Tepoztlan (Morelos, 2021–under construction); and Casa Estudio (with Rozana Montiel, Valle de Bravo, 2021–under construction), all in Mexico. ROZANA MONTIEL was born in Mexico City in 1972. She holds an M.A. in Architectural Theory and Criticism from the Polytechnic University of Cataluña UPC (Spain, 2000), and a B.A. in Architecture and Urban Planning from the Universidad Iberoamericana (Mexico, 1998). She is the founder and director of her own Mexico-based architectural firm Rozana Montiel Estudio de Arquitectura. Her built work includes Common Unity (Mexico City, 2016); Albino Ortega House (Morelos, 2017); Fresnillo Playground (Zacatecas, 2017); Ocuilan Dwelling (Ocuilan, 2018); Nidos House (with Claudia Rodríguez, Valle de Bravo, 2020); and the Encinos House (with Claudia Rodríguez, Valle de Bravo, 2020), all in Mexico.

S-AR
CÉSAR GUERRERO was born in Durango, Mexico, in 1980. He obtained his degree in Architecture from the ITESM (Monterrey Institute of Technology, Monterrey, Mexico, 2004). ANA CECILIA GARZA was born in Monterrey in 1980 and earned a Master's in Urban Planning at the IAAC Institute for Advanced Architecture of Catalonia (Barcelona, Spain, 2005), and the title of architect at the ITESM (2003). Their recent work includes the Cosmos House (Puerto Escondido, Oaxaca, 2019, published here); Caté House (Monterrey, 2020); Gallery AAF (Monterrey, 2020); Miraloma Pavilion (Santiago, Nuevo León, 2020); Glamping Outlands Concentrico (Santiago, Nuevo León, 2021); House in Santiago (Santiago, Nuevo León, 2021); and House in the Arteaga Mountains (Coahuila, 2021), all in Mexico. They also designed Modular Pavilions for the 11th MOMENTUM Biennale (Moss/Jeløya, Norway, 2021).

SAVIOZ FABRIZZI
LAURENT SAVIOZ was born in 1976 and received his degree in Architecture from the Haute École Spécialisée (HES) of Fribourg (1998). He worked in the office of Bonnard & Woeffray in Monthey, Switzerland (1999–2003); cofounded Savioz Meyer Fabrizzi in Sion with François Meyer and Claude Fabrizzi in 2004; and then in 2005 co-created the current firm, an association between Savioz and Fabrizzi. CLAUDE FABRIZZI was born in 1975 in Sierre and is also a graduate of the HES in Fribourg (1995–98). Savioz carried forward the Roduit House (Chamoson, 2005) on his own, and among projects he worked on with Savioz Meyer Fabrizzi is the Hôtel de la Poste (Sierre, 2007). Savioz Fabrizzi has completed a primary school (Vollèges, 2010); a shelter for an archeological site (Saint Maurice, 2010); a sports hall (Viège, 2012); a mountain refuge, Cabane de Tracuit (Zinal, 2013); the Savioz House Renovation (Giète-Délé, 2013); a music hall (Sion, 2014); a commercial building that includes their office (Sion, 2017); the Bornet House (Ollon, 2017, published here); and more recently the Mottet House (Chemin-Dessus, 2024), all in Switzerland.

SELGASCANO
JOSÉ SELGAS was born in Madrid, Spain, in 1965. He received his architecture degree at the ETSA Madrid in 1992 and then worked with Francesco Venezia in Naples, Italy (1994–95). LUCÍA CANO was also born in Madrid in 1965 and received her degree from the ETSA Madrid in 1992. She worked with Julio Cano Lasso from 1997 to 2003. selgascano participated in the "On-Site: New Architecture in Spain" exhibition at the Museum of Modern Art, New York (2006). The architects have completed a Congress Center and Auditorium (Badajoz, 2006); Silicon House (La Florida, Madrid, 2006); Studio in the Woods (Madrid, 2009); Auditorium and Congress Center (Cartagena, 2011); Mérida Factory Youth Movement (Mérida, 2011); and Congress Center and Auditorium (Plasencia, 2012), all in Spain. More recently, their work has included the 2015 Serpentine Gallery Summer Pavilion, Hyde Park (London, UK, 2015); Secondhome offices in Lisbon, London, Los Angeles, and Hollywood (2017/2018); Floating Pavilion in Bruges (Belgium, 2018); Sam First Bar (Los Angeles, 2018); the 2015 Serpentine Gallery Summer Pavilion reinstalled at La Brea Tar Pits Park (Los Angeles, 2018); House in Los Rincones (La Vera, Spain, 2021, published here); La Canaria House (Los Angeles, 2021); Social Center and Cafeteria in Bailuwan Town (Shandong, China, 2021); and the Design District Food Market (London, UK, 2021).

FRAN SILVESTRE
Fran Silvestre Arquitectos was founded in Valencia by the architect FRAN SILVESTRE in 2005. Born in 1976, Silvestre graduated from the ETSA of Valencia in 2001. He then studied urban planning at the Eindhoven Technical University before working in the studio of Álvaro Siza in Porto. The architect acknowledges the influence of Siza and of the sculptor Andreu Alfaro. Fran Silvestre's work includes the Atrium House (Godella, Valencia, 2009); the House on the Castle Mountainside (Ayora, Valencia, 2010); Cliff House (Calpe, Alicante, 2012); and such works as the Blanc L'Antic Colonial Showroom (Villareal, 2013). More recently, he has completed the Hofmann House (Valencia, 2018); Penthouse in Costa Blanca (Alicante, 2019); Pati Blau House (Valencia, 2020); House of Silence (Cañada, 2020); House of Sand (Valencia, 2020); and NIU N70 (Valencia, 2021, published here), all in Spain.

SMALLER ARCHITECTS
MINWOOK CHOI was born in 1981 in Korea. He received a B.Arch degree from Inha University (Incheon, 2000–09) and his Master's from the same university in 2011. He founded Smaller Architects in 2016. As he says: "Smaller means small and better." His work includes Common Ground Art Museum (Seoul, 2017); Seroro (Seoul, 2020, published here); Amista House (Seoul, 2020); Each House (Seoul, 2021); and the Column Tiny Building (Seoul, 2021), all in South Korea.

LINE SOLGAARD
was born in 1967 and received her degree from the Oslo School of Architecture (1996–2002). She created her office in Fredrikstad in 2012. Her work includes the Weekend House (Fredrikstad, 2020, published here); seven new private houses (Oredalstunet, Fredrikstad, 2022); Sjølund House (Fredrikstad, 2022); Granholmene House (Fredrikstad, 2022); Traratoppen, a scheme for 130 apartments and townhouses (Fredrikstad, 2021–ongoing); Kjerringholmen (Fredrikstadt, 2023) and Sjølund (Fredrikstad, 2024). Fredrikstad is in southeastern Norway, with a population of about 82,000 people.

SOTAMAA
KIVI SOTAMAA was born in Finland in 1971. He received his Master's degree from the University of Art and Design Helsinki (now called Aalto University) in 1999. He cofounded Ateljé Sotamaa in 2004 with his twin sister Tuuli Sotamaa. His recent work includes the Finnish Pavilion for the 2017 World Expo in Kazakhstan, entirely fabricated from CLT; the design for the award-winning Michelin star restaurant Finnjävel in Helsinki (2019); the Meteorite (Kontiolahti, 2020, published here); and Usva, a digitally prefabricated timber-frame building (Kontiolahti, 2022), all in Finland unless indicated otherwise.

STUDIO DIAA
SUZANNE STEFAN was born in 1979 in Honolulu. She graduated with a B.Arch degree from Virginia Tech (Blacksburg, Virginia, 2003) and did Master's studies at the Architecture Academy in Mendrisio, Switzerland (2008–09). She worked with Marwan Al-Sayed (Phoenix, Arizona, 2005–08); with MW Works (Seattle, Washington, 2015); and with Studio Rick Joy (Tucson, Arizona, 2017) before creating Studio DIAA in Seattle in 2017. Her work includes the 9th and Thomas Residence (Seattle, Washington, 2017); Xala Tented Luxury Camp (Costa Careyes, Mexico, 2017); Mayakoba Beach Club (Playa del Carmen, Mexico, 2017); Ocean Residence (Miami Beach, Florida, 2018); the Madrona Courtyard Residence (Seattle, Washington, 2018); and Portage Bay Float Home (Seattle, Washington, 2020, published here), all in the USA unless indicated otherwise.

STUDIO PUISTO
Studio Puisto Architects was founded in 2014 by the five partners: MIKKO JAKONEN, born in 1979 in Kajaani; EMMA JOHANSSON, born in 1985 in Lieto; SAMPSA PALVA, born in 1981 in Helsinki; HEIKKI RIITAHUHTA, born in 1980 in Tampere, all of whom completed their studies at the University of Oulu between 2008 and 2012. The fifth partner of the firm, WILLEM VAN BOLDEREN, was born in 1982 in Loo, the Netherlands. He did his studies at the TU Delft (2001–05) and then at Helsinki University of Technology (2005–08). Some of their recent projects include the Arctic TreeHouse Hotel, experiential accommodation units (2016); the Kivijärvi Resort/Niliaitta Prototype (Kivijärvi, 2020, published here); Saunaravintola Kiulu, a multipurpose gathering space on the waterfront of Ähtäri (2020); and Space of Mind, a modular cabin (with Made by Choice + Protos Demos, 2020), all in Finland.

SUMMARY
SAMUEL GONÇALVES was born in Arouca, Portugal, in 1988. He graduated in Architecture from the Faculty of Architecture of the University of Porto in 2013. He worked for a year at the Chilean studio ELEMENTAL, directed by Alejandro Aravena. In 2015, he founded his own practice, SUMMARY, at UPTEC (Science and Technology Park of the University of Porto). SUMMARY created the Gomos building system, for which it was selected as a finalist in the Portuguese National Creative Industries Award. In 2020, SUMMARY was selected as "The Emerging Architect of the Year" by the readers of dezeen.com. His projects include Gomos #1 (Penso, Arouca, 2015); Paradinha (Alvarenga, 2021, published here); Aveiro Sports Center (Taboeira, Aveiro, 2021); and a modular kindergarten (Estrada da Luz, Lisbon, 2021–ongoing), all in Portugal.

SZCZ JAKUB SZCZĘSNY
JAKUB SZCZĘSNY was born in Warsaw, Poland, in 1973. He earned Bachelor's and Master's degrees from the Warsaw Institute of Technology Faculty of Architecture (2001) and a Ph.D. from the Warsaw School of Fine Arts, Faculty of Design (2013). He worked with Centrala Designer's Task Force, a network he cofounded in 2001 with Krzystof Banaszewski, Malgortzara Kuuciewicz, and Jan Strumillo based on the infrastructure of Studio Deco, the office of his father Ryszard Szczęsny. He created his own firm, SZCZ, in 2016. His work includes the Keret House (Warsaw, Poland, 2012, published here); "Polish Refuge in Bom Retiro"—a temporary installation and revitalization of the rooftop of the Casa do Povo, a Jewish leftist urban utopia erected in 1953 (São Paulo, Brazil, 2016); "Gustaw Zieliński Square" (Astana/Nursultan, Kazakhstan, 2018); "SPACE," outdoor NGO infrastructure system for Lechstarter CSR Program (Warsaw, Poland, 2019); "Taburete Towers," temporary installations with double usages (Logrońo, Spain; Bangalore, India; and Warsaw, Poland, 2021); and "The Fifth Space," on the rooftop of the Max Liebling House (with Hadas Tuval, Tel Aviv, Israel, 2021).

HIROYUKI UNEMORI
was born in 1979 in Okayama Prefecture. He received his degrees in Architecture from the Yokohama National University (2002–05) and worked in the office of Taira Nishizawa Architects (Tokyo, 2002–09). He created Unemori Architects in Tokyo in 2009. He was also a design assistant at Yokohama University (2014). His work includes House Tokyo (Tokyo, 2019, published here); the Sukagawa Community Center (Fukushima, 2019); Akishimaensis, Education and Community Center (Akishima, 2020); House in Takaoka (Takaoka, 2020); BASE (Tokyo, 2021); and a health and childcare support complex (Kitakami, 2021), all in Japan.

WONDER
CHONG WANG was born in 1986. He received an M.Arch from Nanjing University, a Master's in Engineering from the University of Tokyo, and a Doctorate in Design (Central Academy of Fine Arts, Beijing). He has translated several Japanese architecture-related books from English into Chinese. Chong Wang, QiPeng Zhu, and SiDi Wang founded Wonder Architects in Beijing, in 2017. Their work includes the South River Tourism Complex (Yueyang, Hunan, 2017); Museum Home in Huajiadi China (Beijing, 2017); Cuó E Guan (Beijing, 2017); House in the Window (Xicheng, Beijing, 2017); The Watcher of Time (Yanqing, Beijing, 2018); Intertwine House (Yanqing, Beijing, 2019, published here); and Step House (Wuhan, 2021), all in China.

YOSHIHIRO YAMAMOTO
was born in 1976 in Nara. He graduated in 2000 in Engineering from Osaka Prefectural University and then studied at Kyoto Institute of Technology (2001–04) before working with Compas Architects (Osaka, 2005–08). He opened his current office in 2018. As well as the Toolbox House (Miyakojima-ku, Osaka, 2021, published here), other significant work includes the Kakko House (Osaka, 2014); Crossroad House (Sakai, 2018); Rowhouse on Showa-koji St. (Kyoto, 2018); Sukima House (Nara, 2019); and more recently H's Residence, (Osaka, 2024), all in Japan.

Marte.Marte, Mountain Cabin, Laterns, Austria, 2011.

CONTACTS

Alphaville Architects 46
32 Kamihanada Saiin, Ukyo-ku
Kyoto 615–0007
Japan
Tel: +81 75 312 6951
E-mail: 001@a-ville.net
Web: www.a-ville.net

Cameron Anderson /
Cameron Anderson Architects 54
5 Lovejoy Street
Mudgee, NSW 2850
Australia
Tel: +61 409 257 688
E-mail: info@caarch.com.au
Web: www.caarch.com.au

Simon Anderson /
Anderson Architecture 64
Studio 101, 4–14 Buckingham Street,
Surry Hills
Sydney, NSW 2010
Australia
Tel: +61 9319 0224
E-mail: info@andersonarchitecture.au
Web: www.andersonarchitecture.com.au

Arbol Design 72
Kyouei Blvd 3F, 2–8–11 Shibatai, Kita-ku
Osaka 530–0012
Japan
Tel: +81 70 2805 2546
E-mail: info@arbol-design.com
Web: www.arbol-design.com

Aranza de Ariño 80
Mexico City
Tel: +52 55 4145 4084
E-mail: aranza.arino@gmail.com

Arte-1 90
4F Kurasawa bldg., 5–12–2 Minamiaoyama
Tokyo 107–0062
Japan
Tel: +81 3 3498 2761
E-mail: info@arte-1.com
Web: www.arte-1.com

baumraum, Andreas Wenning 96
Borchersweg 14
28203 Bremen
Germany
Tel: +49 421 70 51 22
E-mail: a.wenning@baumraum.de
Web: www.baumraum.de

Attila Béres / Béres Architects 102
Római út 36
8360 Keszthely
Hungary
Tel: +36 303 29 13 90
E-mail: mail@beresattila.hu
Web: www.beresattila.hu

Bianchi-Fucile Arquitectos..........................112
56 nro 712, La Plata
1900 Buenos Aires
Argentina
Tel: +54 9 221 566 2216
E-mail: leandrofucile@gmail.com
Instagram: @bianchifucile

BIG-Bjarke Ingels Group............................118
45 Main Street, Floor 9
Brooklyn, NY 11201
USA
Tel: +1 347 549 4141
E-mail: nyc@big.dk
Web: www.big.dk

B.L.U.E. Architecture Studio 124
Room 208-209, Building No. 9,
Langyuan Vintage, 6 Langjiayuan,
Jianguo Road, Chaoyang District
100022 Beijing
China
Tel: +86 10 8589 5003
E-mail: info@b-l-u-e.net
Web: www.b-l-u-e.net

Bureau LADA 130
Parnassusweg 172
1076 AT Amsterdam
The Netherlands
Tel: +31 650 61 78 36
E-mail: info@bureaulada.com
Web: www.bureaulada.com

Casey Brown Architecture 136
Level 1, 63 William Street
East Sydney, NSW 2010
Australia
Tel: +61 2 9360 7977
E-mail: cb@caseybrown.com.au
Web: www.caseybrown.com.au

Jaime Chioco / Chioco Design 146
1306 Rosewood Ave.
Austin, TX 78702
USA
Tel: +1 512 374 0288
E-mail: contact@chiocodesign.com
Web: www.chiocodesign.com

Barry Connor Design 152
2 Cobham Street, Spreydon
Christchurch 8024
New Zealand
Tel: +64 21 203 5992
E-mail: barry@barryconnordesign.co.nz
Web: www.barryconnordesign.co.nz

Croxatto & Opazo Arquitectos 160
Sancho de la Hoz, 3431, Office 4, Vitacura
7630551 Region Metropolitana de Santiago
Chile
Tel: +56 9 8233 0901
E-mail: hola@croxattoyopazo.cl
Web: www.croxattoyopazo.cl

El Sindicato Arquitectura 168
Juan Montalvo N1-21 y Francisco de Orellana
170901 Cumbayá, Quito
Ecuador
Tel: +593 2 289 0579 / +593 9 9522 2863
E-mail: elsindicato.arquitectura@gmail.com
Web: www.elsindicatoarquitectura.com

Takaaki Fuji + Yuko Fuji Architecture 174
1–23–7 Uehara, Shibuya
Tokyo 151–0064
Japan
Tel: +81 90 2632 3700
E-mail: contact@ty-fuji.info
Web: www.ty-fuji.info

Sean Godsell Architects 182
Level 1, 196 Gertrude Street
Fitzroy, VIC 3065
Australia
Tel: +61 3 9654 2677
E-mail: info@seangodsell.com
Web: www.seangodsell.com

H&P Architects 190
Building 10–LK2, 4th floor,
90 Nguyen Tuan Urban zone,
Nguyen Tuan Street, Thanh Xuan District
10000 Hanoi
Vietnam
Tel: +84 9 8360 0606
E-mail: ha.dt@hpa.vn
Web: www.hpa.vn

Takeshi Hosaka Architects 198
Koiso Ohtake Bild. #202, 358 Yamabukicyo,
Shinjuku
Tokyo 162–0801
Japan
Tel: +81 3 5946 8909
E-mail: info@hosakatakeshi.com
Web: www.hosakatakeshi.com

i29 architects 204
Industrieweg 29
1115 AD Ouder-Amstel
The Netherlands
Tel: +31 20 695 61 20
E-mail: info@i29.nl
Web: www.i29.nl

Gustavo Penna Architect & Associates 298
Avenue Álvares Cabral, 414
30170–001 Belo Horizonte, MG
Brazil
Tel: +55 31 3218 2400
E-mail: comunicacao@gustavopenna.com.br
Web: www.gustavopenna.com.br

Charles Pictet Baptiste Broillet Architectes Associés 306
12A Chemin Frank Thomas
1208 Geneva
Switzerland
Tel: +41 22 737 14 14
E-mail: info@pictet-broillet.ch
Web: www.pictet-broillet.ch

Prentiss + Balance + Wickline Architects 314
224 West Galer Street
Seattle, WA 98119
USA
Tel: +1 206 283 9930
E-mail: info@pbwarchitects.com
Web: www.pbwarchitects.com

Reiulf Ramstad Architects AS 322
Josefines Gate 7
0351 Oslo
Norway
Tel: +47 22 80 84 80
E-mail: firma@rra.no
Web: www.reiulframstadarkitekter.com

João Mendes Ribeiro Arquitecto Lda 330
Rua de Tomar 1 esquerdo
3000–401 Coimbra
Portugal
Tel: +351 239 83 37 63
E-mail: info@mendesribeiro.pt
Web: www.joaomendesribeiro.com

Claudia Rodríguez 340
Havre 69 D3, Colonia Juárez
Delegación Cuauhtémoc
Mexico City 06600
Mexico
Tel: +52 55 1849 8015
E-mail: claudia.rdgz.q@gmail.com

Rozana Montiel Estudio de Arquitectura 340
Gral. Juan Cano 93, Col. San Miguel
Chapultepec II Secc. Piso 1,
Delegación Miguel Hidalgo
Mexico City 11850
Mexico
Tel: +52 55 5515 4033
E-mail: info@rozanamontiel.com
Web: www.rozanamontiel.com

S-AR 350
Rio Vistula 208
San Pedro Garza García
Nuevo León 66220
Mexico
Tel: +52 81 1519 6750
E-mail: info@stacion-arquitectura.com
Web: www.s-ar.mx

Savioz Fabrizzi Architectes 358
Route des Ronquos 35
1950 Sion
Switzerland
Tel: +41 27 322 68 81
E-mail: info@sf-ar.ch
Web: www.sf-ar.ch

selgascano 368
Guecho 27
28023 Madrid
Spain
Tel: +34 91 307 64 81
E-mail: selgascano@gmail.com
Web: www.selgascano.net

Fran Silvestre Arquitectos 380
Avenida Escultor Andreu Alfaro 13
Godella, 46110 Valencia
Spain
Tel: +34 963 81 65 61
E-mail: info@fransilvestrearquitectos.com
Web: www.fransilvestrearquitectos.com

Smaller Architects 388
3F, 40, Jahamun-ro 17-gil, Jongno-gu
03035 Seoul
South Korea
Tel: +82 70 8860 4943
E-mail: smallerarchitects@naver.com
Web: www.smallerarchitects.com

Line Solgaard Arkitekter 396
Storgata 23
1607 Fredrikstad
Norway
Tel: +47 91 88 64 37
E-mail: line@linesolgaard.com
Web: www.linesolgaard.com

Ateljé Sotamaa 404
Väinämöisenkatu 19A
00100 Helsinki
Finland
Tel: +358 504 35 01 09
E-mail: info@sotamaa.net
Web: www.sotamaa.net

Studio DIAA 412
3125 Eastlake Ave. E, Suite C
Seattle, WA 98102
USA
Tel: +1 206 788 8838
E-mail: info@studiodiaa.com
Web: www.studiodiaa.com

Studio Puisto Architects 420
Mariankatu 7 A 4
00170 Helsinki
Finland
Tel: +358 404 15 14 33
E-mail: info@studiopuisto.fi
Web: www.studiopuisto.fi

SUMMARY 430
Rua Monte Cativo 258
4050–399 Porto
Portugal
Tel: +351 919 09 32 47
E-mail: info@summary.pt
Web: www.summary.pt

SZCZ Jakub Szczęsny 438
Wandy 9 m 4
03–949 Warsaw
Poland
Tel: +48 602 31 63 74
E-mail: jakub.szczesny@szcz.com.pl
Web: www.szcz.com.pl

Hiroyuki Unemori / Unemori Architects 444
Asakusabashi 3–12–6 BASE, Taito-ku
Tokyo 111–0053
Japan
Tel: +81 3 6261 3708
E-mail: office@unemori-archi.com
Web: www.unemori-archi.com

Wonder Architects 452
Gate 6, No. 28, Yongheng Hutong,
Dongcheng District
100009 Beijing
China
Tel: +86 135 2183 7361
E-mail: office@wonder-architects.com
Web: www.wonder-architects.com

Yoshihiro Yamamoto Architects Atelier 460
14–6–302, Ishigatsuji-cho, Tennoji-ku
Osaka 543–0031
Japan
Tel: +81 6 6771 9039
E-mail: contact@yyaa.jp
Web: www.yyaa.jp

Opposite: *Attila Béres, Cabin Moss, Köszeg, Hungary, 2021.*

Page 487: *Reiulf Ramstad, Breitenbach Landscape Hotel – 48° Nord, Breitenbach, France, 2021.*

Photo Credits — 2 © Kivi Sotamaa / **8/9** © Dennis Radermacher / **11, 43, 199–203** © Koji Fujii/TOREAL / **12, 161–167** © Cristóbal Palma / **14, 221–225** © James Brittain / **15, 47–53** © Toshiyuki Yano / **17, 453–459** © Yumeng Zhu / **18, 26, 131–135 369–379** © Iwan Baan / **19, 175–181** © Masao Nishikawa / **20/21, 289–291** Taj Howe / **23, 31, 293–297, 421–429** © Marc Goodwin, Archmospheres / **24, 137–145** © Andrew Loiterton / **25, 259–263, 479** © Marc Lins Photography / **29, 299–305** © Jomar Bragança / **32/23** © Martin Lukasczyk / **35, 271–277** © www.bitmap.no / **36, 153–159** © Dennis Radermacher / **37, 183–189** / © Earl Carter / **38, 97–101** © André Dogbey / **41, 170–173** © Andrés Villota / **55–63** © Amber Hooper / **44/45, 119–123** © Matthew Carbone / **65–71** © Nick Bowers / **73–79** © Yashunori Shimomura / **81–89, 351, 353–357** © Camila Cossio / **91–95, 445–451** © Kai Nakamura / **103–111, 485** © Tamás Bujnovszky / **113–117** © Santiago Bianchi / **125–129** © Ruijing Photo / **147–151** © Leonid Furmansky / **169** © Pablo Caicedo / **191–197** © Nguyen Tien Thanh / **205–211** © www.ewout.tv / **213–219, 243–249** © Leonardo Finotti / **227–233** © Adam Gibson / **235–241** © Makers of Architecture / **251–257** © Piet-Albert Goethals / **265–269** © Gen Inoue / **279–283** © Will Crocker / **285–291** © Tim Bies/ Olson Kundig / **307–313** © Duccio Malagamba / **315–321** © Taj Howe / **323–329, 487** © 11h45 – Florent Michel / **331–339** © José Campos / **341–349** © Sandra Pereznieto / **352** © Claudio Sodi / **359–367** © Thomas Jatscher / **381–387, 431–437** © Fernando Guerra/FG+SG / **389–395** © Jong-Seok Byeon / **397–403** © Einar Aslaksen/ Pudder Agency / **405–411** © Krista Keltanen / **413–419** © Kevin Scott / **439–441, 443** © Andreas Meichsner / **461–467** © Yohei Sasakura

Credits for Plans / Drawings / CAD Documents — 46, 53 © Alphaville / **54, 59** © Cameron Anderson Architects / **64, 68** © Anderson Architecture/Simon Anderson / **72, 75** © Arbol / **80, 82, 88** © Aranza de Ariño / **90, 92** © Arte-1 / **96** © baumraum/Andreas Wenning / **102, 107** © Béres Architecture / **112, 116, 117** © Bianchi Fucile / **118, 123** © BIG / **124, 126** © B.L.U.E. Architecture Studio / **130, 135** © Bureau LADA / **136, 141, 142** © Casey Brown Architecture / **146, 148** © Jaime Chioco/Chioco Design / **152** © Barry Connor / **160, 166** © Croxatto & Opazo Arquitectos / **168, 171, 173** © El Sindicato Arquitectura / **174, 177, 179, 181** © tyfa/ Takaaki Fuji + Yuko Fuji Architecture / **182** © Sean Godsell Architects / **190, 196** © H&P Architects / **198** © Takeshi Hosaka / **204, 210, 211** © i29 Architects / **212** © Brian MacKay-Lyons / **226, 232** © Maguire + Devine Architects / **234, 241** © Makers of Architecture / **242, 248** © MAPA Architects / **250** © Mar plus Ask / **258, 260** © marte.marte architekten zt gmbh / **264, 267** © Moriya & Partners / **270, 276** © Norgeshus AS / **278, 280, 281** © OJT / **284** © Olson Kundig / **292, 296** © ORTRAUM architects / **298** © Gustavo Penna Architect & Associates / **306, 312** © Charles Pictet / **314, 317** © PBW Architects / **322, 326** © Reiulf Ramstad Arkitekter / **330, 333, 336, 337** © João Mendes Ribeiro / **340, 345, 349** © Rozana Montiel Estudio de Arquitectura / **350, 352** © S-AR / **358, 366, 367** © Savioz Fabrizzi Architects / **368** © selgascano / **380, 385** © FG+SG / **388, 395** © Smaller Architects / **396, 401, 402** © Line Solgaard Arkitekter / **404, 410** © Sotamaa / **412, 415** © Studio DIAA / **420, 428** © Studio Puisto / **430** © SUMMARY / **438, 442** © SZCZ / **444, 446** © Unemori Architects / **452, 455** © WONDER/ Chong Wang / **460** © Yoshihiro Yamamoto

10

IMPRINT

EACH AND EVERY TASCHEN BOOK PLANTS A SEED!
Each year, we offset our annual carbon emissions with carbon credits at the Instituto Terra, a reforestation program in Minas Gerais, Brazil, founded by Lélia and Sebastião Salgado. To find out more about this ecological partnership, please check: *www.taschen.com/institutoterra*
Inspiration: unlimited.
Carbon footprint: (almost) zero.

Want to see more? Visit *taschen.com* to view our current publications, browse our latest magazine, and subscribe to our newsletter.

Hohenzollernring 53, D–50672 Köln
www.taschen.com

Layout: Collaborate, London
German translation: Barbara Thoma, St. Moritz
French translation: Claire Debard, Freiburg

Printed in Bosnia-Herzegovina
ISBN 978-3-8365-9890-3